METAPHORS
for EVALUATION

NEW PERSPECTIVES IN EVALUATION

Series Editor: Nick L. Smith

Northwest Regional Educational Laboratory

THE BOOKS IN THIS SERIES reflect an emerging awareness among evaluation practitioners and theorists that evaluation involves *more* than conducting an experimental study in an applied setting. Evaluation is increasingly recognized as a highly complex technical, economic, political, and social activity requiring the skills of many professionals—lawyers, economists, artists, and scientists, in addition to psychologists, sociologists, political scientists, and other applied social research specialists.

The purpose of this series is to deepen methodological discussions of evaluation and to improve evaluation practice. Beginning with Volume 1, this series strives to provide readers with new ways to view the evaluative enterprise and innovative tools compatible with these emerging perspectives. Written by some of the field's most creative theorists and practitioners, these volumes will share the adventure of uncovering new approaches to an exciting young discipline and disseminate useful guidelines for the expansion and improvement of its practice.

BOOKS IN THIS SERIES:

Volume 1 METAPHORS FOR EVALUATION: Sources of New Methods
Volume 2 NEW TECHNIQUES FOR EVALUATION

Additional titles in preparation

n/2

METAPHORS
for
EVALUATION

Sources of New Methods

Nick L. Smith, editor

NEW PERSPECTIVES IN EVALUATION
Volume 1

*This volume published in cooperation with
the Northwest Regional Educational Laboratory*

 **SAGE PUBLICATIONS** Beverly Hills London

This volume of New Perspectives in Evaluation is published in cooperation with the Northwest Regional Educational Laboratory.

For information address:

SAGE Publications, Inc.
275 South Beverly Drive
Beverly Hills, California 90212

SAGE Publications Ltd.
28 Banner Street
London EC1Y 8QE, England

Printed in the United States of America

Library of Congress Cataloging in Publication Data

Main entry under title:
Metaphors for evaluation.

(New Perspectives in Evaluation ; v. 1)
Bibliography: p.
Contents: Developing evaluation methods / Nick L. Smith — Metaphors for evaluation / Nick L. Smith — Investigative reporting / Egon G. Guba — [etc.]
1. Evaluation — Addresses, essays, lectures.
I. Smith, Nick L. II. Series.
AZ191.M47   001.4'33   81-5344
ISBN 0-8039-1613-2   AACR2

FIRST PRINTING

CONTENTS

Series Introduction

THE EARLY YEARS of the young field of evaluation have been dominated by a heavy emphasis on research and the use of a narrow range of social science methodology, principally testing approaches and experimental studies. As the need and concern for evaluation continues to grow in such areas as education, health, criminal justice, welfare, housing, community development, and state and federal oversight, questions about evaluation's quality and utility are increasingly raised. The clients and funders of evaluation are seeking more cost-effective and timely approaches to their evaluation needs. There is an emerging awareness among evaluation practitioners and theorists that evaluation involves more than conducting an experimental study in an applied setting. Evaluation is being recognized as a highly complex technical, economic, political, and social activity which requires the skills of many professionals — lawyers, economists, artists, scientists, and many others.

A new series of exciting volumes is being launched by Sage Publications in this period of tumultuous expansion of evaluation. The volumes in the *New Perspectives in Evaluation* series will share with the reader the latest discoveries in the search for new means of improving evaluation. The series will include volumes which

- explore areas such as journalism, film criticism, architecture, and philosophy in search of new alternative roles and methods for evaluation;
- translate existing procedures from such fields as economics, geography, law, and photography for use in evaluation, providing readers with support in selecting and using these new methods; and
- report on studies of evaluation practice which shake old assumptions about what really happens in evaluation.

The purpose of this series is to deepen methodological discussion in evaluation and to improve evaluation practice. This volume and those to come will provide readers with new ways of viewing evaluation and innovative tools compatible with these emerging perspectives. Readers will be able to choose from an expanding array of alternative approaches to evaluation. Since methodological faddism is as dangerous as methodological conservatism, however, the authors of these volumes will share insights which enable readers to select judiciously those methods that best complement the nature of the object being evaluated and the purpose of the evaluative study.

This series brings to the evaluation reader the latest findings in the exciting search for dramatic alternatives to evaluation. Written by some of evaluation's most creative theorists and practitioners, these volumes will share the adventure of uncovering new approaches to evaluation and provide practical guides to the expansion and improvement of evaluation practice. We guarantee you will never view evaluation the same way again after you have seen the *New Perspectives in Evaluation.*

Portland, Oregon   *Nick L. Smith*
                                              Series Editor

Foreword

EVALUATION is emerging as a discipline of serious concern to scholars, social policymakers, and practitioners alike. To foster the development of the method and practice of evaluation and free it from often limiting traditional conceptions (for example, strict measurement and experimental model approaches), in 1977 the Northwest Regional Educational Laboratory initiated the Research on Evaluation Program. Under the direction and fine tutelage of Nick L. Smith, and with the sponsorship of the National Institute of Education, this ambitious undertaking has drawn upon a cadre of visiting scholars from various disciplines to help devise new methods of educational evaluation through adaptation of metaphorical paradigms and techniques from other disciplines. These disciplines include law, investigative reporting, architecture, geography, philosophy, literary and film criticism, and watercolor painting. Contributions from these otherwise disparate fields promise to broaden and deepen our understanding of the enterprise of evaluation.

Readers may be almost overwhelmed by the wealth of ideas spread before them in this volume. They may agree or disagree with the potential utility of various metaphors, definitions, ideas, or ideals. But the wise reader will examine carefully, evaluate constantly, and test and apply techniques inherent in the various metaphors before deciding on their relative merit and value.

With respect to the usefulness of this evaluation effort, I am in accord with Michael Scriven, who wrote in a recent issue of *Evaluation News:* "These [metaphors] include a good number of rich contributions to practical evaluation methodology which should affect practice considerably. It is by far the most important effort to upgrade the methodology of evaluation in the short history of the subject."

Daniel P. Antonoplos
National Institute of Education
and Adjunct Professor of Research,
American University

Preface

SHOULD EVALUATORS EXPLORE such fields as journalism, geography, and film criticism in a search for new evaluation methods? How would they identify and translate new methods from these disciplines? What would they find?

This book reports on the results of seven efforts to identify new methods for use in evaluation by studying existing procedures used in other disciplines. This work was performed as part of a programmatic effort to improve the practice of evaluation and includes an examination of the fields of investigative reporting, law, architecture, geography, philosophy, literary and film criticism, and watercolor painting. By using these fields as metaphors for evaluation, it was possible to explore the potential contributions of these fields to evaluation methodology.

A metaphor is a device for using one object to create a new perspective on another. Saying that "electricity flows like water" suggests several possible characteristics of electricity based on our understanding of water. We can ask what the electrical counterparts to water's pressure, volume, and rate of flow are; we can examine electricity as if it were water in order to gain new insights into the nature of electricity. In a similar way, the chapters in this book use other fields as metaphors for evaluation. What new methods are suggested if we view evaluation as "the creation of a journalistic story" (investigative reporting), or as "the study of spatial relations" (geography), or as "the search for conceptual clarity" (philosophy), or as "the illumination of form and style" (literary and film criticism)? What we find is an exciting new array of alternatives for evaluation, including

- *cartographic analysis* from geography for use in dealing with such evaluation issues as the geographic distribution of social services;

- *concept analysis* from philosophy for use in clarifying basic concepts in evaluation such as "value," "impact," "remediation," "effective implementation," "achievement," "improvement," and "benefit";
- *document tracking* from investigative reporting for use in collecting evaluation data from archival systems; and
- *structural analysis* from poetic, literary, and film criticism for use in product evaluation.

We also find new conceptual distinctions for possible use in evaluation, such as

- the legal profession's use of different "levels of evidence," depending on the nature of the case as opposed to the evaluator's universal insistence on irrefutable evidence;
- the architect's use of contextual "fit" as an overall criterion for the evaluation of an architectural solution instead of the reductionistic criteria most often used in evaluating programs; and
- the journalist's use of "fairness" as a basis for judging the quality of a story, since objectivity is not truly possible, instead of the evaluator's reliance on supposedly value-free objectivity.

The work reported in this volume began in 1977 as part of the Research on Evaluation Program at the Northwest Regional Educational Laboratory in Portland, Oregon. Supported by a multiyear contract from the National Institute of Education, the Research on Evaluation Program began to develop new evaluation methods for use principally in state education departments and local school districts. While the research reported here uses examples primarily from education, the implications of the work are much broader. The new methods and perspectives drawn here from fields in the sciences, arts, and world of practical affairs have significant potential for improving evaluation practice in many service areas such as health, criminal justice, social welfare, housing, community development, and federal oversight, as well as in education.

The chapters of this volume report the rationale for this study of evaluation metaphors, the nature of practice within the alternative fields, and new methods for possible use in evaluation. In Chapter 1, "Developing Evaluation Methods," I discuss the need for new methods in evaluation, the nature of methodological improvement of practice, and a programmatic strategy for the development, testing, and acceptance of new methods in evaluation. In Chapter 2, "Metaphors for Evaluation," the concept of metaphor is discussed in more depth. In this chapter I also provide an overview of the seven chapters which follow, including a discussion of some of the common themes which run throughout the chapters. Each of the subsequent seven chapters concerns the use of a different field or discipline as a metaphor for evaluation. These chapters have been prepared by individuals with experience in both evaluation and the fields they are exploring; for example, an evaluator who is also an architect, an evaluation theorist who has also been a watercolorist for 25 years, and a philosopher who has recently been working in evaluation. Each chapter contains

(a) a basic description of the field, including its major methodologies and epistemological tools;

(b) an evaluative analysis of the field as a source of new methods for evaluation; and

(c) a discussion of the specific methods, concepts, and points of view which may be adapted for use in evaluation, as well as including recommended readings for those interested in studying these new tools.

The chapters in Volume 1 were selected and sequenced to range from the more obvious to the less obvious translations to evaluation. Investigative journalism, law, and architecture were selected for study because, like evaluation, they deal with providing social services in the world of practical affairs. Geography was selected because it is one of the few social sciences which does not seem to have played as major a role in the early development of evaluation as have psychology, sociology, political science, and economics. Philosophy was selected because of its traditional attention to questions of value, meaning, and the nature of evidence — important concerns in evaluation. Literary and film criticism and watercolor painting were selected as examples of the arts in which the process of evaluation plays a major role in the improvement of practice.

This book is one in a series of volumes to be published on the development of new evaluation methods. Other volumes will deal with specific new techniques in evaluation, the assessment of new procedures through experience in applied field trials, and the uses of alternative forms of representation in evaluation studies. Through this series we seek to broaden the spectrum of methods available to the evaluation practitioner and to deepen the level of methodological discourse among evaluation theorists.

I welcome this opportunity to acknowledge the widespread support given this work. We appreciate the early enthusiasm and continued encouragement given us by the program staff at the National Institute of Education, especially Daniel Antonoplos and Charles Stalford. We are also grateful for the insightful guidance provided by the members of the project's National Advisory Panel:

Adrianne Bank, University of California at Los Angeles

Joan Bollenbacher, Cincinnati Public Schools (Ret.)

Egon Guba, Indiana University

Vincent Madden, California State Department of Education

Jason Millman, Cornell University

Stacy Rockwood, New Orleans, Louisiana

Blaine Worthen, Utah State University

This work has profited from many discussions and collaborative efforts with my colleague at the Northwest Regional Educational Laboratory, Darrel Caulley. The invaluable secretarial assistance of Judy Turnidge and Vicky Kerr saw this manuscript safely through many revisions. The work owes much to their continued professional assistance. I owe my deepest gratitude to my wife, Denny, not only for her fine editorial assistance, but for her frequent perceptive insights concerning the work reported here, and most of all for her steadfast personal support of my efforts.

To all these individuals and the many others who have helped make this work successful, I express my deep appreciation.

Nick L. Smith
Northwest Regional Educational Laboratory

Acknowledgments

We are grateful for the kind permission granted by the following publishers and individuals to reprint or reproduce from their original works portions of the text, tables, and figures in this volume. Paul N. Williams, INVESTIGATIVE REPORTING AND EDITING, © 1978, pp. 14-15. Reprinted by permission of Prentice-Hall, Inc., Englewood Cliffs, New Jersey. *Architectural Program for the Expansion and Remodeling of Loyola Law School,* Los Angeles, California by Frank O. Gehry and Associates, Inc. "Architects" and Brooks/Collier "Associate Architects," 1979. Figure 6.1 reprinted from the GEOGRAPHICAL REVIEW, Vol. 58, 1968, with the permission of the American Geographical Society. Figure 6.2 used with permission from "Social Change Through Education: Problems of Planning in Rural Australia" by Janice J. Monk appearing in RURAL CHANGE AND PUBLIC POLICY edited by Avery, Lonsdale, and Volgyes (New York: Pergamon Press, © 1980). Figure 6.3 used with permission of Dr. Florence Ladd, Dean of Students, Wellesley College, Wellesley, Massachusetts. Figure 6.5 from A. Robinson, R. Sale, and J. Morrison, *Elements of Cartography* (fourth edition, 1978) used with permission of John Wiley & Sons, Inc. Figures 6.6a and 6.6b from A. Robinson, *Elements of Cartography* (second edition, 1960) used with permission of John Wiley & Sons, Inc. Mark S. Monmonier, *Maps, Distortion and Meaning* (Washington, D.C.: Association of American Geographers, Resource Papers for College Geography No. 75-4), 1977, p. 26, fig. 22; p. 33, fig. 31; p. 29, fig. 26. Reprinted by permission. C.C. Roseman, *Changing Migration Patterns within the United States* (Washington, D.C.: Association of American Geographers, Resource Papers for College Geography No. 77-2), 1977, p. 19. Reprinted by permission.

Nick L. Smith
*Director, Research on Evaluation Program, Northwest
Regional Educational Laboratory*

CHAPTER *1*

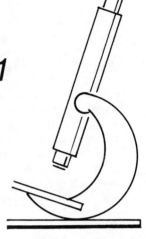

Developing Evaluation Methods

*For the past four years Nick Smith has directed the
Research on Evaluation Program, which conducts
research on the nature of evaluation practice and
researches and develops new evaluation methods.
Through his published methodological research on
evaluation in health, education, and community development, he has sought to ground evaluation
theory in empirical work on evaluation practice. He
won the President's Problem competition of the
Evaluation Network in 1978, served as President of
the Evaluation Network in 1980, and has been evaluation book review editor of* Educational Evaluation
and Policy Analysis *since the journal's inception.*

Prologue

This chapter presents a rationale for the development of new evaluation methods through the adaptation of existing methodologies from
the arts, sciences, and world of practical affairs. Subsequent chapters
provide evidence of the results of employing the strategies suggested
here. Proposing to develop methods on such a grand scale may seem
overly adventurous, even hubristic, but the potential gains far out-
weigh the risk of failure. We respond with the words of Oliver Wendell
Holmes in 1886:

> No man has earned the right to intellectual ambition until he has
> learned to lay his course by a star which he has never seen — to dig

by a divining rod for springs he may never reach. In saying this, I point to that which will make your study heroic. For I say to you in all sadness of conviction, that to think great thoughts you must be heroes as well as idealists. Only when you have worked alone — when you have felt around you the black gulf of solitude more isolating than that which surrounds the dying man, and in hope and despair have trusted to your own unshaken will — then only will you have achieved. Thus only can you gain the secret isolated joy of the thinker, who knows that a hundred years after he is dead and forgotten, men who never heard of him will be moving to the measure of his thought — the subtle rapture of a postponed power, which the world knows not because it has no external trappings, but which to his prophetic vision is more real than that which commands an army. And if this joy should not be yours, still it is only thus that you can know that you have done what it lay in you to do — can say that you have lived, and be ready for the end [quoted in Harrison & Stein, 1973, pp. 1-2].

The authors of this volume did indeed experience the "black gulf of solitude" during their work on the material presented here, but we also felt ample intellectual reward for the effort. We trust you will agree that the result was worth the solitude and risk.

The Need and Nature of Methodological Improvement

The purpose of this chapter is to set the context for the subsequent chapters which explore the fields of investigative reporting, law, architecture, geography, philosophy, literary and film criticism, and watercolor painting, looking for new methods for use in evaluation. The work reported in these subsequent chapters was conducted as part of a multiyear, programmatic effort to identify and develop new alternatives for evaluation practice. In collaborating on this developmental work, the authors were broadly guided by the project's purpose and operational strategy, which are described in this chapter. Although the project provided broad guidelines, the creativity evident in the subsequent chapters is the sole result of the fertile minds of the contributing authors.

The first half of this chapter, then, addresses four questions which provide a background for the work that follows:

- Is there a need for new evaluation methods?
- How is methodological improvement accomplished?

- What is it about the nature of evaluation that suggests a search of other fields for new methods?
- What are the levels of practice at which new methods might be identified?

In the final half of the chapter, we turn to a consideration of the strategies for developing new methods, looking at the following questions:

- How have new methods historically been developed?
- What are the systematic ways to develop new methods?
- How might we assess the quality of new methods?
- What blocks the acceptance of new methods?

This material thus provides a context for viewing the work of the contributing authors.

The Need for New Evaluation Methods

Is there really a need for new evaluation methods, or is this just another example of an esoteric academic interest? In the pages which follow, I will provide evidence that there is a genuine need for new evaluation methods — at least in education — and that this need is recognized not only by evaluation theorists but by evaluation practitioners and educators as well.

Arguments from the literature. Evaluation method is a popular topic in the professional literature, and one can find many clear statements of methodological preference.

> There is almost universal agreement among evaluation researchers that the randomized controlled experiment is the ideal model for evaluating the effectiveness of a public policy. If there is a Bible for evaluation, the Scriptures have been written by Campbell and Stanley (1966), along with a revised version by Cook and Campbell (1976) [sic]. The "gospel" of these popular texts is that all research designs can be compared more or less unfavorably to randomized controlled experiments, departures from which are subject to varying combinations of threats to internal and external validity [Rossi & Wright, 1977, p. 13].

While there is indeed considerable support for the experimental approach to educational evaluation, it is not without opposition. Increasing numbers of evaluators are turning away from experimental approaches and examining alternative paths to the conduct of evaluation.

But what is the nature of this traditional, conventional form of evaluation? Guba (1978), in a splendid comparison of conventional inquiry and naturalistic inquiry in education, describes this traditional view as an approach based on logical positivism and experimental methods which is reductionistic, preordinate and fixed, and interventionistic. It is an approach focused on the verification of stable treatments within controlled settings. He contrasts this traditional view with the naturalistic approach which is based on phenomenology and investigative methods and which is expansionistic, emergent, and variable; an approach focused on discoveries about variable treatments in natural settings.

The traditional view has many proponents, and much has been written on the need for true experiments in educational evaluation and on the dangers of quasi-experiments (for example, Gilbert, Light, & Mosteller, 1975; Campbell & Boruch, 1975; Cook, Cook, & Mark, 1977; Boruch & Rindskopf, 1977). Cooley and Lohnes (1976) even argue that evaluations of major educational systems will *necessarily* be multivariate, longitudinal, large-sample, and expensive.

In the last few years, this traditional view has been much criticized (see, for example, Parlett & Hamilton, 1976; Guba, 1978). It has been argued that the traditional approach

(1) is too preordinate and fixed — it does not allow for the study of open, adapting systems and emergent problems but assumes a static program, at least for the period of study;

(2) is conclusion-oriented when what is needed is decision-oriented methods that allow the use of multiple decision-making frameworks;

(3) is not responsive to information needs of diverse audiences, especially needs for qualitative information;

(4) does not allow the representation of multiple viewpoints and value perspectives;

(5) focuses too heavily on outcomes and does not allow sufficient attention to program activities and issues;

(6) does not provide a means of studying spontaneous events, situations, or crises such as school closures, school levy fights, busing resistance, and student riots;

(7) disregards or attempts to control the role of context and setting in evaluations rather than attempting to understand their influence;

(8) produces artificial results with low external validity because variation is artificially restricted (natural variation is not allowed);

(9) is insensitive to local conditions and unusual effects since emphasis is on large-sample statistics;

(10) is essentially not feasible — procedures such as randomized field experiments simply cannot be implemented in most evaluation settings, due to expense, resistance to randomization, and so on;

(11) results in unethical behavior, such as withholding necessary treatment from control groups.

Traditionalists have countered by providing evidence to show that randomized, controlled experiments are indeed feasible, need not result in unethical treatment of subjects, and do not necessarily preclude qualitative data or attention to local differences (see especially Boruch, 1975; Cook et al., 1977; Boruch & Rindskopf, 1977).

The source of dissatisfaction for the revisionists seems to be the inability of the traditional methods to handle emergent problems in dynamic settings — problems of immediate and prime concern to various evaluation audiences. This dissatisfaction is based on experience with the traditional methods as they have been employed in the past, and it may be that these methods can be interpreted and used differently in the future to obviate the limitations cited by the revisionists. In response to their criticisms, we might begin to see adherents of the traditional methods also emphasizing more process variables, using more audience-defined outcome indicators, and employing more complex designs to account for contextual differences.

Part of the disagreement about the utility of traditional methods also seems to reflect a difference of opinion about whether evaluation is primarily an inquiry-based social service designed to serve clients, or a field-based research activity designed to advance knowledge. Problems of the internal validity, representativeness, generalizability, and replicability of study findings take on a different light, depending on which stance one adopts.[1]

Another basis for disagreement is whether phenomena ought to be manipulated in order to be studied or whether methodology ought to be developed to study phenomena as they exist. Those individuals seeking new approaches fall on the latter side of the issue, while the traditionalists fall on the former. Some traditionalists have even suggested that society itself must change before evaluation can become useful.

If, however, evaluation research is to make its full contribution, substantial changes must be made in society's overall approach to social programming. Legislators and other public officials reflecting widespread public concern must raise significantly their demands for the effectiveness and efficiency of programs. In addition, they must learn to focus more on program goals so that they can assume a more experimental attitude toward specific programming strategies [Caro, 1971, p. 28].

Probably the crux of the disagreement, however, lies in whether one takes evaluation to be a confirmatory or an exploratory endeavor. Listen to some traditionalists:

Successful implementation of a true or a strong quasi-experimental design in an evaluation is a difficult task. The use of such a design must be weighed against its alternatives, which are passive correlational techniques such as path analysis, and qualitative methods such as participant observation. Such qualitative and passive quantitative approaches have properties that can complement well a true or a strong quasi-experimental design. However, it is widely acknowledged that they are not sufficient for drawing causal inferences, and *a causal inference about the impact of a program is the primary goal of a summative evaluation.* Because they allow more confident causal inferences, use of a true or a strong quasi-experimental design is recommended [Cook et al., 1977, p. 135, italics added].

Clearly, most of the theorists searching for new evaluation methods see evaluation as much more exploratory, seeking to identify and describe currently unknown relationships rather than to confirm existing assumptions of treatment impact.

Historically, the social sciences, especially psychology, have been self-critical of their own methodologies (for example, Bakan, 1974; Borgatta & Bohrnstedt, 1974). The same is true in evaluation, where many traditionalists recognize the limitations of their methods; indeed, most of the critics of the traditional approach were themselves well trained in quantitative, experimental methods. Campbell (1976) notes that their criticisms

are often well-grounded in the experimentalist's own framework: experiments implementing a single treatment in a single setting are profoundly ambiguous as to what caused what; there is a precarious rigidity in the measurement system, limiting recorded outcomes to those dimensions anticipated in advance; process is often neglected in an experimental program focused on the overall effect of a complex treatment, and thus knowing such effects has only equivocal implications for program replication or improvement; broadgauge programs are often hopelessly ambiguous as to goals and relevant indicators; changes of treatment program during the course of an ameliorative experiment, while practically essential, make input-output experimental comparisons uninterpretable; social programs are often implemented in ways that are poor from an experimental design point of view; even under well-controlled situations, experimentation is a profoundly tedious and equivocal process; experimentation is too slow to be politically useful; etc. All these are true enough, often enough to motivate a vigorous search for alternatives [pp. 8-9].

Campbell goes on to say that although he finds unpersuasive the qualitative-knowing alternatives suggested so far, he advocates that

one should attempt to systematically tap all the qualitative common-sense program critiques and evaluations that have been generated among the program staff, program clients and their families, and community observers. While quantitative procedures such as questionnaires and rating scales will often be introduced at this stage for reasons of convenience in collecting and summarizing, non-quantitative methods of collection and compiling should also be considered, such as hierarchically organized discussion groups. Where such evaluations are contrary to the quantitative results, the quantitative results should be regarded as suspect until the reasons for the discrepancy are well understood. Neither is infallible, of course. But for many of us, what needs to be emphasized is that the quantitative results may be as mistaken as the qualitative [p. 13].

Thus, even some of the strictest traditionalists support the simultaneous use of qualitative and quantitative methods, relying on accumulated public experience with the methods to illustrate the utility and limitations of each.

There is general agreement among evaluation theorists and practitioners, both traditionalists and revisionists, that the field of evaluation has not yet fulfilled its promise, not yet lived up to its social role as the provider of relevant, useful, timely information for the assessment of educational and social programs and for the establishment of social policy. While the goal is mutually acknowledged, the means to reach it are hotly contested. The traditionalists' response to the challenge is to redouble efforts:

> *if we accept bald criticism of experiments without question, we will compromise our goals without ever having tried to reach them* [Boruch & Rindskopf, 1977, p. 152, italics in original].

The revisionists' response is to

> expand the art and science of evaluation to include crucially important factors that have not really been taken account of in the past [Guba, Note 1, p. 16].

In the final analysis, both camps acknowledge the need for exploring new alternatives in evaluation:

> This is not to say that developing alternatives to randomized experiments is unjustified, of course. There will always be situations in which randomization is physically impossible, politically impractical, or ethically unacceptable. The crucial issue is determining whether these conditions actually prevail and uncovering their nature so that high-quality evaluation — including experiments — can be designed around these constraints [Boruch & Rindskopf, 1977, p. 153].

Practitioner support for new methods. There is evidence to suggest that evaluation practitioners are also looking for new approaches to their work. Although the most pressing problems of evaluation within local school districts and state departments concern the lack of resources and sufficient professional staff, some practitioners have argued for new methods.

Stenzel (Note 2), a state department evaluator, has argued that evaluation methods are needed for use in small school districts where evaluation staff have little time, resources, or expertise. Evaluation methods are needed which do a better job cf identifying and communicating with various groups, methods which incorporate an understanding of their values and data needs. He argues that evaluators need to know more about how educational decisions are made in local school districts and that they need to tie evaluation into that process. Evaluators also need to know more about the political process within which evaluation operates. Stenzel advocates the study of "natural evaluations" in real settings.

Law (Note 3), another state department evaluator, has argued that traditional evaluation methods which emphasize experimental studies often *cannot* be implemented in state department evaluation contexts. Further, such methods lack utility in shaping state policy and in making state-level decisions. Law argues for new approaches to evaluation on the grounds that the current experimental and testing approaches are not sensitive to the political context of state department evaluation practice, a condition which contributes greatly to their lack of utility.

A recent study of local school district evaluation practice by Lyon et al. (1979) included questions concerning how the effectiveness of local evaluation efforts might be increased. Forty-two percent of the respondents indicated that increased computer time and computer facilities would help, while 31% indicated that information about effective school district evaluation practices was needed. Eight percent of the respondents noted the need for resolution of quasi-experimental design limitations in the local context. Lyon (1979) reports that for metropolitan districts having enrollments of 45,000 students or more, information about effective evaluation practices was indicated as one of the top four items which would most improve unit effectiveness. These data suggest the need not only for the development of new methods but also for the study of method effectiveness within naturalistic settings.

In a similar vein, Caulley and Smith (1980) asked 25 state departments of education about the adequacy of their evaluation methods. Twelve states — virtually half — reported that there were evaluations for which they had inadequate methods, while 15 states indicated that there were information needs of decision makers for which they did not have sufficient methods. Eleven states indicated that they were occasionally required to use methods which they thought were unsuitable, and 18 of the 25 states (72 percent) indicated that they would like to try new evaluation methods, suggesting such approaches as goal-free and self-evaluation procedures.

Thus, many practitioners at the state and local level in education have indicated a need for alternative approaches to evaluation and for evidence of the effectiveness of these methods.

Educators' support for new evaluation methods. Educators have also indicated support for alternative approaches to evaluation. Bernard McKenna, giving testimony on behalf of the National Education Association (Note 4), has argued that the federal government should do research and development, and encourage others to do research and development, in evaluation. Among other items, he argues that evaluation research is needed which focuses on conditions and processes of instruction as well as on its outcomes. Evaluation is needed which employs new types of evaluative criteria, such as determining to what extent education is democratic, helpful, humane, wholesome, enjoyable, fulfilling, and reflective of highest American values. He calls for alternatives to the use of standardized measures in evaluation, advocating the use of a broad range of evaluation criteria and assessment devices. Evaluation processes are needed which integrate curriculum, instruction, and assessment activities so that evaluation provides greater benefit in instructional areas. McKenna argues that new methods are needed which involve representatives of all stakeholders in evaluation, as well as methods which work in the naturalistic settings of local schools. He also advocates the study of evaluation success; that is, he urges that more work be done on meta-evaluation and on the study of evaluation utility.

The Northwest Regional Educational Laboratory (Note 5) recently conducted a survey of educators in six northwestern states, asking about educational priorities. Questionnaires were mailed to a random sample of 1800 teachers and administrators, 65% of whom responded. When asked which of 19 different topics they thought *would* be receiving greater emphasis ten years from now (topics such as program evaluation, citizen involvement, declining enrollment, educational equity, and graduation requirements), they chose program evaluation, bargaining/negotiation, and teacher evaluation, respectively, as the top three topics. When asked which of the same topics they felt *should* be receiving greater emphasis in the next ten years, they ranked program evaluation first, staff development second, and teacher evaluation third. Educational evaluation was ranked seventh in a list of 11 areas where improvement over the next ten years would be most important to the individual respondent (school finance and teacher preparation were ranked one and two, respectively).

Thus, we see that many educators, local teachers, and administrators are concerned about the improvement of evaluation. Many of them agree that there is a need for the development of more effective evaluation methods. On theoretical and practical grounds we see theorists, practitioners, and educators arguing for improved methodology in educational evaluation. In fact, the theoretical arguments summarized above are not restricted to evaluation in education but pertain to evaluation in all areas of social service: health, justice, welfare, community development, housing, and so on. There is indeed a considerable need for and interest in the development of new methods of evaluation. But how might new evaluation methods improve evaluation practice? That is the question to which we now turn.

The Nature of Methodological Improvement of Practice

Methodological improvements affect practice mainly by changing the way we think about what we do and how we can do it; such improvements broaden our perspective on evaluation.

> Yes, I think that methodology has a profound if indirect and oblique influence on practice. Methodology is, after all, different ways of doing things for different purposes. Change methodology and you change, to some extent at least, the problems we attack. Perhaps more important for educational research, problems that have seemed intractable because of their complexity are now becoming tractable and amenable to scientific scrutiny for attack [Kerlinger, 1977, pp. 9-10].

A new methodology, of itself, will not produce better evaluations; only evaluation practitioners can produce better evaluations. As Kaplan (1964) notes, methodology provides a reconstructed logic from which the logic-in-use of practitioners may be independent. But methodological advances can remove constraints that prohibit practitioners from optimal performance. As Kaplan (1964, p. 24) says, "the most important contribution methodology can make to science is, in Peirce's phrase, to help unblock the roads of inquiry."

In educational evaluation, both traditionalists and revisionists have argued that new methods are needed to remove evaluation roadblocks. As evaluators, we are not sure which of our methods are of most use in certain situations; in other situations we feel we have no truly effective tools; and at times we are convinced we do not even know the nature of the roadblocks preventing better evaluations. These conditions argue for increased attention to methodology as one means of improving evaluation practice. Furthermore, while we have identified perhaps two major methodological approaches, experimental studies and naturalistic investigations, it would certainly be premature and shortsighted not to look beyond these approaches to other alternatives. What is needed is a tolerant period in which to search for alternative methodological approaches.

Excessive reliance on a given methodology can breed professional conformity which discourages innovative and unconventional approaches — a conformity wherein efforts, though deemed rigorous, remain unproductive. That this is the risk of any single method or approach has long been recognized. In 1890, geologist Thomas C. Chamberlin described a process for guarding against allegiance to a single point of view; his recommendations are of interest here. Chamberlin urged that multiple working hypotheses should simultaneously be kept in mind.

> The effort is to bring up into view every rational explanation of a new phenomena, and to develop every tenable hypothesis respecting their cause and history. The investigator thus becomes the parent of a family of hypotheses; and, by his parental relation to all, he is forbidden to fasten his affections unduly upon any one. . . . Having thus neutralized the partialities of his emotional nature, he proceeds with a certain natural mental attitude which he enforces with erectness toward the investigation, knowing well that some of his intellectual children will die before maturity, yet feeling that several of them may survive the results of final investigation, since it is often the outcome of inquiry that several causes are found to be involved instead of a single one [Chamberlin, 1965, p. 756].

Thus, evaluation methodologists need to develop and consider multiple working methodologies, knowing that some will prove ineffective or untenable but also knowing that several methods are likely to emerge which will be of use in the practice of evaluation. (One would not expect individual evaluators to subsequently employ simultaneous multiple methodologies, but would expect practitioners to become eclectic, as they are in other professional fields.)

As Chamberlin observed, such an approach to the development of new methods should promote thoroughness, parallel complex views of the same phenomena, and the ability to perceive evaluation phenomena both analytically and synthetically. Such an approach would enable the evaluation discipline to advance its methodology on multiple fronts and to clear barriers to the successful practice of evaluation with greater alacrity. *Our goal should thus be optimum*

matches among methodology, the purpose of an individual study, and the nature of the phenomena being studied – not the superiority of a single overarching methodology, nor methodological diversity for its own sake.
Of course, such an approach is not without drawbacks; straightforward solutions would become even more rare, students of evaluation would need to be familiar with even more material, and practitioners would face an expanding array of options. Chamberlin warned that his approach had to be cautiously applied to practical affairs. He reminded us that consistently applying a poorer set of procedures may produce better results than indecisively using a superior set of procedures. Quick decisions, even if slightly in error, are often better than precise decisions which take too long to make.

Therefore, while evaluation theorists should pursue multiple working methodologies, it is not necessary or even desirable that each practitioner be expert in the use of a full array of methodological tools. Methodologists do not aid practitioners by weighing them down with methodological niceties or by distracting their attention from major substantive issues. Kaplan (1964) warns that excessive attention "can be diverted from substantive to methodological problems, so that we are forever perfecting how to do something without ever getting around to doing it even imperfectly" (p. 25). Methodologists', as well as practitioners', attention must ultimately focus on the substantive issues of evaluation. The final test of methodological innovations must be their contribution to clearing the road for better evaluation practice. We should hope our efforts contribute to the same ends which motivated Chamberlin in 1890:

> The total outcome is greater care in ascertaining the facts, and greater discrimination and caution in drawing conclusions. I am confident, therefore, that the general application of this method to the affairs of social and civic life would go far to remove those misunderstandings, misjudgments, and misrepresentations which constitute so pervasive an evil in our social and political atmospheres. . . . The remedy lies, indeed, partly in charity, but more largely in correct intellectual habits, in a predominant, ever-present disposition to see things as they are, and to judge them in the full light of an unbiased weighing of evidence applied to all possible constructions, accompanied by a withholding of judgment when the evidence is insufficient to justify conclusions [1965, p. 759].

Given a need for new approaches to evaluation, then, and the desire to develop a range of alternatives, how does one begin? Since many other areas of human activity employ methods, we might begin by seeing what we can borrow from them.

Searching Other Fields for Methods

The practice of evaluation incorporates elements of inquiry, valuing, and social change and so can be seen to share common attributes with three major areas of human enterprise: the sciences, the arts, and the world of practical affairs.

- Evaluation, as currently conceived, is based on *inquiry* procedures; it thus shares with the sciences a preoccupation with the question "What is True?" and is aimed at increasing understanding.

- Evaluation is also concerned with *value* and shares with the arts an attempt to answer the question "What is Beautiful and Good?" aiming to increase our appreciation and expression of goodness and beauty.

- Evaluations are conducted to facilitate social *change* and share with the world of practical affairs a concern with the question "What is Viable and Fair?" aiming to improve the human condition.

If we are to develop new methods and new points of view for evaluation, then we might begin by examining the methods used in the sciences, arts, and practical affairs to deal with problems of inquiry, value, and change. Evaluation shares (a) a search for understanding with such areas as physics, anthropology, geography, astronomy, biology, and psychology; (b) a search for value with such areas as music, art, poetry, literature, and theater; and (c) a search for social improvement with such areas as law, journalism, medicine, education, and engineering. Upon closer examination, it is clear that areas such as journalism, medicine, literature, and psychology all seek to integrate elements of inquiry, value, and change, just as evaluation does. There is, therefore, a broad range of areas that might serve as models for evaluation.

To date, however, the majority of evaluation method has focused on inquiry and has come from a narrow range of disciplines in the social sciences. Since evaluation shares common interests with a great many other areas, it seems plausible to suggest that evaluation methodology might benefit from a study of these areas and that, in fact, these areas might provide alternative sources of evaluation method (see Hastings, 1969).

Levels of Methodological Discourse

In discussing the methods of areas which range across the sciences, arts, and practical affairs, it is important to be clear about the level of discourse we are using. There is little common-language distinction of the levels of methodology; the terms "method," "technique," "means," and "procedure" are used fairly interchangeably (Random House, 1966; Crowell, 1962). Therefore, the following distinctions, which have been adapted from Gephart (1977), are offered to facilitate subsequent discussions of evaluation methodology.[2]

Methodology, Level I: Point of View. A disciplinary point of view is a constellation of conceptual, value, social, and philosophical elements which define the nature of the phenomena of interest, the purpose and meaningfulness of the discipline's activities, and the social and historical context in which the discipline operates. The point of view establishes the discipline's goals (while levels II, III, and I V relate more to the discipline's means) and tends to provide the unifying commonality for disciplinary membership. For example, educational evaluators generally hold the common point of view that education can and should be understood, evaluated, and improved; poets hold that the recognition, creation, and preservation of beauty and meaning are intrinsic, rather than utilitarian, goods.

Methodology, Level II: Paradigm. A paradigm is a constellation of elements which direct scientific activities. "Law, theory, application, and instrumentation together provide models from which spring particular coherent traditions of scientific research" (Kuhn, 1970, p. 10). It is at the level of paradigm that some of the most serious divisions within a discipline develop, resulting in antagonistic schools of thought. In educational evaluation, one can identify schools devoted to the naturalistic and experimentalist paradigms, schools split along objectivist and subjectivist epistemologies (House, 1978). In art we can identify representational versus nonrepresentational approaches.

Methodology, Level III: Operational Strategy. An operational strategy more or less specifies a general sequence of activities designed to achieve some end. Such strategies operationalize the approaches suggested by the paradigm being used. In educational evaluation, most attention has been directed toward this level of methodology with the generation of numerous evaluation "models" (see, for example, Stake, 1976; Worthen & Sanders, 1973; House, 1978; and Guba, Note 1, for alternative classifications and discussions of these models). In engineering, for example, an operational strategy for equipment construction might include such steps as design, blueprint, materials specification, prototype development, and full production.

Methodology, Level IV: Technique. Techniques are discrete procedural sequences which result in outcomes of specific prespecified form; they are the constituent elements of operational strategies. A narrow range of research techniques on data collection, measurement, and statistical analysis serves as the primary focus of most evaluation training programs. It is at this level that a discipline member is generally considered to have mastered "the trade"; for example, a journalist's skill in using various techniques to check the veracity of an informant's claim.

These four levels of methodology reflect different degrees of abstraction and generality of methodological discourse, although in practice such distinctions are not always clear. When considering the translation of methodologies from areas in the sciences, arts, and practical affairs for use in evaluation, it will be helpful to remember that this translation can take place at four different levels of discourse. This distinction also highlights the levels at which evaluators disagree about their methodology — at the technique level (arguments about the appropriate use of norm-referenced versus criterion-referenced measurement), at the operational strategy level (the competing models of evaluation), and at the paradigm level (the warring epistemologies [Gephart, 1978]). As we begin more seriously to consider evaluation activities as a form of art or practical affairs rather than science, we can expect these differences also to extend to the point-of-view level.

Means to Methodological Development

Thus far we have discussed various background issues related to the development of new evaluation methods: Is there a need for new methods? How is methodological improvement accomplished? Why might we look to other areas for new method? At what levels of discourse might we find new methods? We now turn to the more pragmatic concerns of how we can actually develop, test, and gain acceptance of new methods in evaluation.

What are the possible means of developing alternative methods? How have new methods been developed in the past? Are there specific strategies that will enable us to develop new methods?

We might look to mathematics and the physical sciences for models of how to develop new methods. Since evaluation at present is viewed as an applied form of social science, and since the social sciences have traditionally looked to the physical sciences for guidance, this seems to be a logical place to start. There are, of course, other areas we could look to for direction, such as within social science itself (see, for example, Judson, 1979). Limited time and resources do not permit a search of even the major possibilities. Since the relevant literature in mathematics and physics is most readily available, it provides the most obvious place to begin such a search. There remains the possibility, of course, that some other area might provide more useful models of how to develop new methods.

One of the most popular discussions of the creation of new methods in science is Thomas Kuhn's book (1970), *The Structure of Scientific Revolutions.* Kuhn argues that new discoveries begin with the awareness of anomaly; that is, with the recognition that natural events are not in accord with the expectations created by the discipline's methodology. As the anomaly is explored in detail, it becomes clear that adjustments in existing approaches will not resolve the condition. A whole new way of viewing nature is required. Following a period of professional crisis and frustration based on the inability to resolve the anomaly, a new approach emerges.

Failure of existing rules is the prelude to a search for new ones [p. 68].

Novelty emerges only with difficulty, manifested by resistance, against a background provided by expectation. Initially, only the anticipated and usual are experienced even under circumstances where anomaly is later to be observed. Further acquaintance, however, does result in awareness of something wrong or does relate the effect to something that has gone wrong before. That awareness of anomaly opens a period in which conceptual categories are adjusted until the initially anomalous has become the anticipated. At this point the discovery has been completed [p. 64]. . . .

The proliferation of competing articulations, the willingness to try anything, the expression of explicit discontent, the recourse to philosophy and to debate over fundamentals, all these are symptoms of a transition from normal to extraordinary research [pp. 90-91].

Holton (1973, 1975) traces the development of major scientific breakthroughs to *thematic reversal* within a discipline. A methodological thema is a guiding theme, such as the preference for viewing nature reductionistically rather than holistically. Holton observes that radically new developments have often resulted from adopting a thema antithetical to the discipline's prevailing view, such as:

(a) Newton's establishment of the theme that evidences of chaos could be explained in terms of some underlying order (the apparently erratic motion of planets could be understood to result from overlapping orderly movements);

(b) the reversal occasioned by kinetic theory which suggested that examples of simple order could be explained in terms of an underlying chaos (an air-filled balloon stays at rest as a result of the random motion of an immense number of air molecules);

(c) the re-reversal caused by Einstein's paper on Brownian motion which showed that simple Newtonian laws could be used to explain the action of invisible, submicroscopic molecules bombarding a dust particle;

(d) the subsequent reversal occasioned by Heisenberg's Uncertainty Principle which explained Newtonian order on the basis of a probabilistic sequence of a random number generator.

Since Parmenides and Heraclitus, the members of the thematic dyad of constancy and change have vied for loyalty, and so have, ever since Pythagoras and Thales, the efficacy of mathematics versus the efficacy of materialistic or mechanistic models. The (usually unacknowledged) presuppositions pervading the work of scientists have long included also the thematic couples of experience and symbolic formalism, complexity and simplicity, reductionism and holism, discontinuity and the continuum, hierarchical structure and unity, the use of mechanisms versus teleological or anthropomorphic modes of approach.

These together with others further discussed in the essays and perhaps a few more — a total of fewer than 50 couples or triads — seem historically to have sufficed for negotiating the great variety of discoveries [Holton, 1973, p. 29].

What seems certain is that regardless of temporary victories for one side or another, the dialectic process of this sort between a thema and its antithema, and hence between the adherents of two or more theories embodying them respectively, is almost inevitable, and is perhaps among the most powerful energizers of research. If the past is a guide, this process will last as long as there are scientists interested in putting questions to nature and to one another [1973, p. 26].

These accounts, in the main, only describe methodological innovations as reconstructed from a historical point of view; they suggest little about how an individual might consciously and systematically attempt to develop new methods. Indeed, philosophers of science frequently consider the means by which new theories and new methods are developed to be outside their realm of interest. Karl Popper states:

> My view of this matter for what it is worth is that there is no such thing as a logical model of having new ideas, or a logical reconstruction of this process [quoted in Cohen, 1977, p. 338].

Philosopher R. B. Braithwaite offers the following view:

> The history of a science is the history of the development of scientific systems from those containing . . . few generalizations . . . into imposing structures with a hierarchy of hypotheses. . . . The problems raised by this development are of many different kinds. These are historical problems, both as to what causes the individual scientist to discover a new idea, and as to what causes the general acceptance of scientific ideas. The solution of these historical problems involves the individual psychology of thinking and the sociology of thought. *None of these questions are our business here* [quoted in Holton, 1973, p. 24].

It appears that, historically, all we have to guide us is general surmise and anecdotes. Kuhn attempts a generalized characterization of a scientist working under conditions of "extraordinary science."

> Faced with an admittedly fundamental anomaly in theory, the scientist's first effort will often be to isolate it more precisely and to give it structure. Though now aware that they cannot be quite right, he will push the rules of normal science harder than ever to see . . . just where and how far they can be made to work [1970, pp. 86-87].

Kuhn suggests that during this period the scientist will also be conducting experiments just to see what will happen, "looking for an effect whose nature he cannot quite guess" (p. 87). At the same time, he will be developing speculative theories in an attempt to explain the observed anomaly.

Perhaps studying the behavior of innovative scientists will provide suggestions on how to develop new approaches. We have many autobiographical accounts of the spontaneous emergence of creative insight, one of the most famous being that of the French mathematician Poincaré:

> For fifteen days I struggled to prove that no functions analogous to those I have since called *Fuchsian functions* could exist; I was then very ignorant. Every day I sat down at my work table where I spent an hour or two; I tried a great number of combinations and arrived at no result. One evening, contrary to my custom, I took black coffee; I could not go to sleep; ideas swarmed up in clouds; I sensed them clashing until, to put it so, a pair would hook together to form a stable combination. By morning I had established the existence of a class of Fuchsian functions, those derived from the hypergeometric series. I had only to write up the results, which took me a few hours.
>
> Next, I wished to represent these functions by the quotient of two series; this idea was perfectly conscious and thought out; analogy with elliptic functions guided me. I asked myself what must be the properties of these series if they existed, and without difficulty I constructed the series which I called thetafuchsian. . . .
>
> I then undertook the study of certain arithmetical questions without much apparent success and without suspecting that such matters could have the slightest connection with my previous studies. Disgusted at my lack of success, I went to spend a few days at the seaside and thought of something else. One day, while walking along the cliffs, the idea came to me, again with the same characteristics of brevity, suddenness, and immediate certainty [reprinted in Bell, 1965, pp. 550-551].

This literature not being very prescriptive about how to gain insights concerning new methods, we might look for a moment outside mathematics and physics. For example, after studying 13 famous psychologists, Cohen (1977) reports that most of their creative insights occur while they are writing. Cohen argues that psychologists do not seem to have the kind of insight typical of physical scientists, but have "a much more partial, *post hoc* intuition as they attempt to make sense of results they have already obtained" (p. 341).

In summary, from this brief survey there appear to be no strong historical precedents to follow in constructing a programmatic effort to develop new evaluation methods systematically. Our only hints are that our developmental strategy should try to include features which would enable us to

- identify and reverse prevalent methodological thema;
- isolate, clarify, and highlight the major shortcomings (anomalies) of existing methods;
- speculatively generate new methodologies and employ them to clarify their unknown nature;
- concentrate intensively on methodological problems, trusting to the fruits of analytic work and spontaneous insight; and
- engage in writing as a means of generating further methodological insight.

But a programmatic effort needs more structure than this, and, not having found a model to follow, we have constructed our own as described in the next section.

Systematic Means for Developing Methods

Francis Bacon wrote:

> For the history that I require and design, special care is to be taken that it be of wide range and made to the measure of the universe. For the world is not to be narrowed till it will go into the understanding (which has been done hitherto), but the understanding is to be expanded and opened till it can take in the image of the world [from *The Parasceve*, quoted in Eiseley, 1973].

Such is the breadth of perspective Bacon brought to his formalization to the scientific method of inquiry. Our attempts to develop new evaluation methods can have no narrower a scope, drawing as they do not only on the sciences but on the arts and practical affairs as well.

Since there is little precedent to follow in developing a system for generating new evaluation methodologies, what is needed is a "preconstructed" logic or rationale and an operational plan from which to initiate developmental activities. With the accumulation of experience in formally developing methods and an awareness of the actual logic-in-use employed, it should be possible at some later point to develop a more systematic reconstructed logic to direct subsequent developmental activities.

A fully articulated preconstructed logic is not feasible at this point, nor is it desirable in light of the exploratory nature of the development of new methods, but it would be useful to chart a general course and to highlight some of the more important issues likely to be encountered. Two alternative strategies for the development of new methods are touched upon in the remainder of this section of the chapter. Two subsequent sections then deal, respectively, with issues related to the testing of such methods and their acceptance by evaluation practitioners and theorists.

The two strategies for the development of new evaluation methodologies described below both presume the use of alternative disciplines in the sciences, arts, and world of practical affairs as sources of new methods. These disciplines contain existing methods which in many cases are well articulated, tested, and the product of substantial developmental effort over a period of many years. It would, of course, be possible to attempt to develop new evaluation methodologies *de novo,* but it seems wasteful, inefficient, and parochial to attempt such efforts unless one can argue that these alternative disciplines have little of use to offer. Since that claim cannot yet be made, initial attempts to formally develop new evaluation methods should at least assess the potential contributions of these alternative disciplines.

As Campbell (1976) notes, workers from many social science disciplines (economics, sociology, statistics, psychology, political science, and education) are already involved in the evaluation of social programs. However, very few specialists from outside the social sciences participate in educational and social evaluations at any level. In recent years, the newer evaluation approaches have tended to draw upon some of the arts and practical affairs disciplines. Approaches such as those of Stake (1975a, 1975b), Wolf (1974, 1975), Rippey (1973), Eisner (1975), and Parlett and Hamilton (1976) are based not on the more traditional agronomy/physics/biology models but on law/anthropology/art models. For example, these approaches are more compatible with a naturalistic inquiry paradigm than with an experimental paradigm (Guba, 1978). Although some innovative, pioneering work has been done, most of the possible alternative disciplines have not yet received even cursory inspection.

Analytic procedures. One primary means of developing new methods would be through the use of *analytic* procedures. A developmental system based on analytic procedures could be thought of as containing three phases: structural delineation, isomorphic comparisons, and methodological translations. The purpose of such an analytic system would be to identify similar methods and translate them for use in evaluation.

In Phase I, structural delineation, the alternative discipline would be analyzed into its structural components, including an identification of its (1) point of view, (2) dominant paradigms, (3) operational strategies, (4) techniques, (5) social role and context of use, (6) historical development, and (7) major methodological issues. Procedures such as Gephart and Bartos' (1969) procedure for profiling research or Gowin's (Gowin & Millman, 1978) QUEMAC procedure for creating critical abstracts of evaluation studies might be adapted for delineating the structure of a discipline's methodology.

In Phase II, isomorphic comparisons, the structural elements of the alternative discipline would be compared with similar elements in evaluation to identify areas of overlap and uniqueness. Elements of the alternative discipline which appeared better developed than their evaluation counterparts or which potentially filled an evaluation need could then be singled out for special attention.

In Phase III, methodological translation, adaptations could be made to selected elements of the alternative discipline to make them compatible for use in evaluation; alternatively, changes in conventional evaluation procedures could be made to accommodate the new methods.

The development of such an analytic system can be seen as a design, not a research, problem and as such might be amenable to the design strategies of Nadler (1970) or the metamethodology strategies of Hutchinson (Note 6).

Synthetic procedures. A second primary means of developing new evaluation methodologies would be through the use of *synthetic* approaches. A developmental system based on synthetic approaches would employ such procedures as thematic reversal, metaphoric reasoning, and futuring. The procedural steps for such a system are not as easily specified as are those for the analytic approach, since less is known about formalized synthetic approaches. I have already touched on the nature of thematic reversal, and in the next chapter I will present a discussion written by Egon Guba on the nature of metaphoric adaptation as a technique for the development of new methods. Guba discusses the use of retroduction as a mode of metaphoric reasoning which provides synthetic combinations of both disciplines. Futuring techniques can also be used to project the nature and role of evaluation methodology under various mutual adaptations of the evaluation discipline and the alternative discipline (see Smith, Note 7, for five illustrations of this technique).

Both analytic and synthetic approaches could be used at all four levels of methodological discourse. However, because of their low level of abstraction and their usual specification in concrete details, operational strategies and techniques could more easily be addressed through analytic procedures than could paradigms and points of view. Adaptations at these latter two levels of discourse are more likely to require synthetic approaches due to the relative mutual independence of these elements across disciplines. Diverse operational strategies and techniques can often be ordered along such common substrata as purpose, focus, locus of input, manipulation procedures, and nature of output. The ordering of points of view and paradigms along substrata is less certain because there is less resolution of these elements in the parent disciplines.

This book contains seven examples of attempts to develop new methods, primarily through the use of metaphoric adaptation. The authors also employed some analytic procedures and variously attended to all four levels of methodological discourse. Their primary starting point, however, was to use their alternative field (law, architecture, philosophy, and so on) as a metaphor for evaluation. The next chapter contains a more detailed discussion of this process.

Assessing the Quality of New Methodologies

Once prototype versions of new methods are developed, they need to be subjected to field trial. The purpose of these field trials is to bring empirical, practical, and social value concerns to the fore in continuing the developmental process of creating new methodologies. Having built a prototype based on conceptual and logical concerns, the next step would be to consider practical concerns of feasibility and cost benefit, empirical concerns of effectiveness and utility, and social value concerns of social bias and fairness. These concerns could best be incorporated into the developmental cycle through actual field trials of the proposed methods.

These field trials would therefore be a part of the formative process — tryouts which provide developmental feedback — but they would not be field tests which would validate a method's utility and worth. As has been argued elsewhere (Smith, 1979), the validation of a new evaluation methodology is a long-term, disciplinary process of accumulating public, experience-based knowledge of the utility of the method in diverse settings. The field trials described below would provide suggestive evidence, not definitive conclusions.

The developmental strategy proposed here of initial conceptual development and then immediate field trial in applied settings is similar to Azrin's (1977) proposal that methods for the improvement of clinical practice are best developed by devising new methods based on previous research but then emphasizing clinical outcomes in evaluating the efficacy of the methods. This approach tends to be primarily methods-focused in the early conceptual stages and problem-focused in the field trial stages. The nature of the field trial activities depends on the preexisting state of knowledge regarding the method; highly innovative methods would require much more elaboration and trial in the field than previously well-articulated methods which would need minimal translation for use in evaluation. The purpose of the field trials would not be to determine which is the best possible method in a given setting, but to understand better the unique contribution and incremental utility of each of a complex of possible methods.

The nature of an appropriate field trial would differ depending on the level of methodological discourse. Consider the four levels of discourse discussed earlier from the more concrete to the more abstract.

Techniques are the discrete procedural sequences which result in specific, prespecified outcomes. Field trials of techniques seem fairly straightforward. For example, new methods of data collection (document tracking, photographic descriptions), data analysis (path analysis, geographic displays), or information sharing (congressional hearings, story telling), could be incorporated into conventional evaluation studies as supplemental efforts, providing developmental feedback and comparisons with traditional techniques. The quality of a new technique could be assessed along three major criteria dimensions:

- Effectiveness — Does the technique produce the specified outcomes? What is the quality of the specified outcomes? Are the outcomes useful and of benefit to the evaluation practitioner? What side effects are produced?

- Feasibility — Can the specified procedures be implemented? Are the necessary inputs, agents, and catalysts available? Are the time, personnel, and resource requirements reasonable?

- Compatibility — Can the technique be integrated into ongoing operations? Are special training or arrangements needed? Do practitioners and clients find the technique acceptable? Can the technique be adapted to fit various local conditions?

Technique trials would probably be the easiest to conduct, since the intervention would be discrete and well defined and expectations of its impact and outcomes could be established a priori.

Operational strategies specify a general sequence of events or activities designed to achieve some end. For example, operational strategies imply — if not explicitly state — the timing and use of various techniques or classes of techniques (that is, data collection or reporting techniques). A new operational strategy, therefore, would have a more substantial impact on the operations of a traditional evaluation. Testing of a new strategy (such as when one tries out a new evaluation model) would require design changes in a traditional study. The test intervention would often be less bounded, discrete, or prescriptive than a technique trial; consequently, the assessment of its impact would be more difficult and its conclusions more equivocal. The criterion dimensions for assessing the quality of a new operational strategy would include those named for technique trials, though the focus of the questions would change somewhat:

- Effectiveness — What outcomes does the operational strategy produce? What are the quality of these outcomes? Are the outcomes useful and of benefit to the evaluation practitioners and their clients? What unanticipated effects occur?

- Feasibility — Can the operational strategy be implemented, and in how many different variations? Are the necessary agents, catalysts, and resources available to operationalize the strategy? What range of personnel, time, and resource requirements are needed for the strategy, and are they available? Can the evaluation staff adapt to the use of the new strategy?

- Compatibility — Can the operational strategy be integrated into ongoing operations? What special training and reorientation needs arise? What problems arise in matching the strategy to unit needs and managerial procedures?

A *paradigm* is a constellation of epistemological approaches, theoretical orientations, operational strategies, and sets of techniques employed in the pursuit of some disciplinary activity. To talk of testing a new paradigm strains the common usage we make of the term "field trial." Of course, to the extent that a new paradigm offers new operational strategies and techniques, these elements could be tested as indicated above. The test of a paradigm, however, would involve less a series of discrete studies than the historical evolution — or "revolution" according to Kuhn — of a disciplinary way of thought. Developing a new orientation for evaluation, such as shifting from an experimental to a naturalistic paradigm, involves changes in conceptual categories and value structures as well as changes in operational strategies and techniques. Disciplinary experience, not field trial, tests a paradigm. In studying the implementation of a new paradigm, however, one would need to be attentive not only to the above criteria but also to second-order effects. For example, how does the nature of the evaluation unit change under the new paradigm? Are the purpose and agency role of the unit modified? How do evaluation sponsors and clients react to a drastically different paradigm? What structural, personnel, and managerial aspects of the unit are affected?

A *point of view* is the constellation of conceptual, social, value, and philosophical elements which define a discipline. A new point of view would thus redefine the nature of the phenomena of interest and change the purpose of disciplinary activity; it would constitute a major upheaval in disciplinary activities and thought. For example, to reclassify evaluation as a branch of aesthetics instead of a branch of inquiry would constitute such a change in point of view. Evaluators would no longer be scientists but artists, theologians, or philosophers.

Under such a change, even what constitutes a test would have to be reexamined. The problem of testing a new point of view at this level thus becomes a problem for the historian and perhaps the philosopher. The heuristic value of the new point of view, its impact on the professional disciplines, and the cultural evolution of thought would be of concern. Thus, one could not test the quality of a new point of view in the way one tests the techniques, operational strategies, or even paradigms.

In terms of short-range developmental efforts to create new evaluation methodologies, it makes sense to consider field trials of techniques and operational strategies and perhaps even to document the effects of a paradigm shift. The real assessment of new paradigms and points of view, however, must be left to future historians and philosophers, though their conclusions will be based on the outcomes of our experiences.

Developing a new method and providing positive test results concerning its use do not ensure that individuals will readily adopt it. What prevents theorists and practitioners from conceptually accepting a new approach? That is the topic of the final section of this chapter.

The Acceptance of New Methodologies

The intransigence of man to accept change has long been noted:

> Custom is the principal magistrate of man's life. [Its predominance] is everywhere visible. Men . . . do just as they have done before; as if they were dead images and engines moved only by the wheels of custom [Francis Bacon, quoted in Eiseley, 1973, pp. 73-74].

Such reluctance to leave established views is no less common among scientists. In arguing for a naturalistic rather than an experimental paradigm for evaluation, Guba (1978) reminds us of the following observations.

> The competition between paradigms is not the sort of battle that can be resolved by proofs. . . . The transfer of allegiance from paradigm to paradigm is a conversion experience that cannot be forced. [Thomas S. Kuhn].

> Although I am fully convinced of the truth of the views given in this volume, . . . I by no means expect to convince experienced naturalists whose minds are stocked with a multitude of facts all viewed, during a long course of years, from a point of view directly opposite to mine. . . . But I look with confidence to the future, to young and rising naturalists, who will be able to view both sides of the question with impartiality [Charles Darwin].

The acceptance of a new methodology requires exposure to and familiarity with it, requires experience over time with it, and occasionally requires a new generation of theorists and practitioners.[3] A few observations on the psychology of methodological attachment might suggest why methodological change is so difficult.

It is clear that any traditional methodology provides the unimaginative individual with an established way of proceeding and the insecure individual with a clear means of attaining peer acceptance. Of course, established methodology also serves very useful functions of providing unity, direction, and quality assurance to a discipline's endeavors. However, none of these points would seem to explain the considerable *conceptual* difficulty many members of a discipline have in comprehending a new methodology at an intuitive and subjective level. The source of this difficulty would seem to be that over a period of time a methodology becomes incorporated into the tacit knowledge structure of discipline members. Since its very nature usually makes us unaware of this tacit knowledge, it is difficult for us to modify it and to accept the new tacit structure required by a fundamental methodological shift.

Polanyi (Polanyi & Prosch, 1975) states: "Personal, tacit assessments and evaluations, we see, are required at every step in the acquisition of knowledge — even 'scientific' knowledge" (p. 31). Polanyi argues that these tacit assessments are based on subsidiary awarenesses which provide a framework for integrating the meaning of our focal awareness — that is, the meaning of the current objects of our perception or thought.

> Consider the act of viewing a pair of stereoscopic pictures in the usual way, with one eye on each of the pictures. Their joint image might be regarded as a whole, composed of the two pictures as its parts. But we can get closer to understanding what is going on here if we note that, when looking through a stereo viewer, we see a stereo image at the focus of our attention and are also aware of the two stereo pictures in some peculiar nonfocal way. We seem to look through these two pictures, or past them, while we look straight at their joint image. We are indeed aware of them only as guides to the image on which we focus our attention. We can describe this relationship of the two pictures to the stereo image by saying that the two pictures function as *subsidiaries* to our seeing, their *joint* image, which is their joint meaning. This is the typical structure of tacit knowing [Polanyi & Prosch, 1975, p. 34].

After repeated use of a methodology's conceptual categories, value assumptions, epistemological framework, and operational procedures, we begin to see most of the world through this tacit, subsidiary structure. A major perceptual shift is thus required to assimilate a new methodology, since we must first remodel much of this tacit structure. If this view of "established methodology as crystallized tacit structure" is true, it would help explain why most major methodological breakthroughs are made either by young individuals or those who are new to a particular discipline (Kuhn, 1970).

Given the difficulty, then, in gaining acceptance for a new methodology, is there anything that can be used to facilitate this perceptual change? We might look to interdisciplinary projects where participants are routinely required to shift perceptual frameworks in order to communicate effectively. Petrie (1976, p. 14) suggests the use of metaphor in facilitating perceptual shifts in interdisciplinary work.

Metaphors traditionally have enabled us to gain an insight into a new area by juxtaposing language and concepts familiar in one area with a new area. One begins to see the similarities and differences between the literal uses of the metaphor and the new area to which we have been invited to apply the "lens" or "cognitive maps" supplied by the metaphor.

The use of metaphors may therefore not only provide us with a synthetic means of developing new evaluation methodologies, as discussed above, but also enable us to communicate better the nature of these new methods to evaluation practitioners and theorists, helping them reorder their tacit structures to adopt more flexibly these new methodologies.

This volume illustrates the use of metaphor to develop new connections between evaluation and other areas of human activity and to share the resulting insights with individuals interested in expanding the range of evaluation methods. In the next chapter I treat the topic of metaphor in more depth and then introduce the remaining chapters of the volume which are examples of the use of metaphorical thinking.

Notes

[1] While it is not necessary to forcibly dichotomize the possible social roles of formal evaluation, some writers feel that service versus research is a crucial distinction.

[2] By defining four levels of methodology, subsequent uses of the terms "methodology" and "methods" become ambiguous unless the level of discourse is specified. Thus, to avoid confusion, these two terms will be used only when the level of discourse is clear or when the point being made pertains to all levels of discourse.

[3] It should be noted that while methodological innovation is slow regardless of which of the four levels of discourse one examines, the following comments are most pertinent to the fundamental methodological shifts required by the introduction of new paradigms and disciplinary points of view.

Reference Notes

1. Guba, E. G. Educational evaluation: The state of the art. Invited address at the annual meeting of the Evaluation Network, St. Louis, Missouri, September 1977.
2. Stenzel, N. Critical needs for research and development in evaluation: Mutated or radical evolution? Public testimony given at the American Educational Research Association annual meeting, Boston, April 1980.
3. Law, A. The need for new approaches in state level evaluations. Paper prepared for the Northwest Regional Educational Laboratory, Portland, Oregon, 1980.
4. McKenna, B. Critical needs for research and development in evaluation: Holism versus partialism. Public testimony given at the American Educational Research Association annual meeting, Boston, April 1980.
5. Northwest Regional Educational Laboratory. Regional needs survey results. Portland, Oregon: Northwest Regional Educational Laboratory, 1980.
6. Hutchinson, T. E. Modus operandi for constructing technology transfer methodologies. Paper presented at the annual meeting of the American Educational Research Association, Toronto, Canada, March 1978.
7. Smith, N. L. The progress of educational evaluation: Rounding the first bends in the river. Invited address at the conference on "Educational Evaluation: Recent Progress — Future Needs," University of Minnesota Research and Evaluation Center, Minneapolis, Minnesota, May 1980.

References

Azrin, N. H. A strategy for applied research: Learning based but outcome oriented. *American Psychologist,* 1977, 32, 140-149.

Bakan, D. *On method: Toward a reconstruction of psychological investigation.* San Francisco: Jossey-Bass, 1974.

Bell, E. T. *Men of mathematics.* New York: Simon and Schuster, 1965.

Borgatta, E. F., & Borhnstedt, G. W. Some limitations on generalizability from social psychological experiments. *Sociological Methods & Research* 1974, 3, 111-120.

Boruch, R. F. On common contentions about randomized field experiments. In R. F. Boruch & H. W. Riecken (Eds.), *Experimental tests of public policy,* Boulder, CO: Westview Press, 1975.

Boruch, R. F., & Rinkskopf, D. On randomized experiments. approximations to experiments, and data analysis. In L. Rutman (Ed.), *Evaluation of research methods: A basic guide.* Beverly Hills, CA: Sage, 1977, pp. 143-176.

Brody, B. A. (Ed.). *Readings in the philosophy of science.* Englewood Cliffs, NJ: Prentice-Hall, 1970.

Campbell, D. T. Assessing the impact of planned social change. Occasional Paper No. 8. Kalamazoo: Evaluation Center, Western Michigan University, 1976.

Campbell, D. T., & Boruch, R. F. Making the case for randomized assignment to treatments by considering the alternatives: Six ways in which quasi-experimental evaluations in compensatory education tend to underestimate effects. In C. A. Bennett & A. A. Lumsdaine (Eds.). *Evaluation and experiment.* New York: Academic Press, 1975.

Campbell, D. T., & Stanley, J. C. *Experimental and quasi-experimental designs for research.* Chicago: Rand McNally, 1966.

Caro, F. G. (Ed.). *Readings in evaluation research.* New York: Russell Sage Foundation, 1971.

Caulley, D. N., & Smith, N. L. Program evaluation in state departments of education. *Evaluation News,* 1980, No. 14, 37-38.

Chamberlin, T. C. The method of multiple working hypotheses. *Science,* 1890. (Reprinted in *Science,* 1965, 148, 754-759.)

Cohen, D. *Psychologists on psychology.* New York: Taplinger, 1977.

Cook, T. D., & Campbell, D. T. The design and conduct of quasi-experiments and true experiments in field settings. In M. D. Dannetti (Ed.), *Handbook of industrial and organization psychology.* Chicago: Rand McNally, 1976, pp. 223-326.

Cook, T. D., Cook, F. L., & Mark, M. M. Randomized and quasi-experimental designs in evaluation research: An introduction. In L. Kutman (Ed.), *Evaluation research methods: A basic guide.* Beverly Hills, CA: Sage, 1977, pp. 103-139.

Cooley, W. W., & Lohnes, P. R. *Evaluation research in education.* New York: Irvington, 1976.

Crowell Company. *Roget's international thesaurus.* New York: Thomas Y. Crowell Company, 1962.

Eiseley, L. *The man who saw through time.* New York: Charles Scribner's Sons, 1973.

Eisner, E. W. The perceptive eye: Toward the reformation of educational evaluation. *Occasional Papers of the Stanford Evaluation Consortium.* Stanford, CA: Stanford University, 1975.

Gephart, W. J. Toward a taxonomy of empirically-based problem-solving strategies. *NSPER Notes,* 1977, 1, 3-7.

Gephart, W. J. On truth. *CEDR Quarterly,* 1978, 11, 1-6.

Gephart, W. J., & Bartos, B. B. Profiling instructional package. Occasional Paper No. 7. Bloomington, IN: Center on Evaluation Development and Research, Phi Delta Kappa, 1969.

Gilbert, J. P., Light, R. J., & Mosteller, F. Assessing social innovations: An empirical base for policy. In C. A. Bennett & A. A. Lumsdaine (Eds.), *Evaluation and experiment.* New York: Academic Press, 1975.

Gowin, D. B., & Millman, J. Meta-evaluation and a direction for research on evaluation. *CEDR Quarterly,* 1978, 11, 3-6.

Guba, E. G. *Toward a methodology of naturalistic inquiry in educational evaluation.* C.S.E. Monograph Series in Evaluation, No. 8. Los Angeles: Center for the Study of Evaluation, University of California, 1978.

Harrison, J. M., & Stein, H. H. *Muckraking: Past, present and future.* University Park: Pennsylvania State University Press, 1973.

Hastings, J. T. The kith and kin of educational measurers. *Journal of Educational Measurement,* 1969, 6, 127-130.

Holmes, O. W. Address to an assembly of undergraduates at Harvard College, February 17, 1886 quoted in J. M. Harrison & H. H. Stein, *Muckraking: Past, present and future.* University Park: Pennsylvania State University Press, 1973, pp. 1-2.

Holton, G. *Thematic origins of scientific thought: Kepler to Einstein.* Cambridge, MA: Harvard University Press, 1973.

Holton, G. The humanistic basis of scientific work. *Change,* 1975, 7, 24-29.

House, E. R. Assumptions underlying evaluation models. *Educational Researcher,* 1978, 7, 4-12.

Judson, H. F. *The eighth day of creation: Makers of the revolution in biology.* New York: Simon and Schuster, 1979.

Kaplan, A. *The conduct of inquiry.* San Francisco: Chandler, 1964.

Kerlinger, F. N. The influence of research on educational practice. *Educational Researcher,* 1977, 6, 5-12.

Kuhn, T. S. *The structure of scientific revolutions.* Chicago: University of Chicago Press, 1970.

Lyon, C. New perspectives on school district research and evaluation. In *What do we know about teaching and learning in urban schools?* Vol. 9. St. Louis, MO: CEMREL, Inc., 1979.

Lyon, C., Doscher, L., McGranahan, P., & Williams, R. *Evaluation and school districts.* Los Angeles: Center for the Study of Evaluation, University of California at Los Angeles, 1979.

Nadler, G. *Work design: A systems concept.* Homewood, IL: Richard D. Irwin, 1970.

Parlett, M., & Hamilton, D. Evaluation as illumination: A new approach to the study of innovative programs. In G. V Glass (Ed.), *Evaluation studies review annual,* Vol. 1. Beverly Hills, CA: Sage, 1976.

Petrie, H. G. Do you see what I see? The epistemology of inter-disciplinary inquiry. *Educational Researcher,* 1976, 5, 9-15.

Polanyi, M., & Prosch, H. *Meaning.* Chicago: University of Chicago Press, 1975.

Random House. *Dictionary of the English language: Unabridged edition.* New York: Author, 1966.

Rippey, R. M. *Studies in transactional evaluation.* Berkeley, CA: McCutchan, 1973.

Rossi, P. H., & Wright, S. R. Evaluation research: An evaluation of theory, practice, and politics. *Evaluation Quarterly,* 1977, 1.

Smith, N. L. Requirements for a discipline of evaluation, *Studies in Educational Evaluation,* 1979, 5, 5-12.

Stake, R. E. *Evaluating the arts in education.* Columbus, OH: Charles E. Merrill, 1975. (a)

Stake, R. E. Program evaluation, particularly responsive evaluation. Occasional Paper No. 5. Kalamazoo: Evaluation Center, Western Michigan University, 1975. (b)

Stake, R. E. *Evaluating educational programs.* Paris: Organisation for Economic Co-Operation and Development, 1976.

Wolf, R. L. The application of select legal concepts in educational evaluation. Unpublished doctoral dissertation, University of Illinois, 1974.

Wolf, R. L. Trial by jury: A new evaluation method. *Phi Delta Kappa,* 1975, 57.

Worthen, B. R., & Sanders, J. R. *Educational evaluation: Theory and practice.* Worthington, OH: Charles A. Jones, 1973.

Nick L. Smith
*Director, Research on Evaluation Program, Northwest
Regional Educational Laboratory*

CHAPTER **2**

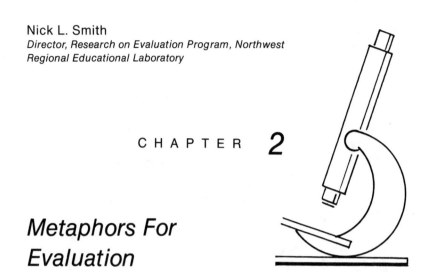

Metaphors For
Evaluation

*For the past four years Nick Smith has directed the
Research on Evaluation Program, which conducts
research on the nature of evaluation practice and
researches and develops new evaluation methods.
Through his published methodological research on
evaluation in health, education, and community development, he has sought to ground evaluation
theory in empirical work on evaluation practice. He
won the President's Problem competition of the
Evaluation Network in 1978, served as President of
the Evaluation Network in 1980, and has been evaluation book review editor of* Educational Evaluation
and Policy Analysis *since the journal's inception.*

IN THE PREVIOUS CHAPTER, I presented a background
rationale for the development of new evaluation methods through the
adaptation of existing tools from other areas. I suggested that the use
of metaphors provided one means of developing new methods, as well
as a means of communicating about methods with evaluation practitioners and theorists. The purpose of the present chapter is to
consider in more depth the concept of metaphor. In the remaining
chapters, the authors have used investigative reporting, law, architecture, geography, philosophy, literary and film criticism, and watercolor painting as metaphors for evaluation. In writing these
"metaphor chapters," they were guided by earlier versions of the
discussion of metaphor which follows. An overview introducing the

major themes of these subsequent chapters follows this presentation on metaphor.

Metaphor

One of the earliest collaborators on this project to develop new evaluation methods was Egon G. Guba of Indiana University. Dr. Guba's early writings on metaphor have been used throughout the years as a basis for work on this topic. A lightly edited excerpt from one of his papers (Guba, Note 1) follows.

A metaphor, as commonly defined, is a figure of speech in which the meaning of a term or phrase is transferred from the object it ordinarily designates to another object so as to provide new insight or perspective on the latter. In a broader sense, the term *metaphor* may also designate a process whereby the meanings and relationships of one theory or model may be used to suggest meanings or relationships in another arena. This possibility was suggested by May Brodbeck (1959) as follows:

Suppose that one area . . . [which has a relatively well-developed theory] is said to be a model for another area, about which little is as yet known. The descriptive terms in the theory of the better-known area are put into one-to-one correspondence with those of the "new" area. By means of this one-to-one correspondence, the laws of one area are "translated" into laws of the other area. The concepts of the better-known theory are replaced in the laws by the concepts of the new area. This replacement results in a set of laws or hypotheses about the variables in the new area. . . . For example, suppose it is wondered whether rumors spread like diseases. That is, can the laws of epidemiology, about which quite a bit is known, be a model for a theory of rumor transmission? Or, to say the same thing differently, do the laws about rumors have the same form as the laws about diseases? The descriptive concepts in the laws of epidemiology are first of all replaced by letter variables. This reveals the form of the laws. The concepts referring to diseases are put into one-to-one correspondence with those referring to rumors. The letter variables in the epidemiological laws are replaced by the descriptive terms referring to rumors. This results in a set of hypotheses about rumors, which may or may not be confirmed. If, optimistically, these laws are confirmed, then the two theories have the same form [p. 379].[1]

The idea that the use of metaphor has utility for generating new insights and providing perspectives has been advanced by many writers. A few examples may suffice to support this contention. Thus, Ortony (1975) argues with respect to pedagogy:

> Metaphors, and their closest relatives, similes and analogies, have been used as teaching devices since the earliest writings of civilized man. The dialogues of Plato are full of them: there is the simile of the sails in *Parmenides* used to explain the nature of the relationship between Platonic Forms and the particular objects partaking of them, or there is the cave metaphor in *The Republic* designed to illuminate various levels of knowledge. The Bible is another good source of metaphor, and, of course, metaphor is the stock-in-trade of poets and writers. The widespread use of metaphor in even the earliest "teaching texts" suggests that metaphor is more than just a literary stylistic device. We shall argue here that metaphor is an essential ingredient of communication and consequently of great educational value [p. 45].

Burke (1969) characterizes the metaphor as one of four "master tropes," describing it as a means for providing perspective:

> Metaphor is a device for seeing something *in terms of* something else. It brings out the thisness of a that, or the thatness of a this. If we employ the word "character" as a general term for whatever can be thought of as distinct (any thing, pattern, situation, structure, nature, person, object, act, role, process, event, etc.), then we could say that metaphor tells us something about one character as considered from the point of view of another character. And to consider A from the point of view of B is, of course, to use B as a *perspective* upon A [pp. 503-504].

Kaplan (1964) observes that metaphors have frequently informed developing theories in the sciences. Thus, for example, there is the

> familiar hydrodynamic metaphor in psychoanalysis, with the id as a reservoir having several "outlets" which can lower internal pressures, which in turn are countered by forces of repression, and so on. Freud also uses a societal analogy, with a "censor," an authoritarian "superego," internal "conflicts" and the like [p. 226].

The utility of metaphors and metaphor-like conceptual translations thus seems to be well-established as a heuristic device [from Guba, Note 1, pp. 1-4].

Selecting Metaphors for Study

Metaphors that have turned out to be fruitful in the past (e.g., the law, as explored by Owens, Wolf, Levine, and others, or art criticism, as explored by Eisner) have emerged for a variety of reasons: their proponents had by virtue of earlier experience or training become immersed in these areas and later, after having turned their interests to evaluation, discovered the utility of these former interests for evaluation. So far as anyone can tell, their utility as metaphors was chiefly intuited.

Yet once the idea of using other fields as metaphors is proposed, it is not difficult to name some likely candidates: investigative journalism, forensic pathology, wine tasting, accounting, even geography. The original proposal for this project listed some eight examples, and many others have occurred to the project staff since. A letter sent to some 120 evaluation theorists and practitioners soliciting other nominations has turned up still others.

Thus the problem seems not so much to be identifying possible candidates, as choosing wisely from among those already proposed. But what criteria might be used for this purpose? Several seem obvious:

1. *Relevance for evaluation functions.* In what way is the proposed field/discipline related to such evaluation functions as valuing, inquiry, data analysis, or communication? On this criterion, for example, political criticism would look promising while auto racing would not. Probably the most important elements are *valuing* and *inquiry,* which encompass the major purpose and mode of evaluative activity. Thus a selected metaphor that is itself a form of inquiry and that relates somehow to the making of value judgments is ideal.

2. *Sufficient definition.* Is the field/discipline sufficiently well defined and explicated to provide a meaningful metaphor for the many facets of evaluation? So, for example, art criticism would meet this criterion but assessment of homes for tax levying purposes probably would not. Put another way, the proposed area should have sufficient scope so that the number of characteristics or facets which can profitably be contrasted to evaluation is reasonably large.

3. *Heuristic value.* What is the probability that the proposed field/discipline is likely to produce new insights? This criterion is related to the preceding two, in that irrelevant or constrained metaphors are not likely to have utility. But some metaphors simply pack more information, suggest more connections, appear to be more innovative, and so on. For example, given the two related

fields of office management and industrial management, the latter appears a good deal more heuristic than the former.

4. *Accessibility.* Is the field/discipline constituted in such a way that its knowledge and expertise are accessible to evaluators? Extremely technical fields such as electrical engineering do not score high on this criterion, nor do areas whose practitioners are extremely limited in number, e.g., U.N. translators. It will probably not be difficult to meet this criterion in most instances, however.

5. *Non-duplicativeness.* Does the field/discipline overlap with others that are already being studied or that might be studied? Thus, the judging of sporting events and art criticism might be thought of as having too much overlap, while art criticism and journalism would probably be thought of as sufficiently different.

The criterion of non-duplicativeness has several aspects that warrant special attention. There are three different forms of duplication that need to be considered:

a. *External to the project.* There is little point in pursuing metaphors that are already being explored elsewhere, e.g., law and art criticism (unless fresh new approaches can be taken or attention focused on different attributes than had formerly been explored).

b. *Internal to the project.* There is little point in expending project resources on closely related paradigms since there will be too little fresh information resulting to warrant the costs.

c. *Categorically.* It seems likely that proposed metaphors might be classifiable into categories on the basis of some taxonomy or other classification system. If so, there seems to be little point in testing more than one exemplar from each class.

A definitive taxonomy that might be used for this latter purpose does not exist, but an example of such a possible category system is shown in [Table 2.1]. This taxonomy is based on an analysis of guiding inquiry paradigms that seem to underlie various fields/disciplines that might be considered as candidates for analysis. Complete explication of the various paradigms is an epistemological exercise well beyond the scope of this paper. However, as an example, the table makes clear the point that is relevant here, namely, that ways of categorizing fields/disciplines can be invented, and that a set of categories would be useful [from Guba, Note 1, pp. 19-22].

The seven authors represented in this book have used other disciplines and fields as metaphors for evaluation. To understand what is involved in this kind of translation activity, consider for a moment the

TABLE 2.1   An Example of a Category System for Metaphor Candidates

Paradigm	Exemplars	Fundamental Techniques	View of Truth (Truth is . . .)
Logical	Mathematics, Philosophy, Computer Science, Language Linguistics, Literary Science, Accounting	Analysis	Demonstrable (QED!)
Scientific	Physics, Chemistry, Geology, Biology, Botany, Zoology, Physiology	Experimentation	Confirmable
Naturalistic	Anthropology, Ethnography, History, Political Science, Counseling, Social Work	Field Study	Ineluctable
Judgmental	Art Forms (Painting, Music, Literature, Film, etc.); Substances (Wine, Cheese, Tobacco, etc.); Performances (Diving, Gymnastics, Dance, etc.); Objects (Architecture, Horticulture, etc.)	Sensing (Seeing, Feeling, Tasting, etc.)	Recognizable
Adversarial	Law, Congressional Hearings, Investigative Journalism.	Cross-examination triangulation	Emergent (on balance)
Modus Operandi	Medical Diagnosis, Checklist, Trouble-Shooting List.	Sequential Test	Trackable
Demographic	Economics, Demography, Geography	Indicators	Macroscopically Determinable

field of engineering. How could one use engineering as a metaphor for evaluation?

"Evaluation is Engineering." What might that statement mean? What do engineers and evaluators have in common? What do engineers do that evaluators do not do but which evaluators might consider doing?

Engineers invent products, build structures, and control processes, to name a few. These activities suggest metaphors such as these:

- "Evaluation researches the products of tomorrow." This statement emphasizes the role of evaluation in providing information to be used as the basis of new programs or products.

- "Evaluators are the builders of programs." This statement suggests the role of formative evaluation in shaping the nature of a developing program.
- "Evaluation is quality control." This last statement is a particularly strong metaphor, especially in education, where many people think of public education as a production-line process for turning out educated, productive citizens. Under this view, it is easy to think of evaluation as quality control and to look to engineering for models of how to perform evaluation. Educational evaluators might, for example, adopt the engineers' general system theory and consider education as a series of inputs (student characteristics) and outputs (scholastic skills) in an ongoing process. Quality control (educational evaluation) is accomplished by setting quality standards (achievement goals) and monitoring every n^{th} product in the line (testing every third and eighth grader). From this example we can see that the field of engineering can provide some strong metaphors for evaluation, and it has already done so in educational evaluation.

The creation of such metaphors requires creativity and insight. Many metaphors are possible; some work well, others do not. This activity also requires considerable familiarity not only with evaluation but with the field or discipline being explored. For that reason, individuals were selected for this work who had practical experience in evaluation and in some other field. In some cases the project staff found people who had spent ten to twenty years working in two different fields. In other cases, collaboration allowed us to fulfill this dual-knowledge requirement — a rather peculiar one in our age of increasing specialization.

The project staff also selected a range of fields for use as evaluation metaphors. Our selections were, of course, restricted by our ability to find people with appropriate backgrounds. For example, we never found anyone with practical evaluation experience and a knowledge of forensic medicine, although that seemed a provocative alternative. We have selected investigative reporting, law, and architecture because, like evaluation, they deal with providing social services in the world of practical affairs. Geography was selected because it is one of the few social sciences which does not seem to have played as major a role in early evaluation efforts as have psychology, sociology, political science, and economics. Philosophy was selected because of its traditional attention to questions of value, meaning, and the nature of evidence — important concerns in evaluation. Literary and film criticism and watercolor painting were selected as examples from the arts in which the process of evaluation plays a major role in the improvement of practice.

Although the remaining chapters in the book need not necessarily be read in any particular order, they have been sequenced in such a way as to lead the reader from the rather more obvious translation to the less obvious. At this point the reader probably feels more comfortable with the idea that evaluators are sometimes like investigative reporters than with the idea that evaluators and watercolorists have much in common. There are interesting parallels to evaluation throughout all seven chapters, however. Some of the more striking ideas were uncovered by the less obvious metaphors.

As acknowledged in Chapter 1, some individuals have already looked at law and literary criticism as sources of new evaluation methods. Our chapters do not repeat or summarize that work, but represent fresh looks at these fields. What one investigator may deem worthy of follow-up another may miss altogether. It is important to remember, therefore, that the chapters which follow do not represent exhaustive searches of the fields under study; they merely provide the strongest metaphors for evaluation which these authors could uncover. These chapters are suggestive, not definitive, and we urge interested colleagues to explore these and other fields for sources of new evaluation methods.

In identifying metaphors for evaluation, each author was asked to cover, in some way, the following points:

- Describe the field so that the reader has an orientation to the field's nature and purpose — a historical perspective would be helpful.

- Describe the characteristic functions and roles within the field, including the predominant epistemologies, methodologies, instruments, and analytic procedures.

- Analyze evaluatively the concepts and methods that might be translated for use in evaluation, including the purposes they might serve and the conditions under which they might be used.

- Suggest which new methods might be tried in evaluation and how their utility to evaluation could be tested.

- Recommend additional material readers might use for follow-up study in the field or discipline.

To the extent possible for the field being studied and within space restrictions, each author has more or less touched upon these points.

Shared Themes

There are some shared themes which run through two or more of the following chapters. I will briefly mention the more obvious ones at this point to make them more readily recognizable. These themes also serve to loosely integrate the chapters which follow. Some of these themes of common elements are not explicitly discussed in the chapters, but they nonetheless provide some continuity of orientation throughout the work. The first four common themes arose because of the nature of the task given the authors. The remaining themes arose because there are common elements which cut across the various fields.

Metaphor

In all the chapters which follow, the authors are, of course, looking for metaphors for evaluation. They deal with the concept of metaphor differently, however. The term is seldom used in the literary and film criticism chapter, but is subjected to philosophic analysis in the philosophy chapter. Readers should ask themselves, "What are the metaphors here, and what do they suggest about new evaluation methods?"

Evaluation

All the authors are also concerned with evaluation, although their definitions differ, ranging from evaluation to increase understanding (geography) to evaluation to aid decision-making (watercolor painting).

Levels of Discourse

The levels of discourse discussed in Chapter 1 are also used in the following chapters. They are used explicitly in the law chapter, where legal constructs are matched with level of discourse:

I. Point of View	— Justice
II. Paradigm	— Justification
	Persuasion
	Systemization
III. Operational Strategy	— Legislative History
	Courtroom Trial

The terms are not mentioned in the geography chapter, although the material presented there can be grouped according to the four levels:

I. Point of View	— Understanding Spatial Aspects of Problems
II. Paradigm	— Behavioral Geography
III. Operational Strategy	— Cartographic Analysis
IV. Technique	— Mental Mapping

Use of Concepts

All of the authors used major concepts from the fields being studied in order to explain the nature of those fields. A field's methodology cannot be fully understood without understanding the conceptual structure to which the methods relate. The concepts used include:

Investigative Reporting	— fairness/balance, tracking, minimum/maximum projections
Law	— justice, precedent, evidence, appeals
Architecture	— milieu, context, retrofit, form
Geography	— location, shape and size, regionalization
Philosophy	— concepts, facts, clear cases, context, metaphor
Literary and Film Criticism	— form, style, criticism, interpretation
Watercolor Painting	— value, texture, gradation, dominance

Study of Exemplary Cases

Several of the authors illustrate how practitioners in their fields study exemplary cases as part of their work. Lawyers study precedent-setting cases to interpret law. Philosophers study "clear cases" to determine the nature and meaning of concepts. Literary critics study exemplary pieces to uncover the creative techniques used by particular writers. Artists study master works in order to improve their own painting. The study of exemplary cases as a means to improved practice is well documented here.

Minor Themes

There are at least six other minor themes which appear in two or more chapters.

- *Study of Product Design* — How architects design buildings and how artists design paintings are examined for insights into how to design evaluations.

- *Study of Written Language* — The study of written language as a way to clarify meaning and experience and as a means to aid others in more fully experiencing the written word is an activity engaged in by both philosophers and literary critics.

- *Study of Space* — Architects and geographers share a common interest in the study of the relationships among space, function, and social meaning. Might this become a theme in evaluation?

- *Meta-Evaluation* — Three of the authors introduce parallels which have implications for meta-evaluation — that is, the evaluation of evaluation. In law, literary criticism, and architecture, individuals study and interpret the products of their profession as a means of understanding the profession's social role and as a means of improving professional practice.

- *Reconstruction of History* — Reconstructing a history of events is important in law and investigative reporting. Legislative histories are needed in order to properly interpret and apply laws. The reconstruction of events is used in journalism as a means of gathering evidence for a story.

- *Characteristics of Practitioners* — All the authors' descriptions indicate that in order to be a competent practitioner in these fields, one needs considerable education and/or experience. Work in all these fields is marked by the need for attention to detail.

These common themes illustrate that there is more similarity across these fields than might first seem apparent. Also, since the fields frequently borrow methods from each other, there is occasionally considerable similarity at the technique level of discourse. Important differences remain, however, especially at the point-of-view level of discourse.

One way to clarify the differences between these fields is to consider what types of questions are most frequently asked in each field. One present difficulty in evaluation which is seldom noted is that evaluators are often unclear about the nature of their questions.

TABLE 2.2 Alternative Modes of Inquiry for Evaluation

Area	Purpose of Area	Role of Inquiry	Historical Foundation	Inquiry Design	Inquiry Techniques	Evaluation Application
Experimental Behavioral Science	To understand the social and individual behaviors of people	To understand the causal links between causes and effects in human behavior	History of experimental approach in science, results of past research, classic methods	Collection of experimental data, statistical analysis and interpretation	Randomized experimental studies with pre-post testing	Conduct controlled studies of programs with emphasis on pre-post testing and statistical analysis
Investigative Reporting	To expose to the public those hidden conditions or behaviors that are inimical to the public interest	To understand and record the chain of events leading to and perpetuating conditions contrary to the public good	History of investigative reporting — especially classic cases, existing legal and financial documentation systems	Field collection of self-report data, conceptual analysis of documentary files	Document "tracking," "key interviews," files-chronologies-summaries	Conduct an evaluation by tracking evidence through existing documents, interviewing key informants, and building a chronology of major events
Law	To ensure equal treatment of all individuals, in resolving social conflict and maintaining social order	To understand what the facts in a given case are and which principles and precedents of law are relevant	History of common law, recorded legislative histories, collections of previous decisions and precedents	Field collection of data, laboratory examination of evidence, conceptual analysis of legal documents	Collection of eye-witness accounts, examination of physical evidence, review of legislative histories and previous court decisions	Study a program through eyewitness accounts and expert testimony on physical evidence; relate judgments to principles identified in relevant past policies, programs, and evaluations
Architectural Design	To define in physical form a solution to functional and psychosocial needs	To understand how elements of form can be combined to meet maximally the needs of a given context	Historical examples of architectural design, accumulated knowledge of materials, structural forms, and human satisfactions with them	Conceptual analysis of alternative form, critique, and analysis of existing structures	Assessment of human needs and structure use, collection of expert and lay criticisms of structures	Perform conceptual analysis of alternative forms of a proposed program, examining existing programs and criticisms of them, collecting information on the needs and context of the program

TABLE 2.2 (cont.)

Area	Purpose of Area	Role of Inquiry	Historical Foundation	Inquiry Design	Inquiry Techniques	Evaluation Application
Geography	To understand the spatial aspects of natural and social phenomena	To understand how spatial distributions and associations relate to specific events, conditions, and behaviors	History of mapping and cartographic analysis, classic studies	Field collection of data, statistical and cartographic analysis	Interview techniques, collection of documentary data, mapping techniques	Collect field data on the spatial distribution of variables relevant to program effects, relate these data to program operations to study the effects of context
Philosophical Analysis	To clarify the meanings of terms basic to philosophical inquiries	To understand how language is used/ can be used to make logical constructions of the immediately given	Historical products of philosophic inquiry, past examples of concept analysis	Conceptual analysis of language use and meaning as it naturally occurs	Use of clear cases, contrary cases, borderline cases, stipulating contexts, use of metaphors, concept maps	Conduct a conceptual analysis of the major terms employed in a program to clarify the nature of the program
Literary and Film Criticism	To heighten experiential understanding through recognition of form and style	To understand the elements of form and style and how they combine to create reader experiences and understandings	History/philosophy of poetry, historical themes and techniques of literature and film criticism	Cognitive analysis of existing poems, writing, and films	Matrix analysis of themes, "accurate, sharp, loving description," formal analysis of representation of reality	Study a program, analyzing how its structure, format, and content interrelate to contribute to the overall "effect" of the piece
Watercolor Painting	To create a representation that can become a shared message or experience	To understand how the elements of line, value, color, texture, shape, size, and direction can be used to create a desired effect	Historical collection of works of past painters and critiques of them	Sustained personal experience in making and critiquing paintings	Trial-and-error experience with design elements (pigments and shapes), study of others' work	Through many years of personal experience and study, become a master in the design and evaluation of a particular type of program

In fact, having been trained as researchers, many evaluators assume that most evaluation questions are causal questions which require experimental designs. For example, in evaluating the effects of a new drug counseling service in several outpatient clinics, the question likely to receive the greatest attention is: "Has the rate of drug use declined as a result of this new service?" Other important noncausal questions are likely to get overlooked — such as these:

> Should the new services have been placed in the current clinics? What is the regional distribution of drug abuse? (a geographic question)
>
> What is the cost-effectiveness of these new services? (an economic question)
>
> What moral obligation does the community have to offer drug rehabilitation care? (a philosophic question)

The preoccupation with causal questions results in evaluators' inadequately attending to these other significant questions (see Smith, 1981, for an extended example). Readers should note, in reading the following chapters, the kinds of questions addressed by each field.

There are many ways to portray the similarities and differences across the seven fields represented in the following chapters. Since evaluation is considered by many to be a form of inquiry, it might be useful to study the role of inquiry in each of the fields discussed here. Table 2.2 contains a summary of the modes of inquiry as represented by chapter authors. Of course, more than a single mode of inquiry is used in any particular field or discipline. Table 2.2 contains only the dominant mode discussed by the authors. It may be helpful to review this table in order to highlight the different modes of inquiry as they are described in the following chapters.

One of the purposes of this book is to share with readers the results of several attempts to use other fields as metaphors for evaluation in order to uncover new evaluation methods. Another purpose is to encourage readers to participate in this stimulating approach to methodological improvement, to search for their own metaphors for evaluation. The authors touch upon more possible metaphors than they can adequately develop in this limited space, and there are undoubtedly many possibilities they have not yet recognized. After all, to coin another metaphor, "Reading is the raw material of intellectual creation." We invite our readers' participation in this intriguing search for new evaluation methods.

Note

[1] The procedures suggested by Brodbeck, of course, establish the *isomorphism* of the two theories. Maccia (1964) has suggested that the same argument holds for substance, resulting in what she terms *isosubstantism*. Metaphor applications discussed in this paper may result in either or both.

Reference Note

1. Guba, E. G. The use of metaphors in constructing theory. Paper and Report Series, No. 3. Portland, OR: Research on Evaluation Program, Northwest Regional Educational Laboratory, 1978.

References

Brodbeck, M. Models, meaning, and theories. In L. Gross (Ed.), *Symposium on sociological theory.* Chicago: Row, Peterson, 1959.

Burke, K. *A grammar of motives.* Berkeley: University of California Press, 1969.

Kaplan, A. *The conduct of inquiry.* San Francisco: Chandler, 1964.

Maccia, E. S. Retroduction: A way of inquiring through models. *Memorias del XIII Congress Internacional de Filosofia,* Mexico: Universidad Nacional Autonoma de Mexico, 1964, 545-562.

Ortony, A. Why metaphors are necessary and not just nice. *Educational Theory,* 1975, 25, 45-53.

Smith, N. L. Non-causal inquiry in education. *Educational Researcher,* 1981, 10, 23.

Egon G. Guba
Professor of Education, Indiana University

CHAPTER **3**

Investigative Reporting

Egon Guba has spent 30 years in the study of evaluation. He has made contributions to the development of the CIPP model and, more recently, to the adaptation of naturalistic methodology to evaluation practice. His interest in journalism dates from his high school and college days as editor of his school paper, but has been stimulated recently by the fact that most evaluations are in some respects adversarial. Investigative reporters have developed special methodologies particularly useful in conflict – as opposed to cooperative – situations.

What is Investigative Journalism?

Thrust into the limelight recently because of the Watergate scandals and their exposure by Washington *Post* reporters Carl Bernstein and Robert Woodward, investigative journalism has a long and distinguished history, dating at least to the time of John Peter Zenger. Although vilified by Theodore Roosevelt as "muckraking," the movement has proved to be peculiarly vital, coming to a climax in the 1960s and '70s in various guises as depth reporting, the "new journalism," the underground press, reform journalism, interpretative reporting, and public affairs reporting. But the term "investigative reporting" seems both most descriptive and most acceptable.

Proponents and practitioners of investigative reporting are not consistent in their descriptions of what investigative journalism is.

Definitions range from the semiserious (for example, "investigative reporting is the canker sore in the official mouth), through the simplistic (investigative reporting is simply the reporting of concealed information), through the public-spirited (investigative journalism is the reporting of concealed, obscure, or complex matters significantly affecting the public). There is a spirited debate about whether investigative reporting is all that different from "plain good reporting," apparently on the assumption that every good reporter must "dig behind the facts in order to provide context, depth, and meaning to his story." Some definitions of investigative journalism insist upon a focus on *processes* rather than merely on *events,* thus making interpretation a key element. Finally, in order to honor the adjective "investigative," some commentators believe that the story must evolve from the reporter's own investigation, not merely reporting on the results of someone else's investigation (as by a congressional committee). All things considered, it is likely that most observers would agree that the following definition embodies most of the elements that have been included in various formulations:

> Investigative journalism is journalism focused on processes that requires the exposure of elements or aspects being kept wholly or partly secret from the general public, that seeks to redress an imbalance inimical to the public interest, and that results from the personal efforts of the journalist involved.

What Do Investigative Journalists Do?

As a group, investigative journalists have not been particularly introspective or reflective about the processes in which they engage. Formulations of what might be called the "logic-in-use" of the profession are rare. Of course, the development of such formulations may lead to a freezing of what are taken to be the legitimate activities in which investigative reporters may engage. The development of an orthodoxy is always a risk that attends efforts to reduce the art of a field to a science. Nevertheless, such formulations are useful; they provide guidance to the neophyte, they permit assessment of performance and guide adjustments on the part of the veteran, and they facilitate communication and conceptualization on the part of students.

One useful formulation of such a reconstructed logic for investigative journalism is reproduced as Figure 3.1. This formulation was proposed by the late Paul N. Williams in his book *Investigative Reporting and Editing* (1978, pp. 12-34). He suggests that most investigative reporting follows 10 steps.

1. Conception. Basic ideas which might be pursued in a journalistic investigation come from somewhere. Williams suggests there are many sources, including tipsters, inside informants, reading, news breaks, legwork, tangential angles from other stories, and personal observations and files.

2. Feasibility study. Williams suggests that the reporter prepare a memo outlining answers to questions such as: Is it possible to do the study? Are people, time, money, and technical skill available to pull it together? Will the study stand still long enough for examination? What will the study mean to my readers? What is likely to happen to the paper (suits, boycotts, etc.) if the story is printed?

3. Go/No-Go decision. Based on the feasibility study, the reporter and his editor make the first of three go/no-go decisions about whether to go ahead with the story. An interesting feature of this decision process is the outlining of "minimum-maximum returns." Decision makers need to be satisfied that even the *minimum* possible return on an investigation will be publishable and useful, and they need to assess what the *maximum* return is likely to be, assuming everything goes perfectly.

4. Planning and base-building. Planning involves projecting the methods, tasks, roles, and schedules needed to carry out the investigation. Base-building (sometimes known as "doing a fast study") involves developing a base of information about the target(s) of the investigation — or, as Bob Greene, editor of Long Island's *Newsday* has put it, developing your "jungle map," as you are about to enter a "jungle."

5. Original research. Virtually all of the investigation takes place with this step. Records searches, observations, and interviews are combined to turn up pieces of the puzzle and put them together. The reporter works by formulating hypotheses about what must be the case *if* what he suspects is true is actually true; then he checks out the consequences of those hypotheses in an effort to prove them. This process, which will be termed "tracking" for want of a better word, is the most essential and characteristic element in investigative reporting.

6. Re-evaluation: the second go/no-go decision. When the original research is finished, the reporter and his editor assess progress with respect to the previously determined minimum and maximum goals. This assessment leads to one of several decisions: drop the story; inactivate it while remaining alert for leaks, tips, or leads that may suggest reactivation; proceed to key interviews (see below) to complete the minimum story; recognize that the minimum story is

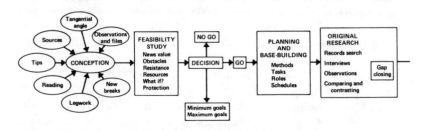

Figure 3.1   The Reconstructed Logic of Investigative Journalism
SOURCE: Williams (1978, pp. 14-15). Reproduced by permission.

already in hand and the maximum story possibly achievable; or, most desirably, proceed with key interviews to complete the maximum story.

7. *Key interviews.* These are interviews with the "target" or other persons close to the target. Ideally, the target has remained unaware of the existence of the investigation until he is actually interviewed. The interview is seen as an opportunity to validate known information, to elicit new information, and to give the target the chance to tell his side of the story.

8. *Final evaluation.* Once the key interview(s) have been conducted, the reporter makes a final evaluation of his work. He tests each point against documents and files to be certain that each can be justified. Other interpretations that can be made from the data are examined; if the data support *them* as well, a sufficient case has not been made. The reporter must be certain that his case cannot reasonably be challenged.

9. *The final decision – the third go/no-go decision.* This decision involves not only the reporter and his editor but most likely also legal counsel, who will be checking for such things as possible libel, the paper's position if the story is challenged in the courts and the reporter is ordered to divulge his sources, and so on. Thus, this decision is based not simply on the merits of the case but also on considerations of whether the paper will be disadvantaged. Moreover, ethical considerations are brought to bear; the case may be clear and the paper protected, but the public good brought about by disclosure must outweigh possible damage to innocents to warrant publication.

10. *Writing and publication.* In this step the reporter casts his story into readable form and sees it through the entire publication process, to be certain that no errors are allowed to creep in.

Figure 3.1 (Continued)

Is Investigative Journalism a Useful Metaphor for Educational Evaluation?

It is difficult to assess the value of one discipline as a metaphor for another when neither is well defined. Educational evaluation is riding the crest of a wave of conceptual change; since 1967 it has been variously estimated that 40 or more models have been proposed in the literature. Which of these shall we mean? Similarly, investigative journalism, after a period of dormancy, has reemerged in the last decade and a half in a variety of forms, as attested in the opening paragraph of this essay (including one form called "precision journalism" by its proponents who seek to base investigative journalism forthrightly on social science research methods, including especially quantitative methods). Which of *these* shall we mean?

Confusions produced by these rapid changes in both areas cannot be resolved; a more eclectic approach must be taken. At a more general level, certain similarities can be noted that suggest it may be useful indeed to view educational evaluation from the investigative journalist's perspective (and probably vice versa):

- Both are processes of inquiry.
- Both utilize many standard data collection and analysis techniques: interview, observation, records analysis, and the like.
- Both take place in a naturalistic setting — that is, the context in which the entity being evaluated (on the one hand) or being investigated (on the other) reside.
- Both depend heavily on the interaction of an inquirer (evaluator or reporter) with people, so that the nature of the outcome is heavily influenced by the nature of that interaction.

There are also some salient differences between the two disciplines:

- They differ in purpose. The purpose of the evaluator is to establish the worth or merit of some entity, while the purpose of the investigative reporter is to expose some situation or condition inimical to the public interest. It is worth noting, however, that both these purposes have a consumer advocacy flavor.

- They differ in degree of secrecy. The investigative reporter lives in an atmosphere of virtual secrecy, while the evaluator is virtually always a public figure.

- They differ in assumptions one can make about cooperation or conflict with the persons with whom one deals. The investigative reporter must assume that he and his subjects have a conflict of interest that may lead them to lie or deceive whenever possible. While it would be naive to assume that the educational evaluator is never in such a situation, it is more generally the case that he can assume he will receive some cooperation from his subjects.

- They differ in the degree to which they rely on available versus newly generated information. The investigative reporter relies heavily on documents, records, and recollections — traces of events or activities *past*. The educational evaluator is more likely to be able and to elect to generate *de novo* information as the basis for his inquiry — for example, test scores.

- They differ in the criteria by which they will judge their work. The investigative reporter is likely to deal in such criteria as warrantability and defensibility, while the educational evaluator is more concerned with scientific criteria such as validity and reliability and practical considerations such as timeliness and relevance. Of course, both groups are concerned about the factualness of their reports and about the cost-effectiveness of their operations.

It is the precise point of a metaphor that there should be sufficient *ground* — that is, elements in common — between the principal subject (in this case, educational evaluation) and the metaphoric term (in this case, investigative journalism) in order to make the metaphor intelligible and interpretable, and also sufficient *tension* — differences in elements between principal subject and metaphoric term — to make the metaphor useful for providing new perspectives and insights. This condition seems to be well met by the extent of similarities and differences between investigative journalism and educational evaluation, so that the likelihood that the former will turn out to be a useful metaphor for the latter is high. The extent to which this prediction is borne out can best be tested in the next section, in which some heuristic parallels between the two disciplines will be explored.

What are Some Parallels Worth Further Exploration?[2]

There are many parallels between educational evaluation and investigative journalism worth exploring; those that follow, while incompletely pursued here, will give the reader an idea of the possibilities that inhere in the metaphor of investigative journalism. The particular topics are not arranged in any order of importance or other priority; each is interesting in its own way.

1. Investigative parallels. Investigative reporting begins with the assumption that the reporter is in a conflict situation with respect to the target of the investigation, who is assumed to be engaged in some form of illegal, unethical, immoral, or otherwise reprehensible behavior. Thus, the reporter does not anticipate cooperation from the target, but instead expects to be lied to and deceived so long as the target continues to believe that such behavior will shelter or protect him.

Of course, the evaluator does not confront such extreme cases, but it would be naive for him to believe that cooperation from those involved in an evaluation can be counted on. Indeed, in most cases the evaluator would be well advised to act within the framework of what Douglas has called the "investigative paradigm":

> The investigative paradigm is based on the assumption that profound conflicts of interest, values, feelings, and actions pervade social life. It is taken for granted that many of the people one deals with, perhaps all people to some extent, have good reason to hide from others what they are doing and even lie to them. Instead of trusting people and expecting trust in return, one suspects others and expects others to suspect him. Conflict is the reality of life; suspicion is the guiding principle [Douglas, 1976, p. 55].

Douglas notes that investigative journalists have developed this paradigm "most explicitly and completely." But while journalists tend to deal with persons whose motives for "hiding from others what they do" may be nefarious, it is clear that *everyone* has something that he or she may wish (and indeed, has a right) to keep private. In an evaluation situation, it would be the rare person who would not feel threatened, who would not wish to put his or her best foot forward, who would rather not have the evaluator discover some aspect of his or her operation that might seem, if not illegal or immoral, at least unusual. To take such a posture is not criminal but simply human; yet the effect on the evaluator's "search for truth" is similarly compromising.

Further, if investigative reporters seek the reform of conditions so that the public interest is better served, the investigative evaluator may also seek the reform of educational conditions so that children and society are better served. In seeking that end, the role of the evaluator is closer to that of investigative reporter than has perhaps been imagined, and in playing out that role the evaluator may find an investigative posture both more realistic and useful than a cooperative one.

2. *Legal parallels.* Several classes of laws that apply to investigative reporters have implications for the practice of educational evaluation as well.

Libel and slander laws are intended to protect a subject against unwarranted and deliberate efforts to present an unflattering or damaging picture of him or her and/or against false statements damaging to his or her character and reputation. That evaluators may also be subject to legal sanctions because of purported libel has hardly begun to be appreciated by the profession; yet it seems clear from the parallels between evaluation and journalism that a reasonable case could probably be made should such an action be brought. It seems unlikely that a court would dismiss such a case as not being legally significant — that is, because the subject had suffered no injury and was patently not entitled to remedy at the bar. These points seem to be especailly significant when one considers the current emphasis on accountability. Who will collect the information on which accountability judgments will be based if not the evaluator? And if decisions are made that are perceived by some as personally or programmatically harmful, will not the evaluator be required to defend the data? To be sure, the best defense against a libel or slander action is to be able to show that what was said or printed is true, but what evaluator is so confident of his data that he is certain they will stand up under courtroom attack from a trialwise and dogged opposing counsel? Conversely, if an evaluator approves a program and the program subsequently fails (for example, a child who fails to learn to read after having been taught by a method warranted as effective by an evaluator), is not the evaluator accountable too?

Shield laws providing special privilege to reporters who shield their sources are porous. The Supreme Court has recently upheld two lower court decisions requiring reporters to disclose their sources. There is little doubt that evaluators have even fewer privileges. At first glance it seems inconsequential whether privilege laws cover evaluators — after all, their information is usually public, and they almost never have a "Deep Throat" whom it is necessary to protect. Yet how often is it the case that an evaluator promises anonymity to a respondent in a questionnaire or interview situation? Can that guarantee be maintained?

Freedom of information laws are intended to guarantee citizen access to information collected as part of any public process, with few exceptions. There are two implications for the evaluator. On one hand, information needed by the evaluator, such as project memos and other documents, may be legally accessible to him because they are produced as part of an activity paid for with public funds. On the other hand, information collected *by* the evaluator may itself be accessible to other people for similar reasons. The evaluator may find, for example, that not only his formal reports but also his individual test scores and even his informal field notes may be subject to subpoena should anyone choose to bring an action. Evaluators need to maintain their files with that possibility in mind.

3. Ethical parallels. There seems to be little doubt that investigative reporters operate in ethical gray areas much of the time. Indeed, as Anderson and Benjaminson point out, "In those cases which are difficult to judge, most reporters tend to err on the side of dishonesty to obtain the information" (1976, p. 7). To justify such actions, reporters commonly fall back on one or more of the following rationalizations:

• moral relativism, argued on the basis of need to follow the subject to his own level of morality to deal with him effectively;

• exemption by guilt, argued on the basis that the preestablished guilt of the subject makes it permissible to pursue him in any way one can;

• moral tradeoffs, argued either on the basis that the public's right to know offsets the subject's right to candor, or that the public has more to gain from good reporting than it has to lose from the discomfort of the corrupt;

• rejection of oppressive laws, argued on the ground that some laws are inherently bad and deserve to be broken as a kind of (surprisingly) moral obligation.

Despite these or other rationalizations, and despite the counterarguments that can be brought to bear against them, reporters still daily face the need to make ethical decisions. Given the admittedly gray area in which they work, it would be unreasonable to demand an absolute adherence to the "purest" standards.

There are very few parallels between the circumstances confronted by the investigative reporter and those in the world of the educational evaluator. The latter typically is not dealing with a covert operation, one in which corruption or illegal or unethical behavior abounds. The entity being evaluated is known to all, and the context in which it exists is reasonably open and accessible. Moreover, the persons relating to the entity being evaluated are usually not disreputable. If they are guilty of anything, that guilt is certainly not apparent, nor is the crime likely to be morally reprehensible. Thus, the usual arguments of the kind made by investigative reporters seem not to apply.

But on close inspection, the differences between the ethical situation of the evaluator and that of the investigative journalist are more matters of degree than of kind. There are situations in which subjects make every effort to keep certain information from the evaluator, to deceive him about the true state of affairs, or to mislead him with respect to what are the important data. Every evaluation has political and human overtones, and to suppose that human foibles will not emerge in such situations is simply naive. When the evaluator finds himself in *his* gray area, will he stoop to the same rationalizations as the reporter? It would be surprising indeed for him to do otherwise.

4. Objectivity/fairness parallels. Journalism in general and investigative journalism in particular are moving away from the criterion of objectivity to an emergent criterion usually labeled "fairness." Objectivity, according to the dictionary, means "determined by and emphasizing the features of the object or thing dealt with rather than the thoughts, feelings, etc., of the artist, writer, or speaker" . . . or journalist or evaluator. Objectivity assumes a single reality to which the story or evaluation must be isomorphic; it is in this sense a one-perspective criterion. It assumes that an agent can deal with an object (or another person) in a nonreactive and noninteractive way. It is an absolute criterion.

Journalists are coming to feel that objectivity in that sense is unattainable. Fact gathering and interpretation are inseparable. Objectivity cannot even be attained, journalists aptly point out, by scientists or IQ testers. There are always multiple perspectives from which to view a story — including the perspective of the subject. And even if objectivity could be attained at the data-collection end of journalism, it cannot be attained in reporting because of the need to compress the story into available space and to phrase it in language comprehensible to the average reader. Distortions inevitably result.

Enter "fairness" as a substitute criterion. In contrast to objectivity, fairness has these features:

- It assumes multiple realities or truths — hence a test of fairness is whether or not "both" sides of the case are presented, and there may even be multiple sides.

- It is adversarial rather than one-perspective in nature. Rather than trying to hew the line with *the* truth, as the objective reporter does, the fair reporter seeks to present each side of the case in the manner of an advocate — as, for example, attorneys do in making a case in court. The presumption is that the public, like a jury, is more likely to reach an equitable decision after having heard each side presented with as much vigor and commitment as possible.

• It is assumed that the subject's reaction to the reporter and interaction between them heavily determines what the reporter perceives. Hence one test of fairness is the length to which the reporter will go to test his own biases and rule them out.

• It is a relative criterion that is measured by *balance* rather than by isomorphism to enduring truth.

Clearly, evaluators have a great deal to learn from this development. For, like journalists, evaluators have sought to be objective. In the case of the evaluator, however, the motivation to objectivity is probably even higher than it is for journalists, because evaluators have so fiercely endeavored to emulate the cool, dispassionate scientist as a model. And like journalism, evaluation is beginning to face up to the fact that objectivity is as unattainable as the Holy Grail — perhaps desirable ideally but a completely impossible achievement in the real world in which they operate. Like journalism, evaluation is beginning to realize that a methodology which assumes singular reality, isomorphism, nonreactivity (or noninteractivity), and absolute scales is simply untenable. Evaluators may be well advised to work out their own form of "fairness," stressing balanced, even adversarial, procedures and reports in which strenuous efforts are made to eliminate — or at least expose — personal biases.

5. *Operational parallels – tracking.* A major source of information for the investigative reporter is the record; indeed, Williams asserts that "the first and great commandment of investigative journalism is this: 'get the record' " (1978, p. 13). Records are important because they are an accessible, stable, and rich resource; they constitute a legally unassailable base; they represent a "natural, in context" source; they are available on a no-cost or low-cost basis; and they are nonreactive. But obviously there is a surfeit of records. How can one know *what* records will be worth consulting in any given case? The answer to that question seems to emerge from a process which will here be called "tracking," by way of analogy to the process by which the hunter stalks his game. Williams suggests that the investigative reporter

has ingrained within himself a special style of reasoning. He knows how things normally work. If he observes a phenomenon, an effect, he wonders what caused it. He develops a hypothesis and begins checking it against observable facts. He works to back up the chain of facts, searching for information that will either support or negate his hypothesis. He tries different combinations of conflicting versions of a story until he finds the one in which salient points overlap [1978, p. 13].

In a similar vein, Locklin comments:

> I have a working theory that if I know something, if I know what the situation is, the date the money went, how much money went, who paid, who got it, if I know that, I can usually prove it [1976, p. 7].

Both these quotations illustrate the salient point that from a knowledge of "how things normally work"; the investigator can deduce what trails or tracks must have been left *if* his suspicions are warranted. Here are several examples from the world of investigative reporting:

- A public administrator is believed to have housed his paramour in a building that fell to him to administer as part of an estate for which there was no will. The reporter's suspicion was verified by recourse to utility bills which showed that this house was in use rather than standing empty. Utility bills were consulted because the reporter reasoned that if someone was living in one of the houses administered by this official, that house ought to show patterns of usage different from other buildings also administered by this official which were standing empty.

- A municipal officer accepts a bribe to sway the city administration to an opinion favorable to the officer's "client." The client cannot pay the bribe directly in cash since it is likely that the IRS would be attracted if the officer were suddenly to spend or deposit a large sum of money otherwise unaccounted for. Instead, the client sells a desirable piece of property to the officer at "bargain basement" rates; the officer in turn resells the property at its true value. The officer pays the capital gains tax, but the remaining money is "clean" and can be deposited without hesitation. But a trail has been left in the recorded transfers of deeds, as well as in the income tax return. The shrewd reporter may uncover these transactions through a search of courthouse records and through the intercession of a "contact" at IRS.

- A businessman has been accumulating funds in a variety of illegal ways, but it has been impossible to demonstrate that the funds are actually in his possession. Unfortunately for the businessman, his wife elects to sue him for divorce, and she, being aware of these hidden resources, will not be denied her share. The property settlement reached between them, a matter of public record in the divorce court hearing the suit, is exploited by a reporter to put him on the track of the funds and, eventually, to their source.

In all three cases the investigative reporter is guided to the precise set of records he needs by a combination of two factors: certain suspicions and a knowledge of "how things work." He knows what kinds of tracks *must* have been left *if* his suspicions are justified, and he goes about looking for them *where they must be found*.

The transfer to educational evaluation is patent. Consider the following hypothetical examples:

- It is asserted that the motivation of pupils to read historical novels has been increased because of the teacher's method of having the class act out segments of such novels in full dress of the period. That assertion can be checked by looking at existing library withdrawal records, records of sales of books at the local bookstore, and so on.

- It is asserted that a certain instructional outcome has occurred because of the serendipitous introduction of certain unplanned teaching techniques. The existence of these techniques and their impact on day-to-day instruction can be at least partially assessed by consulting lesson plans that teachers are required to file.

- It is asserted that evaluation reports have systematically "turned off" certain parent groups in the community. Some insight into the truth of this allegation may be gained by searching minutes and newspaper accounts of recent PTA meetings at which these reports were disseminated.

Again, the key is a combination of assertion (a suspicion) and a knowledge of how things work.

6. *Operational parallels – the key interview.* For the investigative reporter, the key interview is the culmination of the entire investigative process. This interview has a variety of purposes: to confront the subject(s) with the results of the investigation to that point, to elicit the subject's response to the allegations, to test the story for accuracy (while recalling that the subject is motivated to mislead and deceive), to get the subject's side of the story (including motivation for his actions and/or his rationalizations for engaging in them), and, it is hoped, to uncover new information that is available only from this knowledgeable source.

The reconstructed logic of a typical key interview includes these steps: gaining entree, preparing and beginning the interview, controlling the interview, confronting the subject, and recording. Presumably the investigative reporter is well skilled in the specific techniques of each step. Standard textbooks on investigative journalism devote a great deal of space to such techniques, underscoring their importance.

Two applications of these procedures come to mind with respect to educational evaluation. First, it is sometimes the case that the evaluator finds himself confronted by an uncooperative informant — for example, a project or program director who, in a third-party evaluation situation, feels threatened by the evaluation. While the degree of uncooperativeness is never likely to be so severe as in the case of the investigative reporter confronting a subject about to be branded as a thief or an incompetent, there will surely be a temptation for the subject to misdirect, exaggerate, evade, and perhaps even lie. It seems likely that the specific techniques used by the investigative reporter under such circumstances might prove useful to the educational evaluator as well.

Second, there is a possible parallel in the sense of testing a report or an allegation with the person whom it most directly affects. Even when there is no apparent reason (from the point of view of the evaluator) for a subject to feel anxious or threatened by an evaluation, he may nonetheless take exception to some aspect of the report once it has been developed. Evaluation is always dysfunctional to human performance to some extent; moreover, there are always political aspects to be considered (an evaluation report almost always disrupts the existing balance of power from someone's point of view). Subjects alluded to in evaluation reports are likely to be sensitive and may weight the data presented and the interpretations made in quite different ways from the evaluator.

The prudent evaluator will want to test his report with various subjects for reasons similar to those of the investigative reporter — to check on credibility with the subjects, to solicit their reactions, to get further details that may clarify or extenuate, and the like. In such situations evaluators may find themselves beset in ways similar to those experienced by the investigative reporter in the key interview. The tactics which have been devised by such reporters for key interviews may then turn out to be very useful.

7. *Operational parallels – indexes, files, chronologies, and summaries.* Obviously, the investigative reporter develops files on the cases he investigates; they become an important permanent record for him, serve as the basis for the story as he writes it, and may in due course serve as an invaluable back-up in the case of legal action. But files have a great deal more utility than merely convenience in cataloging collected material and serving as a memory aid. They are, in fact, an important tactical tool in their own right.

The general flow of activity for utilizing files as investigatory tools is displayed in Figure 3.2.

Filing begins with the establishment of a folder for each of the individuals involved in the investigation (Stage 1). There may be only one folder if there is no immediate lead to anyone but the major subject, but there soon will be multiple folders as the investigation proceeds.

STAGE

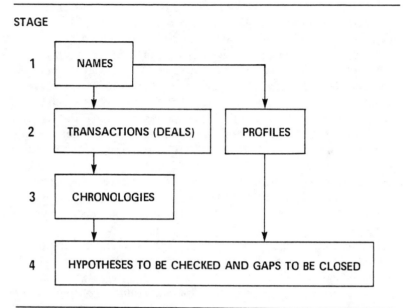

Figure 3.2 The Use of Files in Journalistic Investigations

As the person or persons originally targeted enter into transactions with others, transaction folders are developed relating to each such "deal" (Stage 2). A transaction may range from something as simple as meeting for lunch to something as complex as a real estate purchase.

Simultaneously, profiles — that is, summaries of the subjects' characteristics and lifestyles — are developed for each of the persons for whom a "name" file has been established.

Chronologies are developed for the various transactions. Thus, we may find that on January 5 Mr. Smith had lunch with Mr. Brown, that on January 6 Mr. Smith deposited $2500 in *his* bank account, that on January 8 Mr. Brown was awarded an important contract over which Mr. Smith's office had jurisdiction, and that on January 9 Mr. Smith deposited an additional $2500 in his account (Stage 3).

As the files develop, important items are cross-referenced. Thus, the notation that Mr. Brown withdrew $5000 from his bank account would be referred to in both his name and deals files; a notation about this behavior might also be placed in the profiles file.

Each file is summarized on a systematic basis, so that the investigator need not deal with all the bulky original items whenever he enters the file but rather with a summary of what it contains.

Entries in the several files will give rise to hypotheses to be checked or point to informational gaps that ought to be plugged. So, for example, the chronology on Mr. Smith and Mr. Brown gives rise to the hypothesis that Mr. Brown has bought Mr. Smith's favor for $5000, with $2500 delivered in advance and $2500 after the contract was awarded. If the chronology showed the timing of deposits and withdrawals but the information that Mr. Brown had received a contract mediated by Mr. Smith's office had been missing, the reporter would have been led to hypothesize some illegal activity between the two and would have gone looking for whatever it was the $5000 had bought (Stage 4).

This process of keeping careful files, cross-referencing them, summarizing them, and developing chronologies from them as a means for keeping track of what is going on and suggesting hypotheses or gaps is obviously also a useful one for the evaluator to follow. This approach seems to be especially useful in any evaluation intended primarily to monitor and as an adjunct to the tracking process described earlier.

8. *Operational parallels – minimum-maximum goal projection and aborting.* After a preliminary study has been made of the feasibility of a certain proposed investigation, a decision must be made whether it is worth pursuing — whether the story will be worth the resources necessarily expended to get it. Editors often demand minimum-maximum projections from reporters at this stage. For example, a proposed investigation of the management of an airport whose profits fell enormously after ownership was transferred from private to public agencies might show that, at a minimum, the new management was incompetent (a knowledge gain of some utility to the public interest), but might also show, at a maximum, that the managers were dishonest and systematically bilking the public (a greater gain). The go/no-go decision must be made on the basis of the minimum goals; there must be sufficient payoff to warrant the resource investment. Then, if the story begins to approximate maximum goals, the paper will have reaped an unexpected bonanza — a windfall profit, as it were.

Evaluators have not taken a minimum-maximum approach in specifying the outcomes of their evaluations. But many evaluations have fallen short of the expectations held for them. It seems likely that if evaluators specified modest minimum expectations they were *certain* they could meet and then specified other expectations which they *might* be able to meet if everything fell into place, evaluation outcomes would be received in a more realistic context and evaluator credibility would rise. For examples, the evaluator might specify that,

- at a minimum, he will be able to provide information on achievement of a program's objectives, but that, if things go well, he might also be able to identify the concerns and issues on the minds of the most relevant audiences and perhaps even gather preliminary data responsive to them;

- at a minimum, he would provide a "thick description" of the entity being evaluated, with documentation of every process step, but that, if things go well, he might also be able to provide some judgments or recommendations for improvement;

- at a minimum, he will be able to establish the relationships existing among certain variables of interest, but that, if things go well, he might also be able to pin down some of those relationships with cause/effect data.

Evaluators have often been accused of overpromising; the minimum-maximum strategy is both more realistic and more credible than is current practice.

However, despite the best planning and the most realistic estimates of minimum expectations, sometimes stories, or evaluations, go wrong. It is interesting to note that Williams has identified no fewer than three go/no-go decision stages in his reconstruction of the investigative reporting process, and it is apparently the case that investigative stories can be and are aborted at each of those checkpoints. Evaluators, who one might expect to be sensitive to reviewing their own work, seem not to have incorporated such checkpoints into the reconstructed logic of *their* practice.

To be sure, there has been talk in the evaluation literature of meta-evaluation criteria. The most recent and massive effort to devise such criteria is the current task of the Joint Committee on Evaluation Guidelines and Standards, formed by the American Educational Research Association, the American Psychological Association, the National Council on Measurement in Education, and some nine practitioner groups, among them the National Education Association, the National School Boards Association, and the Education Commission of the States. But these criteria have a very summative flavor — they can be used to examine an evaluation when it is complete, and probably to help to plan it before the fact. There are few criteria, however, and certainly no mechanisms, for examining an ongoing evaluation. Certainly, evaluators do not typically ask whether the evaluations they conduct are making reasonable progress toward minimum and maximum goals; and the possibility of *aborting* an ongoing evaluation is virtually unthinkable.

One can only express surprise at the evaluators' apparent disinterest in self-evaluation and suggest that the example set by investigative reporters might be a useful one to emulate. It might, indeed, be in the best interest of the evaluation profession if an occasional evaluation were aborted, or at least restructured, as a result of such a self-examination.

9. Operational parallels – reporting. The investigative journalist's ultimate purpose is to write a publishable story that will be well received by the readership. Most journalists agree that it takes more than just a startling set of facts or disclosures to accomplish that aim. Of course, qualities of good writing are essential, such as clarity and creativity. But reporters must also provide answers to the questions: What am I trying to prove? Who gives a damn (who is the primary audience for my story)? Why will my primary audience care — to which of their interests does the story appeal?

Evaluation, too, must be reported. But often evaluators do not ask themselves the questions investigative journalists routinely ask. Indeed, the majority of evaluation reports read as though they were written for other evaluators — to fit some kind of reconstructed logic of what the evaluation process entails, or to meet the model of scientific reporting, rather than to communicate to some audience a description and judgment of an entity in which they have a stake.

- Evaluators may well ask, "What am I trying to prove?" One should not take that statement too literally, of course, for the good evaluator does not set out to prove anything. Yet he has a case to make, for or against the entity being evaluated. He needs to be clear in his mind what that case is and to arrange his data in a way that will present that case fairly. In general, the latter condition implies that he will, as would the journalist, present a "balanced" story.

- The "Who gives a damn?" question is intended to require the journalist to identify the audience(s) for which he is writing. The evaluator has a similar problem, and he needs to be aware that among his audiences will be others besides the evaluation's clients or sponsors, and perhaps even some that would prefer to continue in a "low profile" posture. But the evaluator needs to fulfill his responsibility to all such audiences. Of course, it goes without saying that different audiences will profit from different styles and content in reporting; the wise evaluator makes an audience analysis before he starts his report to be sure he finds the "voice, vocabulary, and pace" for each. At times reports will not be written but will take a form most congenial to the audience in question.

- The question "Why will my audience care?" suggests that the evaluator should address himself to the particular concerns, issues, and interests the audiences reading his report will want to know about. Indeed, these audience concerns and issues can become the basis for the entire evaluation, just as, in the case of the investigative journalist, reader concerns, issues, and interests become the basis for focusing the entire investigation. The evaluator who has looked into his audiences ahead of time and organized his evaluation accordingly is ahead of the game when reports are written.

The evaluator is thus well advised to spend time learning how investigative reporters organize their reporting in order to deal with the key audience questions. Analogous procedures in educational evaluation would undoubtedly be productive.

Epilog

The brief narrative presented here was intended to acquaint you with some possibilities inherent in the investigative journalism metaphor and to whet your appetite for further exploration of this fascinating discipline on your own. The examples given here have been only that — they can be and need to be explored in greater depth. Further, there are many other parallels, excluded here for lack of space, which also warrant study. The metaphor is rich indeed; it awaits intelligent mining. Here are some sources to which you might wish to turn for further exploration.

For an expanded discussion of the relationship of investigative journalism to evaluation:

Guba, Egon G. Investigative journalism as a metaphor for educational evaluation. In N.L. Smith (Ed.), *New Techniques for Evaluation*. Beverly Hills, CA: Sage Publications, 1981. This chapter contains an extensive bibliography not only of books and articles but also of source journals which frequently publish articles dealing with investigative journalism, investigative journalism newsletters, and organizations relating to investigative journalism.

For two recent textbooks dealing with investigative journalism:

Anderson, David and Benjaminson, Peter. *Investigative Reporting*. Bloomington: Indiana University Press, 1976.

Williams, Paul N. *Investigative Reporting and Editing*. Englewood Cliffs, NJ: Prentice-Hall, Inc., 1978.

For a brief, popularized account:

Noyes, Dan. *Raising Hell: A Citizen's Guide to the Fine Art of Investigation.* San Francisco, CA: Mother Jones Magazine, 1978. (Copies may be ordered for $2.25 by writing to Raising Hell, 607 Market Street, San Francisco, CA 94105.)

For two organizations that can provide information and fugitive published materials:

Center for Investigative Reporting, Inc.
The Broadway Building
1419 Broadway, Room 600
Oakland, CA 94612

Investigative Journalism Project
Urban Policy Research Institute
321 S. Beverly Drive, Suite W
Beverly Hills, CA 90212

For the national professional organization of investigative journalists:

Ms. Myrta Pulliam
Investigative Reporters and Editors, Inc.
307 N. Pennsylvania Street
Indianapolis, IN 46206

Notes

[1] This paper is a much-abridged version of a monograph, "Investigative Journalism as a Metaphor for Educational Evaluation." The longer work can be found in Volume 2 of *New Perspectives in Evaluation* (Smith, 1981).

[2] The parallels to be considered in this section represent only a sampling of those presented in the larger document of which this is an abstract. See footnote 1.

References

Anderson, D., & Benjaminson, P. *Investigative reporting.* Bloomington: Indiana University Press, 1976.

Douglas, J. D. *Investigative social research.* Beverly Hills, CA: Sage, 1976.

Locklin, B. V. "Transcript of discussion by Bruce V. Locklin." Investigative Reporting Seminar, November 20, 1976. (Available from Urban Policy Research Institute, Beverly Hills, CA)

Smith, N. L. *New Techniques for Evaluation.* Beverly Hills, CA: Sage, 1981.

Williams, P. N. *Investigative reporting and editing.* Englewood Cliffs, NJ: Prentice-Hall, 1978.

Thomas R. Owens
Associate Director, Education and Work Program,
Northwest Regional Educational Laboratory

Thomas R. Owen
Independent Consultant, Portland, Oregon

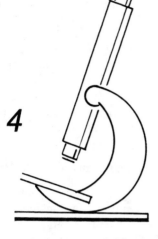

CHAPTER **4**

Law

Thomas R. Owens has been coordinating evaluation and knowledge development activities for NWREL's Education and Work Program for the past seven years. In that time, the program has developed and applied a number of new methodologies for evaluating Experience Based Career Education (EBCE) and other experiential education programs. Tom first adapted and tried the adversary evaluation process in 1969 while working at the University of Hawaii. Since then he has modified the concept with EBCE in 1976 and was a team member in 1978 on NWREL's adversary evaluation of the Hawaii 3 on 2 Program. ● *Thomas R. Owen is an independent educational program and statistical consultant whose evaluation work during the last several years has centered on experientially based programs. His other professional interests include museum evaluation, the application of microcomputers in education, and the problem of incorporating evaluation into program decision-making.*

FOR CENTURIES, law has provided a system of social rules and procedures to regulate behavior of individuals and institutions. The field of law, in our opinion, provides fertile ground as a metaphor for educational evaluation, since both fields involve systematic inquiry, procedures for making judgments, and a valuing of justice. In this chapter we will provide a brief overview of the field of law, describe some similarities and differences between the two fields, provide metaphors at three levels of generality, explore two metaphors in some depth, suggest other parallels between law and educational evaluation, and conclude with some suggested next steps for persons wishing to delve more deeply into these relationships.

Since the purpose of this chapter is to explore law as a metaphor for evaluation and to stimulate others to probe more deeply into the insights that may be presented here, we will not attempt an extended coverage of a single metaphor. Instead, we will provide some brief references that may help the reader begin his or her own investigation.

Overview of the Field of Law

Law has presumably evolved from the social and family customs of our prehistoric ancestors. With the advent of writing and the need for standardization and communication, written laws such as the Code of Hammurabbi and the Ten Commandments were developed. By Roman times, law had become differentiated into public law dealing with citizens' relationships with the state and private law dealing with citizens' relationships with one another. Modern law has become more complex and is seen to operate in several capacities: for effecting grievance remediation, punishment, administrative regulation; for ordering governmental conferral of public benefits; and for facilitating and effectuating private arrangements (Summers, 1972).

Laws are made by legislatures, administrative agencies, and, in common law countries, by judges as well. As society became more complex, it became more difficult for legislative bodies to make adequately comprehensive laws, so administrative and regulatory agencies were often empowered to make laws within prescribed limits. Judge-made law is possible in common law countries and results partly from the lack of a clear distinction between the creation of a law and the creative interpretation of a law as it is applied to a situation that it was not specifically and explicitly designed to cover.

Law is legitimatized by various means from sheer force through appeal to "natural" law. "Might" may not make "right," but it is sufficient to make the law. In democratic societies, of course, we often have legitimation by mutual consent of the governed. Ultimately, law can be criticized from the standpoint of "natural law"; that is, an appeal to a higher law — of God, reason, morality, or justice.

In order to make the metaphorical claim that evaluation is law, we ought to back up one step and determine what law is. In "Law as the Soverign's Command," Austin (1966, pp. 77-78) says that law "may be said to be a rule laid down for the guidance of an intelligent being by an intelligent being having power over him." Similarly, Kelsen (1966, p. 110) says:

> It is the function of every social order . . . to bring about certain reciprocal behavior of human beings: to make them refrain from certain acts which, for some reason, are deemed detrimental to society, and to make them perform others, which, for some reason, are considered useful to society.

These definitions might be said to characterize law as a body of rules and sanctions. Oliver Wendel Holmes, Jr. offers a contrasting definition of law: He sees it as predictive of what courts will do.

> The object of our study (law) then is prediction, the prediction of the incidence of the public force through the instrumentality of the courts. . . . A legal duty so called is nothing but a prediction that if a man does or omits certain things, he will be made to suffer in this or that way by judgement of the court [Holmes, 1966, p. 176].

He goes on to summarize that law is a "body of dogma or systematized prediction" (p. 177).

The field of law appears to us to encompass the written set of regulations of individual and institutional behavior, the handling of issues concerning the justification of those regulations, and the interpretation of them in the process of determining whether compliance is or ought to be achieved. There is in this construction considerable parallel between law and evaluation.

Similarities and Differences Between Law and Evaluation

The field of law shares a number of attributes with that of educational evaluation. Five parallels will be drawn. First, both fields show a valuing of fairness and justice. Rules of evidence in law, for example, are used to help decide the appropriateness of testimony being presented; criteria such as validity and reliability help establish the quality of data in educational evaluation.

A second parallel is that law and educational evaluation involve a systematic inquiry process. Both fields contain a variety of techniques for planning, obtaining, and summarizing information. In both cases, there is usually a rational model that governs what information is to be collected and how it may be used.

Third, both fields focus on communicating information which is considered important for someone else to use in making decisions. In a court hearing, the information is usually presented orally to the judge and jury. In evaluation, the information is more often communicated to decision makers through written reports.

A fourth parallel between the two fields lies in their struggle with similar ethical issues. While both fields espouse justice for all, lawyers face the realization that laws are not always applied fairly to all segments of society. Similarly, in educational evaluation there is a growing concern over test biases against minority students, and there is controversy regarding fair standards for judging programs. Professionals in both fields, in working with their clients, are mindful of potential conflicts of interest, confidentiality of client information, and their responsibilities to the general public as well as to their clients.

A final parallel that can be drawn between the two fields is the disdain many lay persons have for the jargon and technical language used by lawyers and evaluators, language which seems to set these professionals apart from the common man. This disdain increases as people suspect that these professionals use legal technicalities or statistical manipulations for their own ends.

The two fields also differ in a number of ways that are important to consider. For example, in educational evaluation there are no common statutes to determine when effective learning has been violated, no documentation of educational precedent, no cross-examination of witnesses, no naive jury waiting to make a decision based solely on an evaluation report, and no recognized appeals processes.

Levels of Discourse

In an earlier chapter of this book, Nick Smith makes a significant contribution to thinking about methodology by proposing levels of methodological discourse. His four levels, going from general to specific, are (1) point of view, (2) paradigm, (3) operational strategy, and (4) technique. As we considered law as a metaphor for evaluation, it became clear to us that metaphoric translations can and should be made at various levels. At the first level we consider parallels in goals between law and evaluation. At level 2 we propose parallels in the broad functions and tasks in these two fields. Level 3 leads us to translate strategies or models from law to evaluation, while level 4 provides an opportunity to examine techniques from the field of law that may have exciting applications to evaluation. However, level 4 becomes too specific for use as a metaphor. Table 4.1 illustrates one or two metaphors from law at each of the first three levels of methodological discourse. Each metaphor is described more fully in the remainder of this section.

Point of View

To say that evaluation is a process for establishing individual and social justice has important implications for evaluation. Such a statement implies that evaluation must deal with values as well as with facts; that justice applies to each person, not just to those who are most visible; that procedures used in evaluation must themselves be fair; and that the outcomes of an evaluation will lead to a just decision.

Ernest House (1976), who claims to have borrowed heavily from the philosophy of John Rawls, has demonstrated that the underlying value of the utilitarian evaluation commonly practiced in education is that of maximizing test scores. As a substitute, he proposes that "evaluators consider basing value claims on the character of the distribution of benefits rather than on the measurement of net benefits for a group" (p. 75). Thus, it becomes important to determine how a program benefits the least advantaged students rather than merely looking to see if it leads to an overall average gain.

Evaluation as justice implies that measurement instruments and procedures be used that are fair to all those being tested. Not only must instruments not discriminate against minority students and those for whom English is not a first language, but the procedures of data collection and interpretation need also be considered in terms of justice.

Recent trends in the field of law indicate a growing post-Watergate sensitivity to helping ensure justice and equity for all without respect to the wealth or cultural background of clients. In examining a new professional role for lawyers, Marks (1972) discusses the conflicting

TABLE 4.1   Law and Evaluation Metaphors

Levels of Methodological Discourse	Legal Constructs	Evaluation Metaphors
1. Point of View	Justice	Evaluation is a process for establishing individual and social justice.
2. Paradigm	a. Functions of government (legislative, executive, judicial)	a. Evaluation involves making an evaluative claim, using that claim in regulating and administering a practice, and in subjecting that claim to judicial review if the claim becomes contested.
	b. Tasks of lawyers (prediction, justification, persuasion, systematization)	b. Evaluation involves predicting likely program outcomes, providing data to support judgments regarding the achievement of program objectives, persuading others that a program's claims are valid, and writing reports that integrate program findings with prior research.
3. Operation strategy	a. Legislative history	a. A (legislative history) evaluation reconstructs the history of particular federal legislation mandating evaluations for the purpose of interpreting its meaning.
	b. Courtroom trial	b. An (adversary) evaluation consists of two evaluators or evaluation teams employed to plan, implement, and report an evaluation from diametrically opposed viewpoints.

role perceptions between traditional private attorneys and public interest lawyers:

> Unless society finds ways of subsidizing the price of entry into the law forum, or unless the profession as a whole changes its cultural (lifestyle) base and professional outlook enough to drop or reduce that price so that the poor, the unpopular, the isolated, and the abstract or fragmented interests in our society are represented on an equal basis with all others, the public interest responder has identified for himself a professional role which is isolated . . . [p. 248].

> As an institution, the private law firm did not, in the past, include in its definition of professional responsibility a sense of duty to the public which went beyond economic self-interest and loyalty to regular clients [p. 265].

As an alternative to public interest law firms specializing in such cases and thereby having problems of economic survival, Mark discusses the released time program in some private law firms. This involves relieving the lawyer from some portion of responsibility to the firm's regular clients to work on public interest cases.

The desire for involvement by some of the legal profession in public interest activities, and concern over how it should be funded, provide some interesting challenges to the field of evaluation. What are an evaluator's responsibilities for evaluating aspects of education of particular concern to the public? If these concerns are different from those of the project staff and funding agency, how will the concerns of the public be addressed, and who will pay for the work on their behalf? What happens if a concerned citizens group without funds desires an evaluation of a school busing program that a Board of Education may not wish to have evaluated? Would it be possible for a school district to set aside a small portion of its research and evaluation funds for publicly requested studies that may cut across individual programs? Although we do not have answers to such questions, the metaphor of evaluation as a process for establishing individual and social justice suggests we may need to give attention to such ethical issues in the future.

Paradigm

A look at the functions and tasks of law suggests further interesting metaphors for educational evaluation. In our society, law and political order comprise three functions: legislative, executive, and judicial. Bob Gowin, in a critique of an earlier draft of this chapter, has suggested that we could think of evaluation as (a) "making an evaluation claim, (b) using that claim in regulating and administering a practice, and (c) having that claim subject to 'judicial' review if the claim becomes contested." For example, an evaluator of a new career education program might help staff refine an objective which indicated that students would increase their career development skills at a level significantly greater than students in a conventional vocational education program. This claim or objective, if accepted and understood by students and staff, should help focus the instructional content and strategies of the program and could be tested by the evaluator as part of the evaluation design.

In their legal method book, Dowling, Patterson, and Powell (1952) identify four principal legal tasks that make up the lawyer's work: persuasion, prediction, justification, and systematization. The task of the advocate is to persuade the court, by legal arguments, to reach a decision in favor of the client. As a counselor advising a client, the attorney's role is to help clients find the safest ways to conduct their affairs. The attorney has to give a reliable prediction of what the courts are likely to decide. A third task in law, performed by judges, involves reaching a decision and providing a justification for the decision reached. The fourth task of lawyers can be labeled that of "text-writers"; it involves writing treatises, articles, and notes in legal periodicals.

As applied to educational evaluation, the tasks of justification and persuasion seem most relevant. Many evaluators would see their task as providing data to support judgments such as the extent to which a project achieved its objectives or is of social worth. This task of justification becomes especially important when an evaluator makes recommendations as part of an evaluation report. If evaluation audiences paid greater attention to the task of justification, evaluators might be held more accountable for substantiating their recommendations with evaluation data they have accumulated.

In the task of persuasion, an evaluator would need to understand what factors would be most likely to render a favorable verdict for the client in the opinion of the outside judges. This may cause the evaluator to look carefully at costs and ease of program implementation as well as at students' outcomes. In the political realities of education, an evaluator is often hired to collect data to show how effective a program is and to provide program staff with ammunition to persuade outsiders that the program should continue to receive funding. An ethical concern arises at this point if the data indicate to the evaluator that the program is not effective and there is little evidence that the program will become effective. As an ethical professional, the evaluator would have to abandon the legal metaphor of persuasion at that point and portray the findings in a candid way.

The task of prediction has seldom been considered in relation to educational evaluation. There are times, however, when an evaluator can serve a useful role in the proposal-writing or early start-up phase of a program by examining proposed objectives of a program and predicting the likelihood that the objectives would be reached given the nature of the students to be served and the proposed instructional interventions. A sound knowledge of evaluation findings from similar programs can serve as a good basis for making such predictions. In this role, the evaluator might help a program staff avoid stating unreasonable outcome expectations and thereby promising more than can be delivered.

The fourth task of law, systematization, is also seldom applied to evaluation but suggests some interesting parallels. As the field of educational evaluation matures, it will be necessary that evaluation findings from similar programs be written up and synthesized so that readers can retrieve evaluation findings related to a particular content or subject area by consulting journals or reference documents. The establishment and maintenance of such a reference system would allow future evaluators to review findings, instruments, and the like for a particular content area before they undertook to prepare a comprehensive evaluation plan. Such a system would also be useful to evaluators in writing reports and preparing interpretations of their findings.

Operational Strategy

Legislative History

Legislative histories and courtroom trials serve as legal constructs that can provide a metaphor for evaluation at the operational level. A number of conventions have been generated to aid legal interpretation, such as the construction of histories of legislative acts for the purpose of determining the true intent of the legislators. These legislative histories have been used in the United States since its beginning and were modeled on similar practices of the British Parliament. The following quotation from a sixteenth-century publication provides a rationale for this approach.

> The statute shall be taken . . . ex mente legislatorum, for that is chiefe to be considered, which, althoughe it varie in so muche that in maner so manie heads as there were, so manie statute makers, so many myndes; yet, notwithstanding, certen notes there are by which a man maie knowe what it was. . . . And so, in our dayes, have those that were the penners & devisors of statutes bene the grettest lighte for exposicion of statutes [Thorne, 1572, in Folsom, 1972].

Legislative histories are used to limit the scope of application of a law or to impose limitations on the meanings of particular words thought to be ambiguous (Folsom, 1972, p. 13). They can be used to clarify both the purpose of the law and its immediate meaning (Landis, 1930). Interpretive problems stem both from the inevitable ambiguities of language and from the impossibility of anticipating all situations to which the law might apply. Technical and social changes, for example, can create problems of interpretation: Witness the difficulties of the copyright law after the advent of the photo copier.

The use of legislative histories is restricted to interpreting language already in the law. Courts, in theory, may not add new material to the law, and official written documents, not surveys or interviews of legislators, are generally the only allowable sources. The allowable documents include releases, drafts, transcribed testimony, proposals, bills, committee hearings and reports, and general debates.

Folsom (1972, pp. 8-12) describes, in addition to legislative histories as such, other kinds of usable histories for legal interpretation, including histories of external events (the tone of the times), legal history (an examination of previous laws covering the same area), and statutory history (a look at successive wordings of the same piece of code). Although the question of whether there is discoverable legislative intent has not gone unchallenged (pp. 7-8), all of these approaches are generally regarded as legitimate.

The application of the legislative history procedure to program evaluation is twofold and straightforward in both cases. In the first case the application is direct and nonmetaphorical. There are programs which do have legislative histories. ESEA Title I, Title IV, and the new Title I Technical Assistance Centers are examples of programs which have their direct source in federal legislation. In these instances, a formal legislative history might be carried out by — even required of — the evaluator in any study large enough to underwrite the cost of the effort. Whether the legislative history was seen as an audit activity seeking to hold the program(s) to the intents of the legislators or whether it was seen as a means of determining the interests of one potential audience, it might be a very revealing exercise. The study might use legislative sources to test the wording of agency implementation documents such as RFPs (requests for proposals) and contract specifications, and/or to test program objectives and other statements of purpose against both legislative intent and agency guidelines.

The second approach to the use of legislative history-like activities in the evaluation of programs is more general and less technically similar to the "real thing" than the first. This second form tends to be used in situations where legislative antecedents are distant or nonexistent but where the authors of the program may be at hand, as with a local group of proposal writers or with members of an administrative steering committee. The purpose of such a study would be the same as for a more formal legislative history — that is, to bring clarity, or a recognition of divergent viewpoints, to the expressed goals and objectives of the program in question. Methodologically, this study must rely more on surveys and interviews of the original program architects. The problem with these reconstructions, of course, is that they may be a reflection of current interests as much as of past intents. Nevertheless, reconstruction may be the only avenue open, even though the updated interests of legislators would not properly be a part of a historical approach.

One evaluation study used both of the approaches to legislative history described here. In an evaluation conducted by the Northwest Regional Educational Laboratory, Nafziger, Benson, and Worthen (1977) collected and analyzed over 30 legislative and administrative documents related to the origin and purposes of the program being studied, the Hawaii 3 on 2 Program (a state-funded, elementary school team teaching program). These documents included state legislature conference committee reports, correspondence from the Senate committee on education, State Department of Education testimony to the House education committee, House resolutions, and Legislative Auditor's reports. The documents were reviewed by the evaluators, and an annotated bibliography was prepared for each

document. This study also included interviews with former legislators, state superintendents, and former state board of education
members in an effort to determine the purposes for the program.
In a study of the ESEA Title I evaluation system, McLaughlin
(1975) took a partly historical approach that looked at the intents of
the legislators to examine "the congruence between the assumptions
and expectations that generated these notions of evaluation and reform and the dominant incentives that shaped the behavior of individuals and institutions in the Title I policy system" (p. vii). Using
documents of subcommittee hearings, among others, she was able to
show the diversity of opinion among legislators, federal agency, and
local school people.

For those who wish to do a legislative history, Folsom (1972)
provides an extensive set of document sources and a procedure — the
skeleton history — for developing a comprehensive list of documentation leading to a piece of legislation. The best place to begin is with a
reference, obtainable from the funding agency, to the appropriate
piece of legislation. Next, the acquaintance of a government document librarian should be sought, since the reference system for legislative documents is difficult for the uninitiated. Skeleton histories are
compiled for statutes enacted from 1963 onward in *Statutes at Large*,
a publication containing a "Guide to Legislative History of Bills
Enacted into Public Law." *The Digest of Public General Bills and
Resolutions* is also useful for statutes enacted since 1967. With the
skeleton history, investigators can study the documents at any depth
they feel would be worthwhile. The first document sought should be
the committee report recommending the bill to the full legislative
body. This report is legally and practically the most important because it contains the committee's formal and final agreed-upon
rationale for the legislation. Other documents of hearings and even
statements made during floor debates do not carry the weight of the
committee recommendation. The investigator should be aware that
there are often three such committee reports, one each from the
House, the Senate, and from a joint committee. State, as opposed to
federal, legislation may have a more limited legislative history because states often do not publish legislative activities as extensively
as does the federal government. Once the evaluators have the historical documents, they may use them to compare with program and
agency objectives and activities.

There are potential problems with a legislative history-like approach to an evaluation study. As with all goal-based approaches, it is

unclear how closely a developing program should be held to original intents. Another potential problem has already been mentioned: the credibility of reconstructed intents. Perhaps evaluators could develop an oral history methodology. The legal approach to these oral histories would be to test the credibility of the reconstructions through cross-examination of the witnesses.

In situations where circumstances dictate and resources permit, the evaluator may undertake a full legislative history using techniques such as those proposed here. In most cases, however, the rationale for a legislative history would lead an evaluator to spend at least some time exploring the background of the program to be evaluated. By interviewing the project proposal writers, funding agency staff, and local advisors to the project, an evaluator could reconstruct the historical context leading up to the project. Such a historical search could uncover conflicting expectations held by various groups or individuals for the program, needs that led to the program, past attempted solutions and their outcomes, and relationships between the current project and past projects.

Adversary Evaluations

The most powerful legal metaphor to have influenced educational evaluation has been that of a trial or adversary hearing. "Adversary evaluations," as they have come to be called, have borrowed freely from legal procedures used in jury trials and administrative hearings. Worthen and Owens (1978) point out:

> As yet, adversary evaluation offers no unified framework meant to prescribe the course of all such evaluations. However, a simple common thread runs through all emerging conceptions of this approach. In its broad sense, the term refers to all evaluation where there is planned opposition in the viewpoints of different evaluators or evaluation teams. Webster's sense of "contending with, opposing" is central to this general definition. The fact that an evaluation approach includes a planned effort to generate opposing points of view *within* the overall evaluation is the *sine qua non* here [pp. 336-337].

The adversary approach is a relative newcomer in educational evaluation. However, in the past 15 years it has been one of the most widely discussed, implemented, and evaluated models in evaluation. Over a decade ago, Guba (1965) suggested that educational evaluation might well adopt or adapt aspects of the legal paradigm. But five years passed before the first clear-cut example of adversary evaluation in education was conducted (Owens, 1971). Since that time, conceptual work by Wolf (1973), Owens (1973), and Levine (1974) has stimulated further interest in the adversary approach. During the past five years, various evaluation studies have used at least some of the concepts of adversarial proceedings (for example, Wolf, 1975; Hiscox & Owens, 1975; Levine, 1976; Kourilsky & Baker, 1976; Nafziger et al., 1977; Wolf & Tymitz, 1977).

Case studies summarizing six adversary evaluations have been described by Owens and Hiscox (1977). Adversary evaluations have been used to determine the viability of alternative programs or proposals prior to adoption (Wolf & Tymitz, 1977), to evaluate ongoing processes (Levine, 1976), and to conduct a summative evaluation of a program (Nafziger et al., 1977). Criteria for judging adversary evaluations have been treated elsewhere (Worthen & Owens, 1978).

Proponents seem to hold at least eight assumptions regarding adversarial approaches to evaluation (Worthen & Owens, 1978, p. 337):

1. Evaluators are not by definition objective spectators capable of rendering unbiased judgments about programs, based solely on canons of scientific inquiry. Quite the contrary, evaluators are subject to certain biases that should be exposed by an "honest opposition" charged with examining the issue from another point of view.

2. Whenever evaluation studies use multiple variables or data sources, the essence of evaluation lies as much or more in the judgmental decision of how to weigh the evidence as in the collection and analysis of data. The fundamental evaluation instrument remains human intelligence — applied to whatever data are yielded through the evaluation study.

3. Social and educational phenomena are complex and multidimensional; therefore, an effective evaluation must attempt to portray as many dimensions as possible, revealing the interrelationships that exist. Qualitative as well as quantitative data are needed to accomplish this task. Human testimony can be as valid as test scores.

4. Evaluation occurs in a pluralistic society in which differing values must be addressed.

5. Decision makers generally are (or should be) interested in considering various interpretations of evaluation data, rather than being satisfied with the conclusions of a single interpretation.

6. An adversary approach can reveal information that influences decisions, but that would likely be overlooked in a traditional evaluation approach.

7. Important decisions regarding large-scale programs are seldom made by a single individual. Therefore, an effective evaluation must communicate findings and interpretations to a broad audience, including all relevant decision makers.

8. Research on information dissemination (Bettinghaus and Miller, 1973) indicates that two-way communication is usually more effective than one-way communication in spreading new ideas. Adversary evaluation encourages dialogue between evaluators and decision makers, especially during the presentation of evaluation data.

Some may justifiably argue that important assumptions are omitted from this list or are inherent in any adversary model, while other assumptions are more germane to one particular adversary strategy. Yet, those listed here underlie many proposals to expand the adversary approach in educational evaluation (for example, Wright & Sachse, 1977).

So far in this chapter we have discussed legal metaphors that we feel hold promise for improving educational evaluation or for expanding its approach. A look at law, or any other discipline for that matter, can also suggest some metaphors that may be harmful if applied. These are described in the next section.

Moribund and Malignant Metaphors

Raitz (1979), in a recent article on the use of metaphor in the language of education, discusses the risks as well as the advantages of using metaphors. He cites as an illustration of moribund metaphors in education those in the "strength" family used to characterize the mind as "strong or weak." Such metaphors imply that the mind "can be strengthened by exercises such as drill, for example, and it will become weak if it is not used" (p. 198). The risk in such metaphors is that they imply untested or false assumptions that could have negative effects on educational practice. The same concern needs to be raised with legal metaphors applied to evaluation. Two examples will be given: The first deals with concerns over interpreting and manipulating law; the second, with an attorney's overzealous defense of a cause.

Alexander Solzhenitsyn said, in a commencement address in June 1978 at Harvard ("A World Split Apart: The World Demands From Us a Spiritual Blaze"):

> Western society has chosen for itself the organization best suited to its purposes and one I might call legalistic. The limits of human rights and rightness are determined by a system of laws; such limits are very broad. People in the West have acquired considerable skill in using, interpreting and manipulating law (though laws tend to be too complicated for an average person to understand without the help of an expert). Every conflict is solved according to the letter of the law and this is considered to be the ultimate solution. If one is right from a legal point of view, nothing more is required, nobody may mention that one could still not be entirely right, and urge self-restraint or a renunciation of these rights, call for sacrifice and selfless risk: this would simply sound absurd. Voluntary self re-straint is almost unheard of: everybody strives toward further ex-pansion to the extreme limit of the legal frames. . . . It will be simply impossible to bear up to the trials of this threatening century with nothing but the supports of a legalistic structure. . . . It is time in the West, to defend not so much human rights as human obligations.

As a result of their experiences in conducting an adversary evalua-tion of the Hawaii 3 on 2 Program, Popham and Carlson (1978) describe a number of potential pitfalls of the legal trial model when applied to educational evaluation. One of the most serious concerns was that the evaluators on both sides got so entrapped with the challenge of winning the case that, at times, they let that goal out-weigh rational consideration of the findings.

Other Parallels

Three additional legal areas are examined below for their implica-tions when applied to evaluation: (1) the appeals process, (2) levels of evidence required, and (3) professional preparation of lawyers.

Appeals Process

The law has recognized that no system is perfect and that a check is needed to ensure that established trial procedures are not violated or that corrective action occurs if they are. The appeals process is therefore an important aspect of the trial process.

The function of an appellate court is to review the record of a trial to see whether or not the trial court erred in any of its various rulings.

> In actions at law (common law) where there is a constitutional right to jury trial, the appellate court will not disturb the findings of the jury on the facts, even though it disagrees with them, if there is substantial evidence in the record to support the verdict. . . .
> The most frequent grounds for appeal include erroneous rulings of the judge, such as refusing a challenge for cause, sustaining or overruling an objection to evidence, granting or denying a motion for a directed verdict, refusing or granting a requested instruction, or making an erroneous statement of law in the charge [Green, 1965, p. 452].

Jerome Frank (1930) explains that the major cause of legal uncertainty is not uncertainty in the rules but fact uncertainty. That is why the appeals court does not decide the facts. "If a trial court mistakenly takes as true the oral testimony of an honest but inaccurate witness or a lying witness, seldom can an upper court detect this mistake; it therefore usually adopts the facts so found by the trial court" (p. xv).

In the opinion of the American Bar Association, the possibility of appellate review of trial court judgments should exist for every criminal conviction. "It is undesirable to have any class of case in which such trial court determinations are unreviewable" (Sobeloff & Reitz, 1969, p. 7).

Unfortunately, no systematic appeals process exists in evaluation. If project staff feel they have been misrepresented in an evaluation report, or if inappropriate instruments or data analysis procedures were used, there is generally no recourse. Although independent educational audits have been commissioned occasionally in the past, they have seldom been effective in changing erroneous conclusions. For large, summative evaluations it would be prudent to have the procedures reviewed systematically by an independent party, and an independent judgment should be made as to whether the conclusions reached by the evaluator are warranted by the supporting data. In some ways this function is performed by the National Joint Dissemination Review Panel (JDRP), which reviews evaluation findings of projects desiring to receive federal funds for dissemination (Tallmadge, 1977). This panel reviews findings to determine whether they adequately support the claims made. However, the JDRP reviews only a fraction of the number of projects evaluated and bases its judgments on a ten-page summary of the evaluation rather than on a comprehensive report.

Some parts of an appeals system are practiced by individual evaluators. For example, after conducting a student case study, some evaluators will show a draft portrayal to the student to verify its accuracy and to identify any changes, omissions, or additions that may be needed. Similarly, after completing a draft evaluation report for a local project, some evaluators make it a practice to share the draft with the project staff to verify the factual accuracy of the report's contents and interpretations before finalizing the report to present to the school district or funding agency. Such procedures should not be used to enable the project staff to delete legitimate references to program weaknesses or substantiated interpretations.

A practice which resembles aspects of an appeals process and which has become more common in recent years in research and evaluation is the secondary analysis of data. Secondary data analysis usually involves an individual or agency, independent of the one who collected and analyzed the original data, who reanalyzes the data, often using different statistical procedures to reach independent conclusions.

Evidence

The rules of evidence and the procedures for handling, evaluating, creating, and communicating them are important parts of any inquiry-based activity. The evidentiary process of making a legal determination is intricate, well codified, and replete with documented examples of its application. Any number of features of the use of evidence in law might be chosen to explicate here, such as admissibility, use of documentary evidence, opinion as evidence, circumstantial evidence, use of witnesses, use of expert opinion, and the responsibilities and protection of witnesses and defendants. This section will deal with degrees of proof because of its apparent parallels with the level of certainty problems in evaluation.

It is important to note here that the law is not uniform in the level of evidence needed to make a determination. In criminal cases, proof beyond "reasonable doubt" is required (Donigan & Fisher, 1965, pp. 25-26), whereas in civil cases a "preponderance of evidence" is sufficient. The distinction is that "beyond reasonable doubt, requires that the jury feel an abiding conviction, to a moral certainty, of the truth of the charge" (Penal Code of California, 1949). Preponderance of evidence simply requires that "the jury must believe that the facts asserted are more probably true than false" (*Cook* v. *Michael*, 1958). The law here is being pragmatic in allowing a more liberal evidence structure in presumably less serious cases.

Pragmatic relaxations of the rules of evidence also occur in other kinds of cases (Dession, 1957). In antitrust cases, for example, where the arguments tend to be long and ponderous and where the evidence may consist of hundreds or thousands of pages or documents, expert witnesses can sometimes be used to give opinion testimony about the material rather than requiring examination of the documents themselves, as would be required by the "best evidence" rule. In cases tried by judges, evidence can be admitted which would not be permitted in a jury trial because it might confuse or mislead the less sophisticated jurors. Again, a practical consideration, that of speeding up a very lengthy process, leads to a reasoned compromise of some legal protections of the quality of evidence.

The evaluation profession may be able to make similar distinctions in the level of certainty required of evidence in formative and summative evaluation studies. For a program that is very expensive, very important, and/or very controversial, a wrong decision could be harmful and difficult to correct, and high certainty of evidence may be desirable. The recommendations stemming from formative evaluation studies, however, are usually less serious because (a) they may be reversed at a later date if subsequent information proves them wrong and (b) they are under heavy pressure to be timely if they are to be of any value at all. It is both unnecessary and impractical to use the same high standards for evidence in both kinds of evaluations.

Standards of performance for formative studies or studies with low budgets might be relaxed in a number of areas. Levels of statistical significance could be liberalized from the conventional .05 level restriction. Comparison groups, while they might sometimes be desirable in formative evaluation, are more necessary for final proof than for program improvement. Sampling considerations are another area for possible compromise. In formative evaluation and small context-bound studies, consensual validity, credibility by triangulation, collecting evidence from multiple sources, and iterative demonstrations may be more appropriate to the "responsive" task than formal proofs.

Professional Preparation

The case method of teaching in American law schools has been used for over a hundred years. This method of instruction was introduced into American legal education at the Harvard Law School in the fall of 1870 by Professor Christopher Columbus Langdell (Dowling, Patterson, & Powell, 1952, p. 16). Professor Langdell's arguments in favor of the case method were referred to in a report by Professor Josef Redlich. In 1914, Professor Redlich was asked by the Carnegie Foundation to investigate the case method of instruction and to report on its merits. Professor Redlich's report was highly in favor of the case method and had a great influence on American law teachers and lawyers. As a result, the case method was accepted as an essential device of instruction in the American legal educational system.

The case method of instruction has been viewed as scientific, pedagogical, pragmatic, and historical (Dowling et al., 1952, p. 15). While views of the case method have varied under different instructors, in different courses, and in different law schools, three essential aspects of the case method of instruction have emerged: the use of the casebook, student participation in class discussion, and the use of the problem type of examination.

The casebook is designed to help students learn common law as a systematic, rational body of doctrine. Class discussions, using the Socratic method, require students to work out conclusions from questions posed by the instructor. Students must think for themselves, defend their conclusions based on a specific case in the book or other cases, and isolate the significance of the case. The use of hypothetical cases on examinations gives students experience in reaching decisions and justifying them in terms of analysis of the facts and statements of legal propositions.

Although the use of the case method of studying law is intended to help students synthesize material, make independent judgments, and develop critical thinking patterns, there are several major disadvantages associated with this method. It is judged to be inadequate for studying legal history, legislative development, or the philosophical or ethical considerations of law. It is also very time-consuming.

What implications does the case method of study have for training educational evaluators? It could be argued that this method is inappropriate outside of the field of law, since other disciplines lack the systematic collection of factual cases and decisions found in law.

However, if we are willing to apply the principles of case methods at a more informal level, some interesting possibilities emerge. As in law, it is probably wise to admit that some concepts, such as those in statistics, may be taught better without a case method of study. However, once a student has completed basic courses in areas such as statistics, research design, evaluation theory, and research methodology, a case method of study might be a stimulating and effective way of learning to apply these principles to the realities of program evaluation. Imagine for a moment an advanced evaluation course using as a casebook six to ten evaluation reports. Students could be assigned to critique the designs and statistics employed, examine the political context that may have been involved, argue whether the conclusions and recommendations in the reports were adequately supported by the findings, or determine how an individual project's evaluation fits with the findings from studies of similar projects.

Suggested Next Steps

Several approaches can be suggested as next steps for those interested in further investigation of law as a metaphor for evaluation. One approach is to review this chapter to find parallels of interest and then to read the references given in that section. A second approach would be to read a popular book on law, such as Jerome Frank's *Law and the Modern Mind* (1930), or a book on legal philosophy, such as *The Nature of Law* edited by Golding (1966), to allow new parallels for evaluation to emerge. One could also consider a particular problem faced in evaluation, such as that of establishing the credibility of interview data, and consult several lawyers or law schools to determine how lawyers are taught to cross-examine witnesses.

One approach for identifying legal techniques which could be usefully adapted to educational evaluation would be to review general evaluation phases (such as those shown in Table 4.2), select a phase that may be of interest, and then explore one or more of the legal techniques potentially related to that phase.

By starting with the basic evaluation phases shown on this chart, one could easily expand the chart to include techniques from the other disciplines and fields covered in this book. This could then lead to looking across disciplines for ideas that may build upon the interplay of these metaphors. In investigating these or other areas of law, evaluators should be cautioned against becoming entrapped in legal

TABLE 4.2   Legal Techniques Potentially Related to Basic Evaluation Phases

Evaluation Phases	Legal Techniques
Evaluation Planning	Issues formation, design of pretrial interviews, selection of witnesses, establishment of standards, rules of evidence, legal precedent
Data Collection	Pretrial interviewing, ethics regarding confidentiality of data, legislative history
Data Organization and Analysis	Preparation of attorney summary statements, integration of human testimony and statistical data
Reporting	Jury trial, cross-examination of witnesses, use of legal precedent, jury selection and deliberations, appeals process, judge's legal opinion.

technicalities; instead, they should look for generalizing principles or practices that fit existing needs in the field of evaluation.

References

Auerbach, C., Garrison, L., Hurst, W., & Mermin, S. The adversary system. In *The legal process*. San Francisco: Chandler, 1961.

Austin, J. Law as the sovereign's command. In M.P. Golding (Ed.), *The nature of law: Readings in legal philosophy*. New York: Random House, 1966.

Campbell, D.T., & Stanley, J.C. Experimental and quasi-experimental designs for research on teaching. In N.L. Gage (Ed.), *Handbook of research on teaching*. Chicago: Rand McNally, 1963, Pp. 171-246.

Cook v. Michael, 214 Or. 513, 330 P. 2d 1026, 1032 (1958). In R.L. Donigan & E.C. Fisher, *The evidence handbook*. Evanston, IL: Traffic Institute, Northwestern University, 1965.

Dession, G.H. The trial of economic and technological issues of fact: II. In W.T. Fryer (Ed.), *Selected writings on the law of evidence and trial*. St. Paul: West Publishing, 1957.

Donigan, R.L., & Fisher, E.C. *The evidence handbook*. Evanston, IL: Traffic Institute, Northwestern University, 1965.

Dowling, N.T., Patterson, E.W., & Powell, R.R.B. *Materials for legal method* (2nd ed. edited by H.W. Jones). Brooklyn: The Foundation Press, 1952.

Folsom, G.B. *Legal history: Research for the interpretation of laws*. Charlottesville: University Press of Virginia, 1972.

Frank, J. *Law and the modern mind.* New York: Doubleday, 1930.

Golding, M. P. (Ed.). *The nature of law: Readings in legal philosophy.* New York: Random House, 1966.

Green, M. Legal procedure, *Collier's encyclopedia.* Chicago: Cromwell-Collier Publishing, *14,* 1965, Pp. 438-453.

Guba, E. G. Evaluation in field studies. Address presented at an evaluation conference sponsored by the Ohio State Department of Education, Columbus, Ohio, 1965.

Guba, E. G. Toward a methodology of naturalistic inquiry in educational evaluation. In E.L. Baker (Ed.), *CSE Monograph Series in Evaluation,* No. 8. Los Angeles: Center for the Study of Evaluation, UCLA, 1978.

Hiscox, M. D., & Owens, T. R. *Attempts at implementing an educational adversary model.* Paper presented at the Third Annual Pacific Northwest Educational Research and Evaluation Conference, Seattle, 1975.

House, E. R. Justice in evaluation. In G. V Glass (Ed.), *Evaluation studies review annual,* Vol. 1. Beverly Hills, CA: Sage, 1976, Pp. 75-99.

Kelsen, H. The pure theory of law. In M. P. Golding (Ed.), *The nature of law: Readings in legal philosophy.* New York: Random House, 1966.

Kourilsky, M., & Baker, E. L. An experimental comparison of interaction, advocacy and adversary evaluation. *CEDR Quarterly,* 1976, 9, 4-8.

Landis, J. M. A note on "statutory interpretation." *Harvard Law Review,* 1930, 43, 886.

Levine, M. Scientific method and the adversary model, some preliminary thoughts. *American Psychologist,* 1974, 29, 661-677.

Levine, M. *Experiences in adapting the jury trial to the problem of educational program evaluation.* Unpublished manuscript, State University of New York at Buffalo, 1976.

Marks, F. R. *The lawyer, the public and professional responsibility.* Chicago: American Bar Foundation, 1972.

McLaughlin, M. W. *Evaluation and reform: The Elementary and Secondary Education Act of 1965/Title I.* Cambridge, MA: Ballinger, 1975.

Nafziger, D. H., Benson, J., & Worthen, B. R. *3 on 2 evaluation report, 1976-77.* Volume I. Technical Report. Portland, OR: Northwest Regional Educational Laboratory, January 1977.

Owens, T. R. Application of adversary proceedings for educational evaluation and decision-making. Paper presented at the American Educational Research Association annual meeting, New York City, April 1971.

Owens, T. R. Educational evaluation by adversary proceeding. In E. R. House (Ed.), *School evaluation: The politics and process.* Berkeley: McCutchan Publishing, 1973, Pp. 295-305.

Owens, T. R., & Hiscox, M. D. Alternative models for adversary evaluation: Variations on a theme. Paper presented at the American Educational Research Association annual meeting, New York City, April 1977.

Penal Code of California, sec. 1096, (1949). In R. L. Donigan & E. C. Fisher, *The evidence handbook.* Evanston, IL: Traffic Institute, Northwestern University, 1965.

Popham, W. J., & Carlson, D. Deep, dark deficits of adversary evaluation. *Educational Researcher,* 1977, 6, 3-6.

Raitz, K. L. Moribund metaphors in education. *Educational Forum,* 1979, 43, 193-202.

Sobeloff, S., & Reitz, C. *Standards relating to criminal appeals: American Bar Association Project on Minimum Standards for Criminal Justice.* Tentative draft. Institute of Judicial Administration, 1969.

Solzhenitsyn, A. A world split apart: The world demands from us a spiritual blaze. *Vital Speeches,* September 1, 1978, 44, No. 22, 678-684.

Summers, R. S. *Law, its nature, function, and limits.* Englewood Cliffs, NJ: Prentice-Hall, 1972.

Tallmadge, G. *The Joint Dissemination Review Panel: IDEABOOK.* Washington, DC: U.S. Dept. of Health, Education and Welfare, October 1977.

Thorne, S. E. (Ed.). *A discourse upon the exposicion & understandinge of statutes.* 1572. In G. B. Folsom, *Legislative history: Research for the interpretation of laws.* Charlottesville: University Press of Virginia, 1972.

Thurston, P. Revitalizing adversary evaluation: Deep dark deficits or muddled mistaken musings. *Educational Researcher,* 1978, 7, 3-8.

Wolf, R. L. *Application of select legal concepts to educational evaluation.* Unpublished doctoral dissertation, University of Illinois, 1973.

Wolf, R. L. Trial by jury: A new evaluation method, 1. The process. *Phi Delta Kappan,* 1975, November, 185-187.

Wolf, R. L., & Tymitz, B. L. *Enhancing policy formulation through naturalistic judicial inquiry procedures: A study of the individual education program component of Public Law 94-142.* Technical Report. Indiana Center for Evaluation, September 1977.

Worthen, B. R., & Owens, T. R. Adversary evaluation and the school psychologist. *Journal of School Psychology,* 1978, 16, 334-345.

Wright, W. J., & Sachse, T. Payoffs of adversary evaluation. Paper presented at the American Educational Research Association annual meeting, New York City, April 1977.

Geraldine Ferguson
*Professor of Human Development and Research,
Pacific Oaks College*

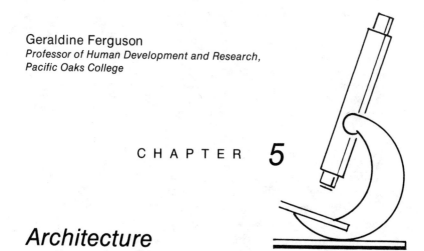

CHAPTER **5**

Architecture

Geraldine Ferguson's chapter reflects her active professional participation as an architect as well as an evaluator. Her current interest is an eminent trip to Japan in order to study the influence of Eastern philosophy on built space, as she feels strongly that we need a better understanding of the relationship which exists among human needs, the cultural context, and physical space.

Overview

Design — and its result in terms of architectural form — is a human product. The function of the architect is to identify or perceive problems in a man/nature context and to define solutions to human needs which exist in a physical context. Norberg-Schulz, in *Intensions in Architecture* (1973), states that architecture has three purposes as a human product: functional-practical, milieu-creating, and symbolizing. His purposes pose a framework within which to discuss the design process.

Functional-Practical

The functional or practical purposes of architecture deal with meeting man's primary needs for shelter and protection. Williams and Williams, in *Craftsmen of Necessity* (1974) state:

When man first began to build, he watched nature's performance and followed it. His ways rested easily in the environment because the environment was his control and reference; he lacked the power to do otherwise. From the surroundings came his materials: the plants and animals, the rock and dirt. He converted the materials into his tools. He learned the vernacular of his materials, the strength of wood, the shapes of clay, the cleavage of stone. He learned the pressures and demands of the biosphere, and he bent to them [p. 3].

Vernacular architecture, or the architecture of noncomplex cultures, deals in a direct way with those primary needs and in direct response to natural, cyclical change. Primitive man was responsive to changes in his environment. Before the agricultural revolution, man's response to these changes was mobility. He built tents and other mobile structures to protect him from the cold and to shield him from the heat. When man learned how to provide his own food without continually following the seasons, he learned to coexist with cyclical changes in his environment. When man first began building permanent shelters, the process must have involved much trial and error. Decisions would have been linked with natural occurrances: rain, snow, wind, flood, and sun. Man, through adaptive responses, gradually developed functional forms to meet his needs. Ralph Knowles describes this process:

When the differentiation of an arrangement occurs in an unselfconscious way over a long period of time and is accompanied by an apparently decreased susceptibility of the arrangement to environmental stress, it may be described as self-organizing. This term may be equally applied to systems in nature and to those made by men under the most primitive circumstances. As long as men remain unaware of a larger purpose, submerged within a continuous environment where the events of nature comprise variation and that variation can only be answered piecemeal, then men remain part of the system; they live "inside" without a really good view of the world beyond. Under these circumstances, it takes a long time to develop an evident direction. Each corrective step along the way is guided by a sense of purpose, but at the same time, each step is discrete and not necessarily related to a general direction in the minds of the builders. They do not initially work from an image of ultimate form. Then, over time, form does emerge and with it the possibility of a correlation with some purpose, seen dimly at first, but nonetheless one that will allow a plan of action. From that point on, men may build machines [1974, p. 17].

In looking at vernacular architecture, one finds many examples of forms which fulfill man's functional-practical needs. The bedouins of the northwestern plains of Syria, because of a lack of rock or wood, built smooth, rounded houses of mud which they called beehives. In Egypt, where wood for beams was available, vernacular, or indigenous, architecture took on a more geometric look, with post and lintel structural members and clay walls. The Williamses (1974) observe:

> Though the structures sometimes appear capricious, they are the solemn resolution of the natural inclination of the material following the lines of stress, the needs of the family to surround and shelter a space and the individuality of the builders' hands. There is little that is arbitrary in indigenous people's lives; decisions are dictated by tradition, the pressures of environment, and the economy of materials [p. 45].

Where rock or stone was available, indigenous architects built within the limitations of that material. In northwestern Bulgaria, buildings were made by fitting loose stone into walls which were wide at the base and narrower at the top. Each stone was fitted to the next, beveled and lapped, without mortar. There were notches for roof beams, which received them exactly. Tiles on the wood beams completed the shell and supplied the compression that kept the structure together.

In the Sahara Desert, in southern Tunisia, the people lived in an elaborate set of hollows and wells below the ground. There is a dramatic change in temperature during the 24-hour period, which precludes the growth of trees for building. There was no mud, no reeds, no animal skins, so the people dug into the earth. Rooms were vaulted to hold the weight, and one could expand the home merely by digging. There were separate rooms for sleeping, cooking, storage, and housing livestock which radiated off the central courtyard and light well.

The people of the Acoma pueblo in New Mexico built on top of a mesa, making them nearly inaccessible to their enemies. In addition to being defensible, the houses were built in response to climatic conditions. The people used adobe packed with grass and sticks, laid over small wood members that spanned timbers. The houses were built on a north-south axis, with common wall construction and tiered so that the open exposure was to the south. Building materials were high in insulating quality, and the orientation and tiered building style maximized the usefulness of the sun's energy for warming the walls and providing light in work spaces.

As indigenous architecture came to be more stylized and other materials and influences became available, the architecture moved away from the close correspondence with natural materials and cycles to include other human needs, which went beyond functional-practical demands.

Milieu-Creating

A second purpose of architecture is to create an environment which has not only an instrumental purpose but also a psychological function. The history of architecture is filled with a variety of forms which, at different times, met the various psychosocial and cultural needs of man. Rapaport hypothesizes possible explanations for form in dwellings:

> The house is an institution, not just a structure, created for a complex set of purposes. Because building a house is a cultural phenomenon, its form and organization are greatly influenced by the cultural milieu to which it belongs. Very early in recorded time the house became more than shelter for primitive man, and almost from the beginning "function" was much more than a physical or utilitarian concept. Religious ceremony has almost always preceded and accompanied its foundation, erection, and occupation. If provision of shelter is the passive function of the house, then its positive purpose is the creation of an environment best suited to the way of life of a people — in other words, a social unit of space [1969, p. 46].

The form of a building is not only determined by the actions of the people within it, but also contributes to the social purposes of those who use it. A milieu extends to people; it also extends to possibilities for social life and differentiation in terms of status, role, or collectivity. Social purposes might include work and its phenomenal context, government and its apparent status, places for public performance — dance, theater, concerts — or enclosures and sites for worship and religious gatherings. Buildings and cities may represent both subgroups of the social system and the social system itself.

Social milieus provide the possibility for activities and also play a part in the regulation of human interaction. Some places are public by design: They are open to large gatherings of people and maximize the possible number of people in a given space. Other places create privacy — a place to be alone or with people of one's own choosing. Paulsson, in discussing this phenomenon, writes:

> A culture is characterized by the common institutions which result from human interaction. When man in early times made an enclosure, he defined a domain different from the free nature, a domain giving visual expression to the community. Gradually, domains of different character were developed according to the purpose they had to serve, and when a roof was put on they became buildings. One particular domain was always of prime importance, which was the public square, where life could unfold in all its variety. The Greek *agora* originally was a meeting place, and only later became connected with commercial activities. The public buildings were joined to the agora but usually they did not open directly onto it, as if to express that the square should be reserved for the citizens. The Greeks distinguished three "qualitatively" different zones in their cities: the acropolis of the gods, the agora of social life, and the enclosed houses of private life. Thus the Greek city had a meaningful architectural form, which corresponded to the social structure. The milieu offered the necessary possibilities, and formed a part of the cultural totality [Paulsson, 1959, pp. 81-90, 121-122].

The practice of differentiating buildings and environments according to psychological needs and social uses is more apparent in a historical context than it is today: architectural practice is presently more inclined to stress the function of the building as a form determinant and as an important variable in the determination of the new aesthetic. In ancient times, however, the sight of the chief's hut being larger than the rest, or that of the king's castle on the hill, was an accepted indication of social hierarchy. In a democratic society, these roles are not as apparent, although different access to money and resources still results in a difference in individual expression in homes in terms of size, location, and appointments. It is hoped that architects will return to using psychosocial data to influence the form of buildings — not in order to develop hierarchies but to extend the possibilities for social interaction.

Cultural Symbolization

Architecture, being a product of man, is a cultural product. In its response to collective need and as an art, it expresses values by its very form. As cultures have evolved value systems and symbols, architecture has evolved to represent these values and symbols in architectural form. Mumford, in *Art and Technics* (1952), indicates that the building of early man, although influenced by physical and site determinants, was much influenced by his predilection toward myth, religion, and ritual. Mumford argues that man was a symbol-making animal before he was a tool-making animal, and that, from the beginning, early man put his energy into symbolic rather than u-tilitarian forms. Religious and sacrificial activities are evidenced by excavation of the most primitive building sites.

Carl Jung said in *Man and His Symbols,*

> what we call a symbol is a term, a name, or even a picture that may be familiar in daily life, yet that possesses specific connotations in addition to its conventional and obvious meaning. . . . Because there are innumerable things beyond the range of human understanding, we constantly use symbolic terms to represent concepts that we cannot define or fully comprehend. This is one reason why all religions employ symbolic language and images [1968, pp. 3-4].

Rapaport (1969), in discussing the development of form in vernacular architecture, feels that sociocultural influences are of great importance in determining form as well as biological needs, technical devices, and climatic conditions:

> Buildings and settlements are the visible expression of the relative importance attached to different aspects of life and the varying ways of perceiving reality. The house, the village, and the town express the fact that societies share certain generally accepted goals and life values. The forms of primitive and vernacular buildings are less the result of individual desires than of the aims and desires of the unified group for an ideal environment. They therefore have symbolic values, since symbols serve a culture by making concrete its ideas and feelings [p. 47].

In seeing architecture as both an art form and a representation of collective cultural values, as evidenced by cultural symbolization, it is evident that architecture is closely tied to the formation of the social milieu. Norbert-Schulz clarifies this issue:

> In the symbol-milieu, which comprises both aspects, the social milieu mediates cultural objects such as common values, empirical

(scientific) constructs, philosophical ideas, moral codes, religious beliefs, ideological convictions, and economical conditions. The objects are manifested through social roles, groups and institutions, and by the physical objects serving social life. We find it convenient, however, to distinguish between the two aspects of the symbol-milieu, as the cultural symbolization may also take place *independently* of the formation of a social milieu. A culture is also characterized by being transmitted in spite of the existing social situation. Thus we are still able to "understand" Michelangelo or Beethoven. The discussion of the symbol-milieu also becomes clearer if we avoid mixing social and cultural objects in a diffuse way. It is important to distinguish between interaction and value, even if they often appear as aspects of the same state of affairs. While the social objects and the social milieu always manifest the cultural objects on which they are founded, the latter have a certain degree of independence [1973, pp. 122-123].

Rapaport (1969) further states: "An indication of the symbolic nature of houses is the fact that many immigrants bring their architecture with them, and persist in its use even though it is often unsuitable for the new area in which they live" (p. 52). A drive down the streets of Beverly Hills, California will illustrate this point in a contemporary context. One sees renditions of Greek temples next to English estates, flanked by French villas. These symbols of European and eastern affluence transferred easily to wealthy American communities.

Whereas early cultural symbolism centered on magic, religion, and ritual, current symbolism appears more as a tribute to production methods and technical advance than to unique cultural innuendoes.

Product Resolution: The Building Task

Standing in equal importance with theoretical and cultural influences on the development of a structure is the actual process — both technical and theoretical — of planning and assembling the building on the chosen site. Wachsmann writes:

Man and his environment are both exposed to processes of modification to the same degree. Thus, man is not necessarily in a position to determine the law of proportion permanently. He will always adapt himself to his environment, which he just as steadily modifies in order to make it useful to him. Similarly, his fundamental ideas, from which the laws of building are derived, will be modified by his awareness of and reactions to technological development [1961, p. 9].

Much could be written on the influence of technology and of new building materials on the design and form of contemporary buildings. Such a discussion is, however, beyond the scope and purpose of this paper: it is sufficient to note the fact that the profession continually adapts, modifies, and redirects its energies in order to maximize the use of new materials and techniques which become available and promise useful or more efficient solutions.

Technical Details

Some Dimensions of Thinking

There exists in architecture a wide range of functions, both in terms of human skills and in the physical manifestations of those skills in the symbolic realm and in the resulting built environment. The concept of architecture concerns itself generically with the "process of design: the process of inventing physical things which display new physical order, organization, form, in response to function" (Alexander, 1964, p. 1). But the human skills represented in those "physical things" encompass that whole range of human skills recognized by our culture and defined by our most advanced technological products and scientific methods. These skills also include intuitive, humanistic, and naturalistic qualities and concerns. D'Arcy Thompson's concern with natural forms in his classic study, *On Growth and Form* (1961), is as much a part of architecture as is Saarienen's St. Louis Arch or Nervi's engineering masterpieces. That concern with natural forms represented by Frei Otto in his study of soap bubbles as a metaphor for minimal structures, which he translated into the tension structures at Munich, are as much a part of architecture as Hartog, who uses natural, cyclic systems — rainfall, wind, and sun — as determinants of form. Computer-generated architecture, extensive use of diagrams, and systems such as critical path analysis, which result in techniques such as fast-tracking, are highly developed, constructive, and efficient examples of linear thinking.

Architectural cognitive functioning draws on two distinct modes. One function is a holistic, intuitive mode. Beveridge, in his *Art of Scientific Investigation* (1950), calls this "intuition." He hypothesizes that intuition is "a clarifying idea which comes suddenly to mind." This mode of knowing complements the logical, rational process which is the basis of much scientific investigation. Ornstein designates this intuitive mode as right brain functioning and sees its function as that of "specialized mentation" (1972). Its function is primarily integrative in nature.

> This hemisphere is primarily responsible for our orientation in space, artistic endeavor, crafts, body image. . . . It processes information more diffusely than does the left hemisphere, and its responsibilities demand a ready integration of many inputs at once. If the left hemisphere can be termed predominantly analytic and sequential in its operation, then the right hemisphere is more holistic and relational, and more simultaneous in its mode of operation [pp. 68-69].

Rollo May, in *Courage to Create* (1975), speaks of this right brain functioning as "unconscious dimensions (or aspects of sources) of experience. I define this unconscious as the *potentialities for awareness or action which the individual cannot or will not actualize*. These potentialities are the source of what can be called 'free creativity' " (p. 58). He indicates that this insight comes to us

> in accordance with a pattern of which one essential element is our own commitment. The break through [sic] does not come by "taking it easy," by "letting the unconscious do it." The insight, rather, is born from unconscious levels exactly in the areas in which we are most intensively consciously committed [p. 65].

This insight comes in the form of a gestalt, which essentially forms a pattern or which connects the elements with which one is struggling in the rational mode. May uses the following quote from Poincare in his autobiography, "Mathematical Creation" to illustrate this point:

> For fifteen days I strove to prove that there could not be any functions like those I have since called Fuchsian functions. I was then very ignorant; every day I seated myself at my work table, stayed an hour or two, tried a great number of combinations and reached no results. One evening, contrary to my custom, I drank black coffee and could not sleep. Ideas rose in crowds; I felt them collide until pairs interlocked, so to speak, making a stable combination. By the next morning I had established the existence of a

class of Fuchsian functions, those which come from the hypergeometric series; I had only to write out the results, which took but a few hours [1952, p. 63].

This intuitive, or holistic, mode of functioning, therefore, is a major integrating principle in architectural design.

A second function is essentially linear in its development and process. Fritjof Capra, in the *Tao of Physics,* defines this mode in the following way:

> Rational knowledge is derived from the experience we have with objects and events in our everyday environment. It belongs to the realm of the intellect whose function is to discriminate, divide, compare, measure and categorize. In this way, a world of intellectual distinctions is created; of opposites which can only exist in relation to each other. . . . Abstraction is a crucial feature of this knowledge, because in order to compare and to classify the immense variety of shapes, structures and phenomena around us we cannot take all their features into account, but have to select a few significant ones. Thus we construct an intellectual map of reality in which things are reduced to their general outlines. Rational knowledge is thus a system of abstract concepts and symbols, characterized by the linear, sequential structure which is typical of our thinking and speaking. In most languages this linear structure is made explicit by the use of alphabets which serve to communicate experience and thought in long lines of letters [1975, p. 27].

Language is the first medium of the rational mind. It is the first linearity in a world controlled by logic, order, sequence, and interdependent structure. As it develops, the ability to deal with symbols also develops. Architects deal in this rational mode, which is filled with signs, symbols, diagrams, and sequences. Albarn and Smith observe:

> The diagram is evidence of an idea being structured — it is not *the idea* but a model of it, intended to clarify characteristics of features of that idea. It is a form of communication which increases the pace of development, or allows an idea to function and develop for the thinker while offering the possibility of transfer of an idea or triggering of notions; finally, through appropriate structuring, it may generate different notions and states of mind in the viewer [1977, p. 7].

Plans which are essentially the concretion of the detailed sequencing of a product are rational and linear in substance. The architect, therefore, combines both the linear and the holistic modes of cognitive functioning. The architect may, initially or at points in the development of a product, pose intuitive solutions to the problems of design. Suddenly the inspiration or solution to the problem will come to the designer's mind; this image must be brought to completion, slowly, by linear methods, by plans and contracts, and then by the actual construction, sequentially, piece by piece.

Architecture is essentially a system in which one must think in wholes but work in a linear fashion in order to produce a physical form. Insofar as architecture may be viewed as art, Norberg-Schulz (1973) explains:

> When the product has a high degree of complexity, the process of creation is characterized by a succession of interconnected intensions. As the structure of the product takes shape, one intension will follow naturally from the other. This may be illustrated by the known fact that a more extensive and complex work of art (e.g., a symphony) cannot be created by starting at the beginning and going on in a "linear" way to the end. On the contrary, it is necessary continuously to keep the totality in mind, and go from the whole to the parts and back to the whole [pp. 77-78].

In dealing with the processes involved in architecture as thought and reason, Albarn and Smith (1977) offer the following:

> We need to re-evaluate the role of reason and our dependence upon those verbal/numerical modes which we traditionally equate with reason. When using reason alone we tend to develop the structure sequentially, brick by brick. Unfortunately, rather than building spaces, this mode often leads us to build roads. A linear approach matches our mundane experience of time but fails to evoke the important counter-model of wholeness which allows for synchronicity. It effectively demonstrates and supports cause and effect but inhibits the use of the additional coordinates to cross-refer spatially outside of the linear time-sense [p. 11].

Holistic and linear modes of thinking and production are, therefore, both integral parts of the architectural domain and process.

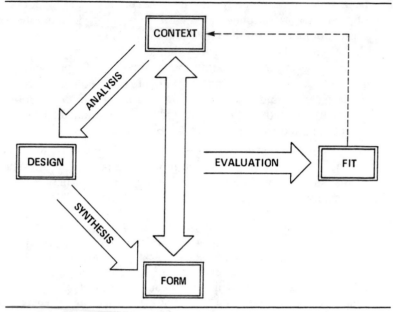

Figure 5.1 Architectural Design Elements and Processes

Architects may use one or the other or each domain in different proportions or combinations, but both holistic and linear thinking remain vital components of architecture.

Architectural Functions and Processes

The design process looks simultaneously at the context and the desired product or form. The architectural product is then designed within the constraints of the context and is evaluated in terms of fit. In diagrammatic form, this process might be conceptualized as occurring in the manner illustrated in Figure 5.1.

Design Elements

Context. The context is anything which makes demands on the form. The context is that which exists, that which is given, or that which defines the boundaries of the solution. One set of constraints might be Norberg-Schulz's (1973) dimensions, as previously stated:

(a) functional or practical needs;

(b) milieu-creating purposes; and

(c) architecture as cultural symbolization.

A less theoretical way of thinking of constraints might be in terms of resources available, such as time, money, labor, and/or building materials. One might think also of laws and codes, existing physical structures, or social or historical precedents. These, in addition to human functional needs to be met, are the demands which determine the context; the context defines the problem.

Design. Architectural design is that process by which one seeks a physical solution to a series of functional and psychosocial needs. One processes information in order to create solutions and then translates those solutions into a physical product.

One of the problems designers have in this process is in defining the problem. Although the constraints essentially define the problem, the designer has rather wide latitude in accepting constraints. A designer may choose to pay a lot of attention to the client's stated desires, or he may negate those in favor of research which purports to have solutions better suited to the client's needs than those the client has designated. The designer might choose to emphasize an ecological concern to which he is sensitive in terms of environmental pressures and for which new materials and processes are not available. The designer might choose to follow a personal line of investigation in which he explores an aesthetic concern or a material concern, such as the variety of uses of glass or brick. The number of variables with which the designer needs to be concerned is enormous; and to the extent that the designer has control over all of the variables, he has a cognitive burden which entails his sorting through the variables, analyzing needs and priorities, and identifying those variables to which he can address solutions.

Form. Form is the realization of the design-building process. It is that human product which has emerged from the analysis of fit between context and design. Although the resultant solution might appear to be a static or finished product, one might think of the form, in an abstract sense, as a hypothesized solution to those variables deemed most in need of attention. The resultant form is not *the* solution; it is one solution among many. It is proposed by the designer to solve the problem he perceived in analyzing the context. His hypothesis is tested, therefore, in the classical sense — not in being the best fit, but in being that solution which minimizes discrepancies between what is necessary and what evolves — that solution in which error is minimized. As new forces or variables become apparent in the context, the discrepancy in fit may deteriorate in such a way that the hypothesized solution (the form) loses some degree of fit. *Fit.* Fit is that dimension of congruence between the context and the form. Fit is a functional description of acceptability. It compares the variables considered in the context with those defined by the physical solution and makes a judgment which designates the degree of mutual compatibility or lack of discrepancy in the hypothesized solution.

Analytical Processes

In conceptualizing the design process, I have also alluded to analytical processes, which in the previous model were represented by arrows. In order to further clarify the model, I would like now to define those processes.

Analysis. Analysis is that process in which one gathers information and then separates that information into its constituent parts or elements. In the process of analyzing component parts, one may look at them separately or in their relation to the whole. In terms of architectural process, analysis is that phase in which the designer looks at all of the component parts which define the problem. He looks, for example, at the site and analyzes its separate components and influences: topography, soil, vegetation, orientation to the sun and wind, seasonal variations, access, and possibilities for views. He might next analyze client needs in terms of function. He might find that the structure functions as an art center which has a determined number of students, faculty, and administration; space requirements for equipment and various activities; special lighting and ventilation problems; and a specific materials delivery problem. The designer might then look at resources available. In this analysis, he might look at time requirements, the amount of money involved, and possibly the availability of labor and materials. The designer, in using the analytical process, may at this point look at these variables as independent, or he may begin to prioritize them and consider the possibility of tradeoffs — for example, if the building is down off the top of a hill, wind protection is achieved but to the detriment of view. At this time, the designer still is analyzing the problem, testing the limits, defining the scope, and prioritizing in order to establish those parameters to which he must pay attention and for which he must provide a physical solution. The result of this phase, the process of problem identification, is the design program.

The following description is included to clarify the process known as programming. Programming is the operation which is preliminary to specific design, in which the designer and client clarify the conditions precedent to construction and describe the requirements to be met by the proposed project. The owner furnishes the basic data and the architect formulates the program. In looking at the *Architectural Program for the Expansion and Remodeling of Loyola Law School,* Frank Gehry indicates:

> The program addresses issues from a performance, or functional standpoint; it prescribes *what the project should do.* The design process will subsequently determine what the project *should be* in order to address the requirements presented in the program [1979, introduction].

Those people who are the ultimate users of the facility are important participants in the process of defining the problem. Gehry (1979) further states, "If the problem is not cogently stated in the program, the potential for a responsive design solution will be seriously limited."

The first phase in programming is the development of project goals. Goals may be concerned with the *process* of planning and construction in terms of people, cost, and time, and also with the *product* in terms of form, function, economy, and time. Gehry states: "Goal statements are those performance requirements which need to be tested during the programming process" (1979, p. A-1). Size goals might include parameters such as the number of students to be served, while cost might prescribe either a total budget or a square foot cost. Other goals might deal with design parameters, ambience, philosophy, function, or humanistic needs. For example, goals might be

> to create a sense of place and physical identity;
>
> to create an environment which expresses a tradition of excellence;
>
> to address the operational and functional needs of students, faculty, and staff;
>
> to reinforce the student's self-esteem within the context of a necessarily demanding and sometimes intimidating educational experience [Gehry, 1979, pp. A-3, A-4].

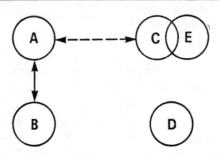

Figure 5.2   Bubble Diagram of Design Relationships
SOURCE: Gehry & Assoc. and Brooks/Collier Associate Architects. **Architectural Program for the Expansion & Remodeling of Loyola Law School.** Los Angeles, California, 1979. Reproduced by permission.

In order to translate goals into the beginning analysis for a physical plan, concepts are delineated which deal with the organization of spaces, the interaction or isolation of people, and movement systems or the flow of people and materials. In defining the interrelationship of concepts, designers develop conceptual diagrams which are representations of functional and operational relationships which are to be respected in the planning of physical space. An example of a conceptual diagram or "bubble" diagram is shown in Figure 5.2.

Gehry describes this diagram as follows:

> In the example diagram the solid arrow shown between functions A and B indicates a primary relationship that suggests either direct physical or communicative connection. The arrow may be used to show direction of flow of people, materials, or information. The dashed arrow between function A and C reflects a secondary relation implying need for a communicative connection but not necessarily a physical connection. The absence of an arrow between the functions C and D means that the two have no function or operational relationship that would influence planning. The overlapping of functions E and C signifies that certain functional or operational features may be common to each or are shared [1979, p. B-2].

After the conceptual diagrams have been delineated (see Figure 5.3), a needs analysis is done which relates actual space needs to budget, existing facilities, scope of the project, construction costs, and quality considerations. Data used to generate this material might

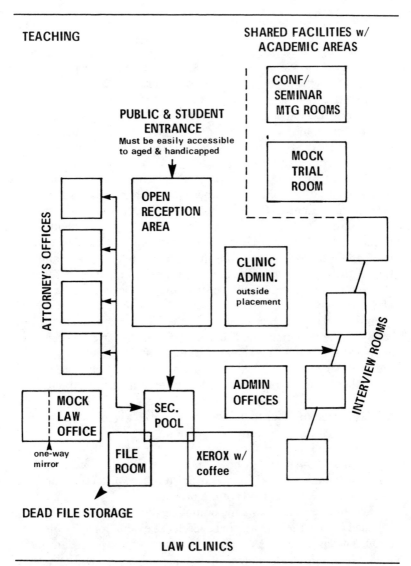

Figure 5.3 Law Clinics

SOURCE: Gehry & Assoc. and Brooks/Collier Associate Architects. **Architectural Program for the Expansion & Remodeling of Loyola Law School.** Los Angeles, California, 1979. Reproduced by permission.

be class sizes, furnishings or functional requirements, legal regulations, or projections for future growth and use.

Synthesis. Synthesis is the composition or combination of parts or
elements to form a whole. During this phase of the process, the
designer finds those physical solutions which meet the demands of the
program. He combines the various components into a unique solution
in order to establish a whole which meets the various needs. In
making this combination, he considers all of those requirements he
has separated out, which in this phase he recombines in order to make
a new and complex whole.

The diagram enables the designer to conceptually explore the
dimensions of the problem, to experiment with the relationship of the
parts to each other and to the whole. The diagram is a nonverbal way
of translating verbalized input and mathematical requirements into a
form which can be translated into spatial components. The diagram
may represent, for example, physical size, the relationship or interaction of the parts to or with each other, or the influence of forces or
stresses on the composition. Through the synthesis of these subsets
of requirements, the designer builds a more complex diagram which is
eventually converted into a model, which in turn begins to give the
solution a three-dimensional quality, and begins a series of successive
approximations in terms of physical form. Throughout this process,
the designer monitors his own process in terms of criteria, such as
internal coherence, logical consistency, integrity, and aesthetics.

Evaluation. Evaluation is that process in which the solution or
form is judged in order to find out how useful it is to the people who
will use it — its utility in terms of function, and its merit in terms of the
larger physical and psychosocial context of which it has become a
part. This judgment about fit is made relative to how well the form
meets the demands of the context or, in other words, how well the
solution meets the demands of the problem.

The architect, in evaluating or making judgments about his work,
is joined by the client in making usefulness evaluations, by his peers
through design awards, by professional journals and juries, and by the
society in general in comments in public publications and by word of
mouth. In time, architecture is also looked at from a historical
perspective. Evaluations are made in terms of both quantitative and
qualitative data. Quantity judgments might include elements such as
cost-effectiveness or efficiency (the ratio of net or functional space to

gross space). While quantity judgments are fairly objective, quality judgments are more subjective. Heyer goes into more detail:

> When an architect talks of quality values in a building, he means many vital concerns. The building must enhance and dignify the lives of those who use it; to do this it must embrace its social purpose. It must develop a rapport with its site, be aware of its environment. It must have functional integrity and structural honesty, while making an expressive statement. It must be more than a slick facade, and must avoid fads, to achieve a forthright statement of purpose without degenerating into depressing sterility or exhibitionistic vulgarity. Its appropriateness and relevance will come from a rational, common-sense disciplining that, coupled with the architect's sensitivity, will integrate and unify the whole. It must have a sense of timeliness and a sense of tradition: timeliness because it expresses its age — a century whose processes and techniques should usher in one of the great architectural epochs — and tradition because architecture, with its continuing concern for space, light and texture, is a great and enduring art [1978, p. 14].

Multiple judgments must therefore be made. Each judgment along the quantity/quality continuum is made by looking at the form in relation to its context in terms of fit. Some of the terms one might use in describing a bad fit would be "arbitrary," "obsolete," "incongruous," or "dysfunctional." Descriptions which might be used in reflecting a positive judgment would be "energy-efficient," "economical," "compatible," or "proportionate." In either case, the goal in design is to reduce the error in meeting needs in order to maximize the fit between the demands of the problem and the solution. There are multiple continua, both quantitative and qualitative, which ultimately pool to form the value judgment.

Evaluative Analysis

I feel that there are two intersecting metaphors available to educational evaluation from the field of architecture. One metaphor concerns the range of human functioning which is used in the design process. The second metaphor comes from the application of those processes within the constraints of the architectural model.

Metaphor 1: The Architect as Inventor of Physical Reality

The architect uses the broad range of mental functioning which includes both holistic and linear thinking. The stability and logic that are a part of the rational mind are surely an important part of what we would hope to reflect in meeting the needs of an advanced, complex society. In dealing with logic, sequence, mathematics, and diagrams, the architect uses those tools which have been developed by civilization and which are unique to man. With these tools, he can build structures and cities which meet the needs of and define the culture we have devised for ourselves.

In terms of holistic thinking, the architect uses various modes, as described by Bob Samples. Samples (1978) writes of four holistic or metaphoric modes:

1. *Symbolic,* in which a symbol, which may be either abstract or visual, is substituted for an object, a process, or a condition;

2. *Synergic-Comparative,* in which objects, processes, or conditions are compared in such a way that the combination or unity which evolves is more than any element alone, because of the comparison of parts being judged;

3. *Integrative,* in which the physical and psychic attributes of the person are extended into direct experience with objects or processes; and

4. *Inventive,* in which the person assumes a new level of awareness, as a result of his involvement and exploration of objects, processes, or conditions.

Architects engage in the whole range of holistic modes in the process of designing and assessing fit. Architects use arrows as symbols of force or to indicate direction. Textures or shading may symbolically indicate shadows, indentations, or juxtapositions. The synergic-comparative mode is an integral part of the development of even the simplest structure, in which hallways, doors, and rooms create movement systems which go beyond the simple attributes of rectangular spaces or openings through vertical planes. Architects function in the integrative mode in terms of actual involvement with models and mock-ups, sometimes becoming involved in the building process itself. The architect reflects the inventive mode through his awareness of "knowing" of the totality of the project, which unites both linear and holistic processes into an integrated whole.

The architect operates in a childlike manner, in that he is immersed in the total sensory, aesthetic, rhythmic totality of the problem, as well as in that rational, logical manner which is the product of our sophisticated civilization. The architect, therefore, combines his total functioning into an invention which exists, physically, in time and space. He is one who evolves a product through an interactive process in which he serially and cyclically engages in analysis, synthesis, and evaluation. He moves through levels of language in which preprogrammed ideas are clarified (the client hears the word roof and pictures the Cape Cod shingles of his childhood; the architect hears roof and thinks of pitch, cost, and materials availability). In doing this, he teaches and educates about relevant issues, concepts, and processes which in turn increases the sensibilities of those he works for and with.

Metaphor 2: The Process of Architectural Design

The second metaphor stems from the model developed in the previous section and displayed in Figure 5.1.

The metaphor is that architecture is the development of a physical gestalt. This gestalt is the result of analysis of the total situation in which the solution can only be judged relative to its fit measured against the context. In education, intelligence testing took out one small piece of human functioning and, using a select population, proceeded to look minutely at that academic process to which schools purport to address themselves. The fact that the measure was neither stable over a person's lifetime nor cross-cultural at first seemed incidental. Evaluators looked only at quantitative measurements, not qualitative values such as social purpose, the dignity of the individual, the uniqueness of the individual, psychosocial relevance, or the physical context (existing conditions).

The gestalt was ignored; only one piece of the problem was attended to. The metaphor for architecture in being the development of a physical gestalt concerns itself with the resulting entity as a whole, made of bits and pieces, pipes, halls, concrete, functional parameters, social expectations; but nevertheless, and in whatever form, a whole which exists in a context, in time and space.

I feel that Alexander's (1964) statement of criteria for the fit of forms in a culture deserves serious consideration in terms of its potential usefulness to educational evaluation. He says that the fit of forms is "a dynamic process in which both form and context change continuously and yet stay mutually well adjusted all the time" (p. 37). I feel we need to consider this "fit of forms" in terms of our changing social context. The development of culture and the enculturation process are products of man's evolution. As such, they represent an ever-changing context to which the form or process of human functioning must stay adjusted. Since both are products of man, man has the responsibility of evaluating, monitoring, and maintaining the mutual adjustment.

Evaluation Methodology

Much of our present evaluation methodology is exclusive: It filters out, systematically, those elements that are gestalt/intuitive in order to be logical, rational, and unbiased. The goal is to condense to numbers (abstract symbols), with the ultimate goal being the zero-based ratio scale.

I feel that few of the important behaviors of humans are reduceable to this kind of scale and that evaluation techniques should aim at being inclusive/expansive in order to increase the evaluator's perception of the total situation and that human behavior imbedded in it. The aim would be to increase the evaluator's perception of the problem, increase his sensitivity to the multilayered complexity of relevant variables in order to make that data available in a mutual contest between evaluator and client, thus enabling the product to benefit from the expertise, needs, and processes of both. Rather than evaluate education or the educational process as a static condition, one should document it as a process with a perceivable rate and direction of change. The immediate target of inquiry should be evaluated within that changing context. Rather than developing judgments, one might try to develop measures of congruence within and relative to the quality and direction of change. Our goal would then be richness, depth, and complexity rather than simplicity and clarity.

We in the behavioral sciences have taken as our own the scientific phrase "elegant" and have prided ourselves on elegant, clean solutions. I postulate, however, that human behavior may not be elegant and simple, but complex and deep. Architecture, lately (such as The Beauberg, Paris), has admitted that buildings contain ventilating systems, sewer pipes, light fixtures, movement systems, and other things that used to be covered by walls and ceilings. Architects are discovering a new integrity in saying "We will expose not only the elegant, clean lines, but also those things which are integral to making the place functional for human beings." I feel that in evaluation, by simplifying and objectifying our measures, we are dropping out much of the richness that makes our behavior and behavioral contexts human. Just as we do not tend to reduce our structures to meet just the basic shelter needs, but rather delight in the idiosyncratic solutions of different human needs in context, I believe our evaluation strategies must reflect our acknowledgement of situation-specific as well as sociocultural human needs and solutions.

How, then, can we help analysts make good intuitive judgments instead of relying solely on quantitative methods? According to House (1978):

> Good insights are often derived from quantitative studies, but they usually result from the analyst making the right intuitive judgments rather than the right calculations. Those successes are often attributed to the quantitative methodology itself rather than to judgment. Critiques usually focus on the technical quality of the mathematical analysis rather than on the quality of judgments associated with formulation and interpretation. When quality of judgment is challenged, justification must rely on the kind of reasoning common to all argumentation.
>
> One result of underplaying the role of judgment is what might be called "method-oriented analysis," according to Strauch. The analyst ignores the complexities of the context and plunges ahead with his favorite method. With superficial thought the methodology is applied in a straightforward manner as if at the end suggesting that it is the readers' problem to decide whether the fit is a good one [p. 15].

Campbell (1974), in his discussion of qualitative knowing, states that knowing is dependent on common sense. Knowledge of any detail is context-dependent. I feel, however, that knowing is more than simply common sense.

The strength of the architectural metaphor is not, therefore, in suggesting a major change in methodology as much as a change in the scope of what is measured. One would assume that a multiplicity of information is a necessary part of a dependable basis for decision-making. An adequate range of data may not be available for the qualitative decisions needed to deal with context and fit. We also need to proceed with an assumption that there is a multiplicity of solutions, with "best" being an arbitrary designation based on situational choice of focus, in terms of the constraints with which the designer/educator chooses to deal. For example, if he chooses to give greatest emphasis in terms of solution-seeking to the first five of ten variables, he can more readily justify some solutions over others. If, on the other hand, he feels the last five are the most critical (or of highest priority), his "best fit" solution may vary considerably from the first solution. An important process, then, becomes the task of making visible the options and the decision-making procedure that led to both the definition of the problem and the design and fit of the particular solution. I would like to see evaluators begin to treat solutions as hypotheses testing a set of chosen variables rather than dealing with them as if they were facts, as has been done in the past. A particular solution may then be viewed as one link in a network which begins to build substance around an idea but which is fluid in form and structure, able to change shape when conditions or perceptions change, much as individual structures and directions of movement in a city grow, develop, and are modified in order to accommodate the changing needs and perceptions of its inhabitants. Solutions which are *proven* to be right can never be seen as other than obsolete or incongruous when the methodologies and values change and leave these proofs behind, whereas hypotheses are invitations to dialogue and further testing. How much more useful it might be to make apparent that choice of emphasis and the hypothesized solution. Rather than ending the dialogue with a quantified statement, one would *begin the dialogue* with, "How's this for a solution?"

References

Albarn, K., & Smith, J. M. *Diagram, the instrument of thought*. London: Thames and Hudson, 1977.

Alexander, C. *Notes on the synthesis of form*. Cambridge, MA: Harvard University Press, 1964.

Beveridge, W. I. B. *The art of scientific investigation*. New York: Random House, 1950.

Bruner, J. *On knowing*. Cambrige, MA: Harvard University Press, 1963.

Campbell, D. T. Qualitative knowing in action research. Paper presented at the American Psychological Association annual meeting, New Orleans, 1974.

Capra, F. *The tao of physics*. Berkeley, CA: Shambhala, 1975.

Churchman, C. W. *The design of inquiring systems*. New York: Basic Books, 1971.

Gehry, F. O. & Associates, & Brooks/Collier Associate Architects. *Architectural program for the expansion and remodeling of Loyola Law School.* Unpublished manuscript, Los Angeles, California, 1979.

Guba, E. G. Toward a methodology of naturalistic inquiry in educational evaluation. In E. L. Baker (Ed.), *CSE monograph series in evaluation,* No. 8. Los Angeles: Center for the Study of Evaluation, UCLA, 1978.

Hartog, I. L. *Design with nature.* Garden City, NY: American Museum of Natural History, Doubleday/Natural History Press, 1971.

Heyer, P. *Architects on architecture.* New York: Walker and Co., 1978.

House, E. R. The logic of evaluative argument. In E. L. Baker (Ed.), *CSE monograph series in evaluation,* No. 7. Los Angeles: Center for the Study of Evaluation, UCLA, 1978.

Jung, C. G. *Man and his symbols.* New York: Dell, 1968.

Knowles, R. *Energy and form.* Cambridge: MIT Press, 1974.

May, R. *The courage to create.* New York: W. W. Norton, 1975.

Moholy-Nagy, S. *Matrix of man.* New York: Praeger, 1968.

Mumford, L. *Art and technics.* New York: Columbia University Press, 1952.

Norberg-Schulz, C. *Intensions in architecture.* Cambridge: MIT Press, 1973.

Ornstein, R. E. *The psychology of consciousness.* New York: Penguin, 1972.

Otto, F. (Ed.). *Tensile structures,* Vols. 1 and 2. Cambridge: MIT Press, 1962, 1966.

Paulsson, G. *The study of cities.* Kobenhavn, 1959.

Poincare, H. Mathematical creation, from *The foundation of science* (B. Holstead, trans.). In Brewster (Ed.), *The creative process.* New York: Gheselin, 1952.

Rand, P. *Thoughts on design.* New York: Van Nostrand Reinhold, 1970.

Rapaport, A. *House form and culture.* Englewood Cliffs, NJ: Prentice-Hall, 1969.

Rudofsky, B. *Architecture without architects.* Garden City, NY: Doubleday, 1964.

Samples, B. *The metaphoric mind.* Reading, MA: Addison-Wesley, 1978.

Thompson, D. W. *On growth and form.* New York: Cambridge University Press, 1961.

Venturi, R. *Complexity and contradiction in architecture.* New York: Museum of Modern Art, 1977.

Wachsmann, K. *The turning point of building, structure and design.* New York: Reinhold, 1961.

Williams, C., & Williams, C. *Craftsmen of necessity.* New York: Random House, 1974.

Janice J. Monk
Associate Director, Southwest Institute for Research on Women, Adjunct Associate Professor of Geography, University of Arizona

J. Thomas Hastings
Professor Emeritus of Educational Psychology, University of Illinois at Urbana-Champaign

CHAPTER **6**

Geography

Janice Monk holds a Ph.D. in geography from the University of Illinois at Urbana-Champaign and served there as a Research Associate in Measurement & Evaluation and Course Development in the Office of Instructional Resources and as Assistant Professor of Geography. Her published work in social geography deals with minority groups, women, and rural social change and with field research in Australia and Puerto Rico. She has also been involved in research and curriculum projects in geographic education. She is a National Councillor of the Association of American Geographers and a member of the Executive Board of the National Council for Geographic Education. • Thomas Hastings has been involved in educational evaluation (student, curriculum, and program evaluation) at the University of Illinois since 1942. He was Director of the Center for Instructional Research and Curriculum Evaluation, CIRCE, at Illinois for 33 years. He has been involved in geography projects as an evaluation consultant from the early 1960s through 1976. This included being an elected member of the Committee on College Geography, an NSF-funded project of the Association of American Geographers to improve geography at the college level.

GEOGRAPHY, perhaps more than most content areas, has looked to evaluation practice in education for help in developing geographic education (Helburn, 1968; Hastings, Wardrop, & Gooler, 1970, for examples). There is at least one excellent example of education looking to geography for help in explaining some phenomena in educational innovation (House, 1974). However, except for one small corner of cartography — geocoding (Smith, 1979) — evaluation specialists seem not to have seriously looked at techniques and methods from geography for possible adaptation to educational (or health sciences, crime and justice, social welfare) program evaluation. This chapter has that "serious look" and suggested use as its purposes.

Overview

Geography has drawn methodologies and techniques from various social, behavioral, and natural sciences from which educational evaluators also have captured some approaches. Multivariate analysis is a set of techniques used by positivist researchers in geography as well as by evaluators and researchers in education. The cultural geographer uses methods similar to those used in history, anthropology, and sociology. So have a few evaluators in the past decade. However, the geographer has carried further concepts such as place and space, scale and regionalization which of themselves may be useful to the evaluator in education. Also, the geographer has used some of the methods a bit differently than has the evaluator in education. Hence, we believe it will benefit evaluators to study some examples from research by geographers. At the very least, the former will gain new understandings or perspectives concerning methods and techniques which they — or some members of their guild — are endeavoring to use in evaluation at the present.

To accomplish this study of geography the remainder of this chapter contains the following:

- A general view of things current in geographic inquiry which is a brief summary of some notable characteristics of the field so that the reader will have a setting for what follows. It is brief, but we do not intend it for developing geographers. Rather, it is written as a "setting" for those evaluators who wish to broaden or better understand their own approaches.

- We have followed this "backdrop" with more detailed treatments of two examples of global approaches to geographic inquiry, each including a number of separate approaches, techniques, or methods. These global approaches are identified as "humanistic geography" and "behavioral geography." We next include a section on cartography, reviewing a mode of data analysis and representation common to all forms of geographic research.

- The setting and each section contain many references to actual inquiries and to essays on approaches. These are not intended to be inclusive, but they should help the evaluator who is interested in further pursuing the work on his or her own.

- The material on geography is interspersed with discussions of application to evaluation in education. In some cases, these are mere suggestions about using a certain perspective. In other situations, an attempt is made to illustrate how a given technique or method might work in a real (or hypothetical) evaluation case. At times we cite actual evaluations in education which are parallel to approaches in geographic inquiry and in which either group of inquirers might study the other for a firmer understanding of the assumptions, payoffs, and risks.

We know, of course, that many of our geographer friends will say we did not go far enough or we left out significant points. Likewise, a number of our evaluation friends (or nonfriends!) will claim there is nothing new here. However, we hope this review helps some evaluators to think more deeply and/or more broadly about educational evaluation. The theory *and* the practice of evaluation need help.

Geography and Geographic Inquiry

Geography is distinguished by its perspectives and by the questions it asks perhaps more than by the phenomena it studies. The dominant concerns are with the spatial aspects of a problem and the significance of place or context in understanding events and behavior. Several basic assumptions underlie geographic investigations. There is a belief that spatial distributions and associations have meaning and that areas are interrelated. There is a holistic perspective which accepts the concept of interacting systems within human and biophysical domains and in the relationship between them. Scale as well as time dimensions set the framework for study. Among the typical questions asked are: "Where is it? What else is there too? How did it get there? What else is there that makes a difference? How is it connected to things in other places? What difference does it make to society that it is there?" (Helburn, 1968, p. 281).

A wide variety of topics is studied within this framework, and individual geographers are usually known by their topical interests —

for example, as urban, historical, or economic geographers or as climatologists, geomorphologists, or biogeographers. Some bridge the human and physical domains, for example, by studying resource management or environmental hazards. Others specialize in the study of a particular region of the world. Four major traditions have been identified in the discipline, to some degree cutting across the topical divisions (Pattison, 1964). The spatial tradition, dominant in the urban and economic geography of the 1960s, is most concerned with problems of distance, direction, form, and movement. It has long used mapping as a method of analysis and has become closely identified with the application of quantitative techniques. Geographers in this tradition study processes such as the spatial diffusion of innovations (Hagerstrand, 1967; Gould, 1969), migration (Wolpert, 1967), the spatial patterns of settlement evolution and distribution (Borchert, 1976; Hudson, 1969; Morrill, 1963), and the spatial aspects of social structure in urban areas (Johnston, 1971).

Holistic focus on the character of places dominates the area studies or regional tradition. Here the concern is more with individuality and uniqueness, and the approach is likely to be humanistic. Examples of such work are studies describing and interpreting the character of major American regions such as the Middle West, the Great Plains, and the Colorado Plateau (Hart, 1972; Mather, 1972; Durrenberger, 1972). There is a tendency to think places should be understood within a comparative perspective by examining similarities and differences and to look at changes over time as well as space. Thus, Meinig explores the evolution of American "Wests" by comparing subregions within the western states at different time periods, focusing on changes in four categories of regional features — population, circulation, political areas, and culture (Meinig, 1972).

The third, or man-land tradition, is also mostly historical and cultural in approach. It deals with the ways in which humanity has modified the natural environment and with the significance of habitat in human affairs. Work in this tradition has emphasized the visible landscape, which is seen as a document revealing the actions and values of the people who have occupied it. In this tradition Sauer (1963) traces a century of settlement in the Middle West showing how different cultural groups such as Anglo-Saxon hunters and livestock raisers and German and Scandinavian farmers successively imprinted their values and technology on the landscape.

Finally, there is an earth science tradition, akin to the natural sciences in method, dependent on field observation and measurement as principal data-collection techniques. The overarching concept of this tradition is the interaction of parts in creating the whole. Knox, for example, has studied the morphology of stream channels and flood-plains in southwestern Wisconsin, considering the influence of climatic fluctuations, vegetation patterns, and human land use on surface runoff and sediment yield which regulate the form of the land surface (1972).

Up to this point we have introduced several different categories of geographic inquiry. Two approaches to inquiry — humanistic and behavioral — have been mentioned. It was also stated that there are a number of topical intersts which differentiate individual researchers. Those mentioned, not all-inclusive, were urban, historical, economic, climatic, geomorphologic, and biogeographic. In addition, we pointed out that four traditions (spatial, regional, man-land, and earth science) can be used as descriptors to talk about differences across geographic studies. The reader needs to recognize that no single category would ordinarily be used alone to "place" a set of inquiries. Rather, one would probably speak of the studies of two geographers in terms such as: Geographer A's studies are behavioral/economic/spatial, whereas B's are humanistic/historical/man-land. As stated earlier, most studies use cartographic techniques.

A number of concepts recur throughout geographic work despite differences in emphases and methodologies between traditions. Among them are direction; distance; shape and size; location, in both its absolute and relative senses; scale; and the idea of regionalization, or the unity of an area defined by chosen criteria.[1] These concepts may be used in both objective and subjective ways. Distance, for example, may be measured in an arithmetic sense but also treated in terms of individual perceptions (such as far or close), and refer not only to space but also to human relations. Location represents much more than identification by a set of coordinates. Although some geographers use "location" and "place" interchangeably, there are those who use "location" as an objective statement based on coordinates and "place" as a more subjective statement about what various actors perceive and value among the many objects and characteristics of the location. The locational attributes of interest may be the "site" — that is, local characteristics or internal forces or processes — or the "situation" — the external relationships of a place with others. Scale is critical in that it influences the application of other concepts. Thus, in studying a school, the movement of students between rooms is a site or internal characteristic, whereas the pattern of movement from home to school is an aspect of situation. If we are studying on a city rather than a school scale, the pattern of travel to school is an internal attribute of the city and thus an aspect of the city's site rather than its situation.

Recent Trends in Geography

The thrust of much geographical work in the 1960's was a concern for the development of spatial theory via the use of scientific method, emphasizing statistical techniques and mathematical modeling. Some important assumptions underlying this work are that human behavior is predictable, that decisions are based on perfect information, rational and motivated by a desire to maximize benefits. As work of this type accumulated, early arguments over the appropriateness of quantitative techniques were replaced by questions of the reality of the assumptions about human behavior and society. Recent approaches are focusing on more complex views of humanity and society. Attention is being paid to individual behavior rather than principally to aggregates. One consequence is a resurgence of humanistic geography, investigating the personal meanings of place and space and the importance of the perceptual and symbolic in human affairs (Tuan, 1976).

A second consequence is that quantitative geographers using the scientific method began exploring behavior at the individual level, examining decision-making processes and the roles of perceptions and cognition in decision-making (Golledge, Brown, & Williams, 1972). Among topics of recurring interest have been residential selection, urban travel, consumer behavior, and the diffusion of innovations. Hall (1978) has developed a synopsis of scientific and humanist approaches in which the former is identified as "positivist-behaviourist" and the latter as "phenomenological-existential," reflecting their respective philosophical underpinnings. Hall's synopsis appears in Table 6.1. Hall says in the footnote for the table, referring to the item-4 examples:

This confusing example is chosen deliberately to illustrate the lack of distinction geographers have drawn between the two approaches. Kirk's [1963] phenomenal environment corresponds closely with the behaviorist's perspective, whilst his behavioral environment tends toward the phenomenological.

TABLE 6.1 "Scientific" and "Humanist" Positions in Contemporary Geography

Positivist-Behaviourist Concept	Example	Phenomenological-Existential Concept	Example
1. Description of behaviour	Factor analytic regionalization	1. Description of consciousness	Regional consciousness
2. People are predictable	Gravity model of migration	2. People are unpredictable	Failure of regional population projections
3. People are information transmitters	Imitators in diffusion theory	3. People are information generators	Innovators in diffusion theory
4. People occupy an objective world	Kirk's Phenomenal Environment	4. People occupy a subjective world	Kirk's Behavioural Environment
5. People are rational	Economic Man	5. People are arational	Geographies of religion
6. People are sufficiently alike for their behaviour to be described by general laws	Basic needs of food and water and maybe shelter and clothing	6. The differences among people are small but very important	Some people(s) dispose of waste carefully, others carelessly
7. Descriptions may be absolute	High population densities may produce pathological behaviour	7. Descriptions may be relative	How is pathological behaviour defined?
8. Investigation of characteristics independently	Regional analysis	8. Holistic approaches are feasible	Regional synthesis
9. People have objective existence and are real and actual	Social class characteristics	9. People are potentialities in the act of becoming	Life cycle characteristics
10. People are knowable in scientific terms	Social physics	10. People are more than we can ever know about them	Evolutionary processes

SOURCE: Hall (1978). Reproduced by permission.

Other geographers are questioning the ends of geographic research as well as the methodologies, claiming that the theories developed imply a static view of society and do not contribute to understanding or solving social problems. Their new approaches are diverse. Harvey (1973) advocates Marxist analysis of urban society in a quest for spatial justice and equity. King (1976) argues for a "value-critical" approach, which would elucidate the spatial implications of alternative goals and values in public policies. Cox (1978) and Wolpert et al. (1972) direct attention to the role of social conflict in locational problems. Smith (1977) draws on welfare economics in attempting to turn geographers' attention to social well-being. Others (Herbert & Johnston, 1976) have begun to examine the institutional constraints on spatial choice and their implications for the spatial aspects of social policies.

Much of this new work is in an exploratory stage, with clearer ideas of the questions to be asked and the concepts which might be used than of the analytical methods to employ. In the sections which follow, we will review the elements of the emerging methodologies in humanistic and behavioral approaches. We will then turn to a classical geographic tool — the map — a medium which facilitates both data analysis and representation.

From this brief but wide-ranging look at geographic inquiry, what seems useful or related to evaluation? First and foremost, there exist clear parallels between the two fields in inquiry (using Hall's terminology). Table 6.1, together with our previous discussion, shows the interaction between the "scientific" approaches and the "humanistic" approaches to inquiry — the latter undergoing a revival in the past decade or so. Literature in evaluation over the past decade reveals the same (or a very similar) phenomenon in that field. One need only study Volumes 1-7 of the American Educational Research Association Monograph Series on Curriculum Evaluation (1967-1974) to see the rise in (or resurgence of) more complex views of educational problems and the growth of studies of individual perceptions as opposed to the exclusive use of aggregated scores. Increasing belief in the usefulness of naturalistic approaches seems to parallel a like development in geographic inquiry. For support of the claim of increased interest in naturalistic approaches among evaluators, see Glass (1976), Eisner (1975), Guba (1978), Parlett and Hamilton (1976), and House (1978), to name a few.

It therefore behooves evaluators of social service programs, including those in education, to study carefully these more recent inquiries in geography *in order to understand better their own applications of these humanistic/naturalistic approaches.* In so doing evaluators could learn more about the possible payoffs and risks and about the underlying assumptions of such approaches.

Several "new" perspectives in geographic research have been mentioned. The concern with spatial justice reminds one of a similar concern with "justice in evaluation" (House, 1976). Harvey suggests Marxist analysis; House uses philosophy from Rawls. In geography King argues for a "value-critical" approach in research, discussed earlier. The influence of differing values on evaluation results has been a concern of educational evaluators during the past decade or so (see, for example, Smith, 1980).

Thus, the list of issues and concerns common to geographic research and social-service program evaluation (emphasis on education) grows. We have already noted that, in geography, "much of this new work is in an exploratory stage, with clearer ideas of the questions to be asked and the concepts which might be used than of the analytical methods to employ." To a notable degree, the same thing can be said for many of the newer conceptualizations in evaluation of educational programs. Because of the commonalities between the two and the apparently similar phases of development, it should be useful for evaluators systematically to study examples of geographic research which use these questions and concepts in helping them develop their own methods and techniques of analysis.

The tension in geographic research as a metaphor for educational program evaluation appears in at least two domains. First, more geographic investigations than program evaluations use ratio measures such as dollars (economic geography) or area and distance measures (spatial geography), although geographers use all four scales: nominal, ordinal, interval, and ratio. Educational program evaluation uses mostly ordinal or interval measures such as questionnaire responses and test scores (except in comparative cost studies). A relatively few evaluation cost studies utilize ratio scales. The tension lies in the application of geographic inquiry to a different type of measurement or in reassessing the possible alternative measures to be used in educational program evaluation. The second domain of tension, and perhaps the more important one, lies in the use of geographic "primitives" (location, distance, space) which, for the most part, are currently foreign to evaluation language and thought. Educational program evaluators can profit, we believe, by focusing on the tensions *and* on the common evolutions.

Humanistic Geography

The fundamental aim of the geographer as humanist is to promote understanding by revealing the richness and complexity of human experience. In this quest, the perspectives of the people involved are of critical importance — their feelings, perceptions, and conceptions (Tuan, 1974). But an understanding of these perspectives can be derived only through knowledge of the context of action (Harris, 1978; Ley & Samuels, 1978a). Thus, the humanist is deeply concerned with both actors and their environment. Inevitably, the work deals with uniqueness. In this and other respects it is unlike what many geographers call "scientific study." Humanistic geography requires synthesis rather than reductionism. It tries to be holistic (Ley & Samuels, 1978a). To convey the nature of experience requires representation of the concrete rather than of the abstract, but in a reconstituted form so that the meaning of the experience and the thoughts behind the actions are revealed (Harris, 1978; Ley & Samuels, 1978a).

There are no standard methodological rules for such study. Of prime importance is some form of encounter with the participants. This implies heavy reliance on field data collection using methods of observation, participant observation, various forms of interviewing, and unobtrusive indicators (Ley & Samuels, 1978b). The combination of such source material is well illustrated by Ley's study of a black neighborhood in North Philadelphia (Ley, 1974). He conducted fieldwork over a six-month period while living in the neighborhood and working as a proposal writer and program developer at a neighborhood community center. This position placed him in regular contact with most community leaders and with residents in many contexts — in their homes, at work, in school, at play, and on the streets. As leader of a high school class in a community church, he was able to develop close relationships with a small group of teenagers. In addition to the period of intensive contact, he visited in the area over a period of 30 months.

Ley's work gave him ample opportunity to observe the local landscape as well as to interact with the residents. For example, he was able to collect data to establish the distribution pattern of graffiti obscenities which served as good indicators of gang territories and predictors of locations where aggressive acts would most likely occur.[2] The interactions with residents supplied not only critical anecdotal material but also assistance in constructing and validating a survey questionnaire applied near the end of his field period.

The importance of substantial interaction with subjects is corroborated by Rowles (1978) in a work on the spatial world of the elderly. He notes that some important points emerged in fleeting moments within the flow of everyday conversation. For example, a chance remark from Marie, an elderly woman he had known over six months, concerning a firearm she possessed resulted in a conversation yielding insights into the fear that suffused her image of neighborhood space.

Data for the study of contexts can be derived from many sources. This range is demonstrated by reference to Lewis's attempt to understand the meaning of the small town in American life through a study of Bellefonte, Pennsylvania (1972). His primary sources include personal interviews with residents; correspondence; observations of the landscape of the town and spatial patterns; architectural details of building age, style, functions, and transformations; census materials; clipping files; public opinion poll data; historical and current maps; ground and aerial photographs; the city phone directory (to identify ethnic groups by analysis of names); and literature of an earlier period.

We realize that some readers may wish to argue against looking at geography for help, since the foregoing description and explication sounds like any field-oriented inquiry from cultural anthropology and certain areas of sociology. But those readers must take into account what has been said to this point about geographic perspectives in the questions asked and in the geographic primitives.

Perhaps a key concept in this section on humanistic geography is the first sentence: "The fundamental aim of the geographer as humanist is to develop understanding by revealing the richness and complexity of human experience." With few alterations the sentence becomes: "The fundamental aim of the evaluator as humanist is to develop understanding (of a particular education program) by revealing the richness and complexity of treatments, external pressures, transactions, outcomes, and perceptions of various participants." Examples of this approach include Stake and Gjerde (1971), Rippey (1973), and Stake (1975). For example, if the evaluation of Head Start by Williams and Evans (1969) had been done with this aim (understanding richness and complexity), and therefore with a different methodology, Head Start *might* have looked much different. This is not to say that the Williams-Evans approach (much quantification, the use of comparatively few variables — and those determined prior to field work — heavy dependence on aggregates, and little if any attention to unique contexts or participant perceptions) is wrong. Rather, the point is that the aim of such an evaluation and the underlying assumptions (House, 1978) are quite different from those we find in the humanistic inquiry of the geographers we have cited.

As we noted previously, Tuan (1974) and Ley and Samuels (1978a) reveal important elements necessary to accomplish this aim of understanding: (1) the perspectives of the people involved and (2) the context of the action. The geographer in this mode is concerned with actors and their environment. If we were to translate this view to the evaluation of, for example, a literacy program in grades 4-6 of Jedbar Elementary School, the concerns and focuses would be not only on the feelings, perceptions, and conceptions of students, teachers, administrators, parents (and possibly the local press), but also on the context of the program. How does it fit with other class and nonclass programs of Jedbar? What supportive (or nonsupportive) activities go on in the school, the school district, and the larger community? How are teachers trained and supported for the new program? Test scores might be displayed or aggregated, but they would play a minor part. Certainly they would add little to understanding the program or in revealing its richness and complexity.

The work by Lewis (1972) in understanding the meaning of the small Pennsylvania town seems somewhat difficult to apply immediately to educational program evaluation because of the content of his study. However, the data sources — with the exception of architectural details of building age and his ground and aerial maps — could all be relevant to certain education program understandings. We feel that the major gain for the evaluator in looking at the Lewis study is seeing the wide range of sources and the way all of the data were put together to provide a very real portrayal of American life in a small town. Smith and Pohland (1974) did a somewhat similar study in educational program evaluation. However, such approaches in evaluation are rare indeed. Evaluators have reason to study geographers' approaches further.

The interpretation and understanding of the data collected require immersion in the context and recognition that actions and objects can be viewed on different levels of meaning. Ley and Samuels (1978b) identify actions as having, first, objective or functional meanings; second, expressive meanings, or those intended by the actor; and third, documentary meanings which reveal influences and contexts beyond the actor. Lowenthal's interpretations of English and American scenes demonstrate the ways in which landscapes can reveal cultural values and preferences (Lowenthal & Prince, 1965; Lowenthal, 1968). For example, he draws attention to the American preoccupation with future glories by noting signs at a construction site extolling the elegance of what is to come (Figure 6.1). Living in the future, he suggests, predisposes Americans to accept

Figure 6.1 The present yields to the envisaged future. The Embarcadero, San Francisco, California

SOURCE: Lowenthal (1968, p. 74). Reproduced by permission.

present structures that are makeshift, flimsy, and transient, obsolete from the start. . . . But the habit of discarding buildings almost as soon as they are put up has its compensations. "If something is built wrong," writes an observer of Los Angeles, "it doesn't matter much. Everyone expects it to come down in a decade or two. Because we invest so lightly in our buildings, we can, and do, experiment. Innovations embellish the whole countryside" [Lowenthal, 1968, p. 76].

The three levels of meaning identified by Ley and Samuels (1978b) add another facet to the process of interpreting the broad range of field data collected by the humanist inquirer in geography or by the evaluator in education. In educational programs a given slogan or a certain teacher-student transaction has a functional meaning of import to the valuing of the program. But the slogan or act will frequently have several "expressive" meanings, as different actors have somewhat different intents. These meanings also are important to increasing an understanding of the program. The third level, a documentary meaning (which comes out in the total picture) will reveal influences on the program beyond the single actor.

Lowenthal (1968) and Lowenthal and Prince (1965) present what seems to be a usable technique for evaluators; they show how landscapes can reveal values (such as the importance of future in Figure 6.1). Surely it would be useful for program evaluators to use, in a similar fashion, "school-scapes" and public commentaries about schooling, education, and related matters if the aim is to understand the phenomena of the program. Patricia Templin (1978), among others, has used photography as part of program evaluation, but not for quite the same purpose as has Lowenthal.

Invariably, in humanistic geography there is a problem of dealing with great accumulations of qualitative data, and the task becomes one of identifying the themes emerging from it. Rowles (1978) has described the means by which he transcribed conversations, recording observations and impressions onto hundreds of index cards, sorting and resorting them into piles representing emergent themes. He struggled for generalized conceptions which could then be verified in further explorations with the subjects. To transmit their interpretations, humanist geographers rely on extensive direct quotations from their sources (personal and documentary). This gives their writing authenticity as subjects "speak for themselves." Yet, despite the richness and satisfying character of much of the writing in conveying the insider's view, there are difficulties with using the humanistic method. Establishing rapport with subjects and the process of data collection can be time-consuming. The inductive approach can result in exploring blind alleys. Personal involvement with subjects may create feelings of ambiguity for the researcher and concerns of reciprocity (Rowles, 1978). Tuan (1976) has identified the dangers of seeing design which might not exist in actions and overemphasizing "beginnings" and conscious design in interpretations of behavior which might, in fact, result from habit. Perhaps the greatest problems are the subjectivity of interpretation and the question of the representativeness of the data. Yet the humanist thinks the abstractions of scientific simplification represent another form of subjectivity and that in-depth insights counter problems of breadth.

Rowles' reflections on experiential fieldwork (1978) tell us quite a bit about his methods of data interpretation and analysis in the humanistic approach. His use of further explorations with subjects to verify his own generalized conceptions is useful for evaluators who wish to use these humanistic approaches. Certainly, many of our colleagues in sociology and cultural anthropology have used these techniques in their research, but their use in program evaluation is still rare.

Finally, in this section on humanist geographic inquiry the caveats presented by Rowles and Tuan (for geographers) are important for the program evaluator. It should also be useful to the latter to see what responses the geographers make to charges of bias and subjectivity.

Behavioral Geography

Since the mid 1960s, geographers who have become identified with a behavioral perspective have focused on the decision-making processes influencing the development of spatial patterns, rather than dealing mainly with spatial patterns and inferring processes from patterns. Behavioral interpretations of migration, for example, emphasize why people choose to migrate. Concepts such as "place utility" are introduced to elucidate the ways people evaluate their degree of satisfaction with a location in terms of their aspirations and perceptions of alternatives (Wolpert, 1965). Such work contrasts with pattern analyses of migration which develop explanations of population movements in terms of characteristics of places of origin and destination, the distances between them, and the magnitude of aggregate flows.

Common to both humanistic and behavioral geographers is their concern with the "images" in people's minds which shape decisions, rather than with an objective world (Golledge & Rushton, 1976). Frequently, they also share the goal of "understanding" rather than "predicting" in the manner of geographers who have worked with techniques such as regression modeling (Clark, 1976). Behavioralists differ from humanists, however, in pursuing a scientific approach, striving to develop an objective and quantitative understanding of people's preferences and choices (Golledge & Rushton, 1976). In investigating locational decision-making, major attention has been paid to the ways in which environmental learning occurs and to processes of information diffusion.

There are certain points of view and emphases in the "behavioral" geographic research which we believe could be useful to the program evaluator in education. Since geographers in this mode tend to use the "scientific" approaches — quantification, regression techniques, scaling techniques — their actual methodologies are not new to most educational evaluators. The fact, however, that they focus on or emphasize the individual's decision-making which affects spatial patterns rather than analyzing spatial patterns and inferring processes should be interesting to the evaluator. If we substitute words in the sentence "Behavioral interpretations of migration, for example, emphasize why people choose to migrate," we get a sentence such as this: "Behavioral evaluations of an educational program emphasize why various persons choose certain transactions over others." Again, this point of view, or emphasis, contrasts with that of looking at outcomes of a program and inferring whether the decisions were meritorious. In this sense, the behavioral geographer is seeking understanding, as does the humanist geographer.

The evaluator adopting this point of view would emphasize the "images" in people's minds which shape decisions about treatments and transactions in a program. The various "meanings" of the program (desegregating, building competencies, developing problem-solving skills) to various persons involved would be the focus of the evaluations. These might be tied to outcome measures later, but the evaluator would not start with the outcome data.

The development of appropriate postulates has been critical in the evolution of behavioral geography and underlies the methodological approaches. Wolpert's work has been seminal, with his introduction to geography of the concept of "satisficing" rather than "optimizing" behavior in economic decision-making, and with the notion of "bounded rationality." He points to a number of reasons for nonoptimal decision-making, including differences in goals between individuals (ranging from survival to maximization), differences in their levels of knowledge of relevant information, and personal variations in aversion to risk and uncertainty (Wolpert, 1964).

Another important advance introduced by Wolpert is the concept that decisions are not made in a passive environment (Wolpert, 1970). He considers this particularly significant in cases involving controversial facilities such as urban renewal or expressway projects.

Sometimes the location finally chosen for a new development, or the site chosen for the relocation of an existing facility, comes out to be the site around which the least protest can be generated by those to be displaced. Rather than being an optimal, a rational, or even a satisfactory locational decision produced by the resolution of conflicting judgments, the decision is perhaps merely the expression of rejection by elements powerful enough to enforce their decision that another location must not be used; alternatively, the locational decision may result in a choice against which no strong argument can be raised since such elements are either inarticulate or command too little power to render their argument effective [Wolpert, 1970, p. 220].

The concept of "satisficing" rather than "optimizing" or "maximizing" outcomes is one many program evaluations should consider. This would be particularly true for a number of our socioeducational programs. Certainly, in many educational programs the reasons Wolpert cites for "nonoptimal" behavior exist. There are "differences in goals between individuals . . . differences in their levels of knowledge . . . and personal variations in aversion to risk and uncertainty." Evaluations which focus on these differences could improve the picture of reality in the classroom.

Many educational programs are predicated on a belief that there *should be* a year's gain in grade-equivalent scores (in reading or in math) for a year of schooling. The evaluation of such programs is then based on this optimizing of gain scores: a year's or more increase equals good; less than a year's increase equals low worth. However, the teachers (and the students) in the program may see optimizing on this one production as detracting from other goals. They therefore engage in enough activity to bring about some noticeable gain so that "something was accomplished" — not necessarily the predicated optimum or maximum. In this case we see Wolpert's "satisficing behavior." If the evaluator looks for factors which influence satisficing, we may learn more about the worths of the program than we would by retaining only the notion of optimizing as the desired end.

Evaluations of educational programs directed at the educationally disadvantaged or multilingual/multicultural groups might do well to study Wolpert's approach to analysis of the relocation of an existing facility. He notes that sometimes the site chosen (substitute "treatment" chosen) turns out to be the site around which the least protest can be generated by those displaced (substitute "by those treated"). One is reminded here of the paper by House, "Justice in Evaluation" (1976). Many school districts today are planning to close one or more elementary or junior high school attendance units because of tight budgets and decreased enrollments. In many cases boards of education require an evaluation aimed at improving the decision concerning which school or schools to close.

Operationalizing concepts identified by Wolpert and other behavioral geographers in empirical studies has been difficult and problems remain, but some methodologies recur. Simulation models have been used to generate outcomes based on specified assumptions and probabilities, and then reality is compared with the solutions from the simulations. In his study of satisficing behavior by Swedish farmers, for example, Wolpert compared actual productivity with that which would have resulted from optimal decisions, generating the latter through a linear programming solution (Wolpert, 1964). If the evaluator were to attempt to make certain that Wolpert's concept of "least protest" were *not* the basis of decision, more justice would be done. This could be done in part by making certain that *all* parties had equal knowledge of consequences and equal access (even encouragement) to real input. Although their limitations are recognized, simulation models still appear to yield better results than other techniques (Brown & Moore, 1969; Golledge et al., 1972). Wolpert has also used a Monte Carlo simulation to project changes which might occur in neighborhood land use over time as property owners, local government authorities, and neighborhood residents pursue their various goals (Wolpert, Mumphrey, & Seley, 1972). His operational technique in this kind of study is to pit an individual against a computer to generate patterns of responsiveness to contrived stresses and to explore patterns of cooperation. The simulations can generate questions for study in actual situations. Such a question might be: "What is the effect of unequal power distribution between policy makers and impacted groups?" (Wolpert, 1970, p. 228).

Not all simulations of behavior are as complex as those noted above. In a simpler case, Adams compared actual spatial patterns of intraurban migration over time with the patterns which would have resulted had the moves been random in direction. He demonstrated the occurrence of a marked directional bias which appears to indicate that people develop a limited spatial image of the city, sharply in focus for places close to home and in their own sector of the urban area but blurry or blank for places on the other side of town (Adams, 1969).

Most evaluators of educational programs are aware of the use of simulations to collect information about an individual's goals and perceptions. The actual methodology has been used in psychoeducational research. However, it would be useful to study Wolpert's and Adams' applications to understand their bases for making inferences about individual decision processes. The techniques of simulation have not been widely used in program evaluation; and if the methods described by Wolpert, Mumphrey, and Seley are useful in projecting changes which might occur in land use over time, perhaps they can be useful in projecting changes in educational programs as various groups pursue their goals.

Several educational programs offer likely situations in which to use these approaches. For example, the "budget-enrollment" initiated program (mentioned a few pages earlier) lends itself to the study of changing neighborhoods and to questions of future land use. The evaluation of a program (or of alternative programs) of school busing could use the simulation approach and the geographer's concern with space. An evaluation of a desegregation plan should be amenable to the approach used by Adams in studying intraurban migration.

Another characteristic of behavioral work is reliance on case studies, since adequate data can be obtained only at this level. Again, research by Wolpert and his associates on locational conflicts in land use provides examples of the method in use (Wolpert, et al., 1972). Initial analysis involves definition of the relevant *attributes* of land use in a neighborhood under study — for example, its stability, variety, and the degree of neighborhood pride and satisfaction. The second concern is with the principal *participant roles with discretion* over land use change. The studies are presented as narratives derived from documentary and observational data analyzed in the framework of concepts and questions developed from simulation studies or from behavioral theories originating in other fields, such as psychology or political science (Wolpert, 1970; Wolpert et al., 1972).

Behavioral research on environmental learning has followed somewhat different methodological routes from those described above. In studies of preferences and choice, a principal concern has been to develop objective methods for extracting a person's environmental knowledge. In early studies, subjects were commonly asked to provide self-reports in prose or sketch-map form which were then analyzed for content or recurring patterns. Such maps are identified as mental maps and will be discussed in more detail later in this chapter.[3] As the research has developed, a wider array of techniques has come into use, with particular interest in experimenting with ways of scaling nonmetric data. In a concise review article Golledge (1976) outlines the methods used to extract cognitive information from individuals about large-scale external environments, the ways of manifesting such information in others, and the means of analyzing it. His review includes research by environmental psychologists, architects, planners, as well as by geographers. Table 6.2 summarizes the methods associated with geographers' work.

It is not possible in this context to consider each of the methods cited; however, discussion of a selection can indicate the kinds of

TABLE 6.2   Some Methods for Extracting Environmental Cognition
Information

Method	Procedure	External Representational Form	Example
Experimenter observation in naturalistic or controlled situations	Experimenter observes or tracks movements through actual environments (e.g., search behavior, overt spatial activity, actual way finding)	Observations Reports Maps Tables	Zannaras (1973- cited in Golledge, 1976)
	Subjects reveal environmental knowledge in the process of sorting or grouping elements of actual or simulated environments	Lists Tables Composite Maps	Golledge, et al. (1975) Zannaras (1976)
Analysis of external representations — participatory activities	Subjects are asked to write descriptions of what they are aware of in environments	Written reports Content analysis Item analysis	Lynch & Rivkin (1959) Appleyard (1969)
	Subjects are asked to decribe orally a given environment	Oral report Transcriptions Interview Protocols	Lynch (1960) Zannaras (1976)
	Subjects draw sketches or sketch maps representing environments	Pictorial sketches Sketch maps Quantitative & structural Analyses	Lynch (1960) Stea (1969)
	Subjects show existence, location proximity or other spacial relations of environmental elements; use of symbols to represent such elements	Base maps with overlays Notation systems	Lynch (1960) Appleyard (1969)

TABLE 6.2 (Continued)

Method	Procedure	External Representational Form	Example
	Subjects asked to identify photographs models, etc.	Verbal Protocols	Stea & Blaut (1973) Zannaras (1976)
Indirect judgmental tasks	Selection of constructs which reveal environmental information; adjective check lists, semantic differentials, repetory grid test, etc.	Word lists Tables Graphs Grids	Harrison & Sarre (1976) Golant & Burton (1976)
	Paired proximity judgments & other scaling devices that allow specification of latent structure in environmental information	Maps Tables	Briggs (1976) Golledge, et al. (1975) Cadwallader (1976) Golant & Burton (1976)
	Projective tests (e.g., Thematic Apperception Tests)	Verbal Stories	Burton, et al. (1969) Saarinen (1973)

SOURCE: Moore and Golledge (1976). Reproduced by permission of the publisher.

procedures involved. Zannaras' work is regarded as particularly interesting because she has explored the same problem with a variety of techniques (1976). Her research deals with the relation between cognitive structures and urban form. She presented subjects with the task of finding their way from the urban periphery to the center, examining the cues they used to select a path. The experiment was conducted in the field; Zannaras observed and subjects recorded the cues they used. It was repeated with the use of slides, scale models, and maps. She noted that subjects did not appear to have difficulty working with the more abstract map and model displays and that the tests with these tools were more easily administered than the field trials. Agreement of results on some hypotheses was found across methods, although specific values of the importance of cues varied (Zannaras, 1976).

Self-report methods have been used to elicit not only what subjects know about their environment but also what they know indirectly. Here Golledge points to the work of Ley (1974) in Philadelphia, discussed earlier, showing that black youths would name areas of stress or repulsion in parts of the city they had never visited but knew of through secondary sources (Golledge, 1976).

Indirect measures have been widely used to deduce subjects' environmental knowledge. Such measures as semantic differential scales and projective tests (for example, the Thematic Apperception Test) have been used in research on people's perceptions of such natural hazards as flooding and drought (Golant & Burton, 1976; Saarinen, 1973). Other researchers, concerned with people's perceptions of distance between places, have asked subjects to make estimates in relation to given scales (Cadwallader, 1976; Briggs, 1976), or have drawn on multidimensional scaling techniques to impose a spatial structure on subjects' judgments of paired stimuli (Golledge, Rivizzigno, & Spector, 1975). This latter technique has received considerable attention but presents problems in interpreting the substantive meaning of the dimensions revealed by the analysis. There are also difficulties associated with determining when the "best" solution has been reached (Golledge & Rusthon, 1972).

The methodologies used in behavioral work have been such that the results are not readily communicated to audiences lacking appropriate technical understanding. Wolpert has approached this task by writing brief scenarios which embody the major issues and present contrasting cases. For example, he describes the response of a poorly organized and declining community to the threats of development by an outside entrepreneur, then contrasts this with the reactions to a similar situation in a neighborhood where a community organization is in the process of development (Wolpert et al., 1972). Maps can also serve as effective means for communicating perceptions. Their strength in this regard may outweigh some of the limitations of mapping as a means of data collection and analysis.

Although case study methodology has not been widely used in the evaluation of educational programs, there is a growing literature concerning methods and applications in this area. (See the Case Study Bibliography included at the end of this chapter.) Again, since the approach is fairly new in both geographic inquiry and evaluation, it might be profitable for evaluators to compare case study techniques and interpretations in both fields. We could at least learn more about the development of methods of case study inquiry.

In geographic study of environmental learning, there may be some parallels to those parts of educational evaluation which deal with preferences and choice. At this point, however, further work is needed by evaluators with Golledge's review of methods (1976) and with Zannaras's applications of several methods (1976). If we change the wording of one of Zannaras's tasks for subjects — "finding their way from the urban periphery to the center" in order to examine the cues they use to select a path — to something like "moving from some general social-educational goals (both positive and negative) to an educational program for implementing those goals" in order to study the cues they use, we may have something useful for evaluation. In bilingual-multicultural programs, a general goal is frequently expressed as "helping 'limited English students' in reading comprehension in English and improving their self-concepts." If an evaluator of such a program had teachers (or curriculum developers) start with this goal and "move" to implementation strategies (telling how they got there), the evaluator could study the cues they used for the journey.

For the most part, the "behavioral" geographic researcher has used methods from psychology, educational psychology, and sociology, which is not surprising since these are behavioral sciences. Program evaluators in general know and use many of these same techniques. Still, we think it would be useful to evaluators to investigate how the methodology (including interpretation and presentation) was adapted for use in geographic research. As evaluators, we might better understand how new methodology develops in our own field.

Having looked at geographic research in general in the first section of this chapter and then examined two seemingly relevant approaches — humanism and behavioralism — we now turn to an area which most people would see as fundamentally "geographic": cartography.

Introduction to Cartography

This section is not a parallel to the sections headed "Humanistic Geography" and "Behavioral Geography." Regardless of the approach (humanistic or behavioral) or the content focus (economic, land use, political), geographers use cartography for both data analysis and communication.

The following material on mapping consists of 12 maps, some grouped for comparison purposes, and a number of pages of explanation. We have dealt with maps more as representation than as analytic tools. For example, the basic analysis was done before Figures 6.2, 6.5, and 6.6 were prepared for presentation of the data. On the other hand, the mental maps of Figure 6.3 are basic data for analysis.

Most of our treatment in this section focuses on caveats concerning such things as scale and symbolization. Maps, like statistical tables, can be very misleading, especially to people who are less familiar with techniques of cartography. We believe it is exceedingly important for persons in program evaluation in education to be highly aware of this.

Anyone in evaluation interested in mapping as a means of analysis should read the paper by N.L. Smith (1979). He treats three forms of analysis by mapping. These techniques have been used in studies of education, health delivery, and crime/justice.

Certainly there are many educational programs, such as school location, relocation of students across schools, or implementation of special education programs for certain subgroups of the school population, which really are at least partly geographic research problems for which the geographer would use cartography for analysis or reporting. Evaluators should be sensitive to these. Since an evaluator charged with studying such programs many times will not be able to have a qualified geographer (or economist or political scientist) present on the project, some attempt should be made to do a reasonable job with that specialist's set of concepts and tools.

Any type of educational program evaluation which deals with spatial distribution (such as Head Start, Follow Through, busing, minimal competence for graduation) can and probably should use cartography for representation or for purposes of analysis. Evaluators should learn to use maps whenever the treatment or the outcomes may vary across locations. However, one can "lie with maps" as one can "lie with statistics." This section includes some caveats for such misuse. There are currently very few examples in evaluation of good use of cartography; among these are Smith (1979). Any type of data — survey, interview, observation, tests — can be mapped if they can be quantified or put in qualitative categories. The maps which follow attest to this. Mental maps of perceived distance from "authority" can be helpful in both analysis and communication.

Cartographic Representation and Analysis

Among disciplines, geography is distinctive for its use of maps. They may depict objective data or may be mental maps, the product of our ability to collect, organize, store, recall, and manipulate information about the spatial environment (Downs & Stea, 1977).

Two important concepts in any consideration of mapping are scale and symbolization. In a narrow sense, map scale means the ratio of the distance on the map to the corresponding distance on the ground. More broadly, scale influences the amount of detail which can be included on a map and determines whether symbols will be visually effective. Most important, it constrains the inferences which can be drawn from a map.

The map of educational attainment in Australia (Figure 6.2) was prepared at the scale of the "statistical division," an areal unit used by the Australian Bureau of Statistics for aggregating census data. One can infer from the map (assuming knowledge of the location of Australian metropolitan areas and state boundaries) that educational attainment is higher in metropolitan statistical divisions than outside and that it tends to vary more between states than within (Monk, 1980). However, one cannot infer that there are differences between rural and urban levels, since most statistical divisions contain both towns and rural areas. In regions of sparse population, the statistical divisions are larger areal units, and the map creates an unwarranted impression of a substantial extent of relatively well-educated people. The data refer only to people who have completed schooling; thus, in those few divisions where abnormally high percentages of the population have never attended school, the extent of educational attainment also appears inflated. Some of the deficiencies in the map could be remedied by using a finer scale, but this would reduce legibility. It is thus essential to recognize that while a map can reveal some generalizations, it must usually be accompanied by qualifying commentary and must be interpreted with knowledge of the data base.

Analysis of the scale used by subjects in sketching mental maps can yield useful insights into perceptions. For example, almost one-fourth of a neighborhood map drawn by Ernest, a black child in Boston, is devoted to Parker Street, the territorial barrier between black and white areas (Figure 6.3). A map by Ralph, another black child in the same neighborhood, but one who attends Boston Latin School, shows a smaller Parker Street and includes much more territory. On Dave's map, Parker Street is also narrow, but all the detail is on the side of the street where Dave lives, and the Mission Hill Project white area appears as a large blank space (Gould & White, 1974).

Knowledge of symbolization is also important in cartographic representation and analysis. As indicated in Figure 6.4, symbols can portray data on nominal, ordinal, and interval-ratio scales. Maps may represent point, line, or areal patterns in space (Robinson, Sale &

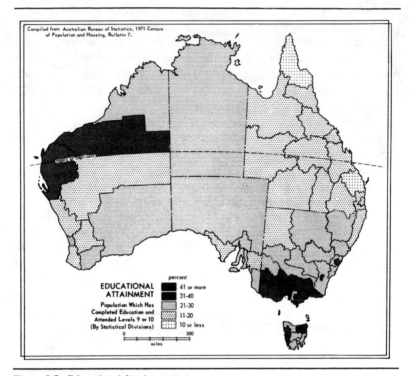

Figure 6.2   Educational Attainment
SOURCE: Monk (1980). Reproduced by permission.

Morrison, 1978). Problems most commonly occur in making decisions about grouping data into categories for representation. Com-
pact classes are generally desirable, but categories may need to be
based on some quantile measure, on equal intervals, on standard
deviations, and the like. The purpose of the map and the inherent
nature of the data are important criteria in decision-making. Figures
6.5 and 6.6 show examples of ways in which symbolization decisions
can affect map interpretation. Information overload is another potential problem in map construction, which can generally be solved by
developing map series, rather than attempting to portray an excessive
amount of information on one map (Figure 6.7).

Maps can be used to show changes through time as well as space
and to indicate correlations. Figure 6.8, for example, shows how
migration patterns have changed over 25 years in various nonmetropolitan regions of the United States. Some regions (for example,
Florida and the West Coast) have experienced growth in each decade;

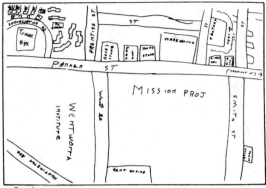

a. Dave's map

b. Ernest's map

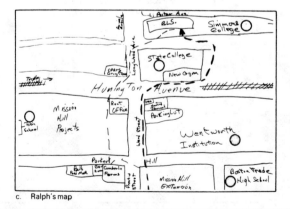

c. Ralph's map

Figure 6.3 Dave's Map/Ernest's Map/Ralph's Map
SOURCE: Gould & White (1974, pp. 32-33). Reproduced by permission.

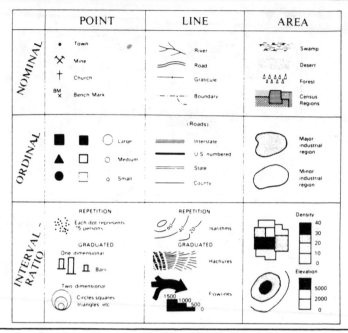

Figure 6.4 Some Examples of the Three Classes of Representation (Point, Line, Area) and How They Might be Used to Portray Nominal, Ordinal, and Interval-Ration Data

SOURCE: Robinson, Sale, & Morrison (1978). Reproduced by permission.

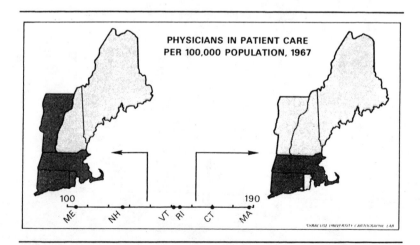

Figure 6.5 Influence of Class Breaks on Map Pattern

SOURCE: Monmonier (1977, p. 26, fig. 22). Reproduced by permission.

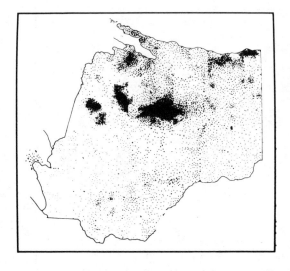

Figure 6.6b A dot map in which the dot size and dot value have been more wisely chosen than in the preceding example. Each dot in this example represents 40 acres of potato production.

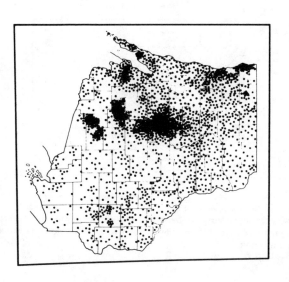

Figure 6.6a A dot map in which the dots are too large so that an excessively "heavy" map is produced. An erroneous impression of excessive potato production is given.

SOURCE: Robinson (1960). Reproduced by permission.

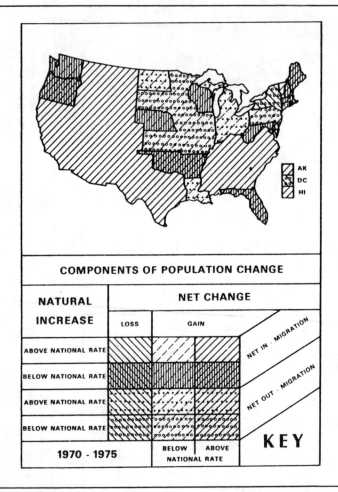

Figure 6.7 Portraying the association among three variables with a complex mul-
tiple-variable map. Note that the legend occupies more space than the
actual map and that many of the area symbols in the legend are not even
used on the map.

SOURCE: Monmonier (1977, p. 33, fig. 31). Reproduced by permission.

others (for example, Regions 14, 15, and 16 in the South and South-
east) have declined in each decade; but most have undergone a
reversal, with nonmetropolitan areas gaining population in the 1970s
after two decades of loss (Roseman, 1977).

Two forms of simple symbolization can be combined to reveal a
correlation (Figure 6.9). These two maps are selected from a time

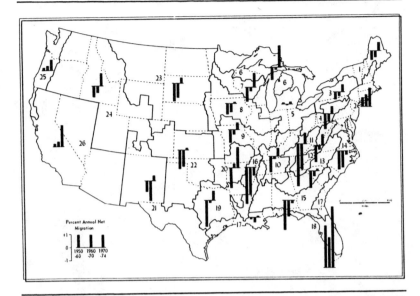

Figure 6.8 Net migration for nonmetropolitan counties in twenty-six regions, 1950-1960, 1960-1970, and 1970-1973

NOTE: See Beale and Fuguitt (1975: 3) for data sources used in compiling this map.
Source: redrawn from Beale and Fuguitt (1975: Map 3, p. 30) with permission of the Center for Demography and Ecology, University of Wisconsin-Madison.
SOURCE: Roseman (1977, p. 19). Reproduced by permission of Association of American Geographers.

series which demonstrates the impact of black migration on voting behavior in Flint, Michigan. The series (mapped at two-year intervals) indicates not only a shift over time in black allegiance from Republican to Democratic parties but that the changes occurred in different parts of the city at different times. The cartographic mode of analysis is parsimonious in this instance since statistical analyses are handicapped by lack of congruence between census tract boundaries and precinct boundaries (Lewis, 1965). Again, the cartographic technique has hazards in correlational work, as shown in Figure 6.10 by Monmonier (1977). Because of the large areas in the northern and eastern units, which fall in the middle-value category (between X_1 & X_2 and between Y_1 & Y_2), the maps convey an impression of a positive correlation between the variables X and Y. However, the smaller areal units might be of equal importance with the larger units — for example, in terms of populations. If all units are of equal population, the correlation, as indicated on the scatter diagram, is negative.

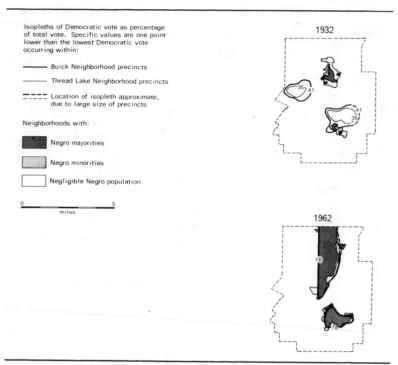

Figure 6.9 Democratic Voting and Negro Neighborhoods, Flint, Michigan: 1932-1962

SOURCE: **Annals of the Association of American Geographers** (1965, pp. 14, 15, fig. 6, P. F. Lewis). Reproduced by permission.

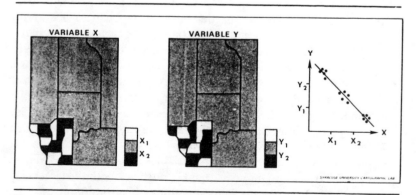

Figure 6.10   Paired maps and a scatter diagram representing the correlation between variables X and Y. Note that variation in the size of the areal units produces an invalid visual association between X and Y.

SOURCE: Monmonier (1977, p. 29, fig. 26). Reproduced by permission.

Problems also occur with the use of mental maps. Subjects, especially children, will vary in their cartographic skills and the development of their abilities to deal with abstract representations (Moore & Golledge, 1976). There are, however, analytical possibilities beyond the level of examining perceptions in simple sketch maps. Saarinen (1969), for example, shows levels of agreement between subjects in images of the Chicago Loop area by tabulating the frequency of inclusion of specific streets, landmarks, and areas on maps made by Loop workers. Comparison of a composite map for this population with a similar composite map of the images of students mainly from Chicago's western and southwestern suburbs shows how the two groups differ in their perceptions (Figure 6.11 and 6.12). Composite maps of students' perceptions of the residential desirability of various parts of their homelands have been constructed by Gould and White (1974) employing principal components analysis of ranked preference data.

What should be recognized in using maps is that the level of analysis cannot be as precise as might be attained with statistical methods. On the other hand, the map can serve as a highly effective means of visual communication as well as an analytical tool, and has advantages over graphs and tables in being able to represent spatial as well as temporal patterns.

This chapter was intended to explore two questions: (1) Does geographic research in terms of aims, points of view, methods, and techniques have anything to offer evaluators of educational programs? (2) If there is a vein of profit here for evaluation, is it rich enough to justify going farther with the digging? At this point, we believe that the answer to each question is affirmative.

First, we described (briefly but broadly) the current nature of geographic inquiry — general purposes, subdivisions, inquiry approaches, and types of questions. Then we focused on two current approaches (humanism and behaviorism, which have some overlap and some distinctions). Finally, we briefly discussed a geographic research tool: the map.

Out of all this we see four things which could be of use to the evaluator of educational programs (and programs in other social service domains).

(1) There are certain perspectives and aims of some researchers in geography which, if adopted by more evaluators, could be an asset to developers and to policy makers.

(2) We found a notable number of techniques or methods which are very similar, if not identical, to those used in a few evaluations.

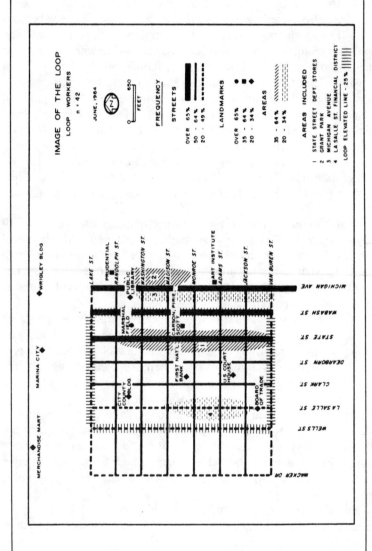

Figure 6.11 Image of the Loop—Loop Workers

SOURCE: Saarinen (1969, p. 16, fig. 2). Reproduced by permission.

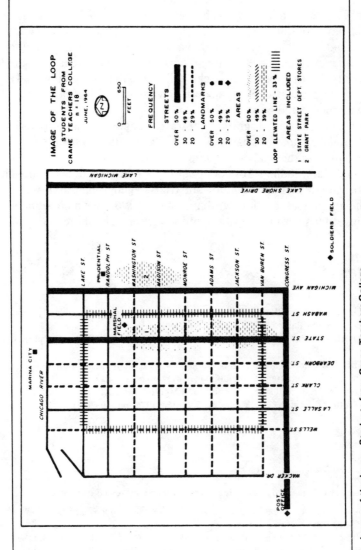

Figure 6.12   Image of the Loop—Students from Crane Teachers College
SOURCE: Saarinen (1969, p. 16, fig. 3). Reproduced by permission.

Study of the geographers' use of these should help evaluators better understand their own assumptions and interpretations.

(3) Certainly there are some techniques used by geographic researchers which might be useful in some evaluations. Evaluators would have to study these further and then apply (adapt) them to educational evaluations. We believe we see programs in education which have aspects calling for geographic inquiry. It is not good enough to say that for these we can call in qualified geographers. The educational evaluator must gain more awareness of these aspects and the way they could be studied.

(4) The area of cartography, central to geography, can be of use to educational evaluation, particularly in presentation of results. It can be also used in the analysis of data.

Those four findings from our exploratory study should be enough to motivate further investigation and trials of geographic approaches. In the references section we have starred works which someone starting on his/her investigation into geography should read first.

Notes

[1] These have been identified as geographic primitives and are succinctly defined by Lanegran and Palm (1978).

[2] Another example of the meaning of graffiti is the article by Ley and Cybriwsky (1974).

[3] The term "mental map" is not confined to a graphic representation but is used more broadly to connote the spatial images in people's minds.

[4] Modified from Golledge, "Methods and Methodological Issues in Environmental Cognition Research," (in Moore & Golledge, 1976, pp. 303-305).

References

(Starred entries are good "beginning places" for the interested evaluator.)

Adams, J. Directional bias in intra-urban migration. *Economic Geography,* 1969, *45,* 302-323.

Appleyard, D. Why buildings are known. *Environment and Behavior,* 1969, 1, 131-156.

Borchert, J. American's changing metropolitan regions. *Annals, Association of American Geographers,* 1972, *62,* 352-373.

Briggs, R. Methodologies for the measurement of cognitive distance. In G. T. Moore & R. G. Golledge (Eds.), *Environmental knowing.* Stroudsburg, PA: Dowden, Hutchinson & Ross, 1976, pp. 325-334.

Brown, L. A., & Moore, E. G. Diffusion research in geography: A perspective. *Progress in Geography,* 1969, *1,* 119-157.

Burton, I., Kates, R., & Snead, R. *The human ecology of coastal flood hazard in Megalopolis.* Chicago: Department of Geography, University of Chicago Research Paper No. 115, 1969.

Cadwallader, M. T. Cognitive distance in intraurban space. In G. T. Moore & R. G. Golledge (Eds.), *Environmental knowing.* Stroudsburg, PA: Dowden, Hutchinson & Ross, 1976, pp. 316-324.

Clark, W. A. V. Technical and substantive approaches to spatial behavior: A commentary. In R. G. Golledge & G. Ruston (Eds.), *Spatial choice and spatial behavior.* Columbus: Ohio State University Press, 1976, pp. 303-311.

Cox, K. R. (Ed.). *Urbanization and conflict in market societies.* Chicago: Maaroufa Press, 1978.

Downs, R. M., & Stea, D. *Maps in minds.* New York: Harper & Row, 1977.

Durrenberger, R. The Colorado plateau. *Annals, Association of American Geographers,* 1972, *62,* 211-236.

Eisner, E. W. The perceptive eye: Toward the reformation of educational evaluation. *Occasional Papers of the Stanford Evaluation Consortium.* Stanford, CA: Stanford University, 1975. (mimeo)

Glass, Gene V (Ed.). *Evaluation studies review annual, vol. 1.* Beverly Hills, CA: Sage, 1976.

Golant, S., & Burton, I. A semantic differential experiment in the interpretation and grouping of environmental hazards. In G. T. Moore & R. G. Golledge (Eds.), *Environmental knowing.* Stroudsburg, PA: Dowden, Hutchinson & Ross, 1976, pp. 364-374.

*Golledge, R. G., Brown, L. A., & Williamson, F. Behavioral approaches in geography: An overview. *The Australian Geographer,* 1972, *12,* 59-79.

*Golledge, R. G. Methods and methodological issues in environmental cognition research. In G. T. Moore & R. G. Golledge (Eds.), *Environmental knowing.* Stroudsburg, PA: Dowden, Hutchinson & Ross, 1976, pp. 300-313.

Golledge, R. G., Rivizzigno, V. L., & Spector, A. Learning about a city: Analysis by multidimentional scaling. In R. G. Golledge & G. Rushton (Eds.), *Spatial choice and spatial behavior.* Columbus: Ohio State University Press, 1975, pp. 95-116.

Golledge, R. G., & Rushton, G. *Multidimensional scaling: Review and geographic applications.* Commission of College Geography Technical Paper No. 10. Washington, DC: Association of American Geographers, 1972.

Golledge, R. G., & Rushton, G. R. Introduction. In R. G. Golledge & G. R. Rushton (Eds.), *Spatial choice and spatial behavior.* Columbus: Ohio State University Press, 1976, pp. vii-xiii.

Gould, P. *Spatial diffusion,* Commission on College Geography Resource Paper No. 4, Washington, DC: Association of American Geographers, 1969.

Gould, P., & White, R. *Mental maps.* Baltimore: Penguin, 1974.

Guba, E. G. *Toward a methodology of naturalistic inquiry.* Monograph Series in Evaluation, #8. Los Angeles: Center for the Study of Evaluation, University of California, 1978.

Hagerstrand, T. *Innovation diffusion as a spatial process.* Chicago: University of Chicago Press, 1967.

Hall, R. Teaching humanistic geography. *The Australian Geographer,* 1978, *14,* 7-13.

Harris, C. The historical mind and the practice of geography. In D. Ley & M. S. Samuels (Eds.), *Humanistic geography*. Chicago: Maaroufa Press, 1978, pp. 123-137.

Harrison, J., & Sarre, P. Personal construct theory, the repertory grid and environmental cognition. In G. T. Moore & R. G. Golledge (Eds.), *Environmental knowing*. Stroudsburg, PA: Dowden, Hutchinson & Ross, 1976, pp. 375-384.

Hart, J. F. The middle west. *Annals, Association of American Geographers*, 1972, *62*, 258-282.

Harvey, D. W. *Social justice and the city*. London: Edward Arnold, 1973.

Hastings, J. T., Wardrop, J. L., & Gooler, D. *Evaluating geography courses: A model with illustrative applications*. Washington, DC: Commission on College Geography, Association of American Geographers, 1970.

Helburn, N. The educational objectives of high school geography. *The Journal of Geography*, 1968, *67*, 274-281.

Herbert, D., & Johnston, R. J. *Spatial perspectives on problems and policies*. London: John Wiley, 1976. (2 vols.)

House, E. R. *The politics of educational innovation*. Berkeley, CA: McCutchan, 1974.

House, E. R. Justice in evaluation. In G. V Glass (Ed.), *Evaluation studies review annual, vol. 1*. Beverly Hills, CA: Sage, 1976, pp. 75-100.

House, E. R. Assumptions underlying evaluation models. *Educational Researcher*. 1978, *7*, 4-12.

Hudson, J. C. A location theory for rural settlement. *Annals, Association of American Geographers*, 1969, *59*, 365-381.

Johnston, R. J. *Urban residential patterns*. London: G. Bell & Sons Ltd., 1971.

King, L. Alternatives to a positive economic geography. *Annals, Association of American Geographers*, 1976, *66*, 293-308.

Kirk, W. Some problems in geography. *Geography*, 1963, *48*, 357-371.

Knox, J. C. Valley alluviation in southwestern Wisconsin. *Annals, Association of American Geographers*, 1972, *62*, 401-410.

*Lanegran, D., & Palm, R. *Invitation to geography*. New York: McGraw-Hill, 1978.

Lewis, P. F. Impact of Negro migration on the electoral geography of Flint, Michigan, 1932-1962: A cartographic analysis. *Annals, Association of American Geographers*, 1965, *55*, 1-25.

Lewis, P. F. Small town in Pennsylvania. *Annals, Association of American Geographers*, 1972, *62*, 323-351.

Ley, D. *The Black inner city as frontier outpost*. Washington, DC: Association of American Geographers, 1974.

Ley, D., & Cybriwsky, R. Urban graffiti as territorial markers. *Annals, Association of American Geographers*, 1974, *64*, 491-505.

*Ley, D., & Samuels, M. Introduction: Contexts of modern humanism in geography. In D. Ley & M. Samuels (Eds.), *Humanistic geography: Prospects and problems*. Chicago: Maaoufa Press, 1978, pp. 1-17. (a)

Ley, D., & Samuels, M. Methodological implications, overview. In D. Ley & M. Samuels (Eds.), *Humanistic geography: Prospects and problems*. Chicago: Maaroufa Press, 1978, pp. 121-122. (b)

Lowenthal, D. The American scene. *Geographical Review*, 1968, *58*, 61-88.

Lowenthal, D., & Prince, H. English landscape tastes. *Geographical Review*, 1965, *55*, 186-222.

Lynch, K. *The image of the city*. Cambridge: MIT Press, 1960.

Lynch, K., & Rivkin, M. A walk around the block. *Landscape*, 1959, *8*, 24-34.

Mather, E. C. The American great plains. *Annals, Association of American Geographers*, 1972, *62*, 237-257.

Meinig, D. American Wests: Preface to a geographical introduction. *Annals, Association of American Geographers*, 1972, *62*.

Monk, J. Social change through education: Problems and planning in rural Australia. In W. P. Avery, R. E. Lonsdale, & I. Volgyes (Eds.), *Rural change and public policy in Eastern Europe, Latin America and Australia*. New York: Pergamon Press, 1980.

*Monmonier, M. *Maps, distortion and meaning*. Resource Paper for College Geography No. 75-4. Washington, DC: Association of American Geographers, 1977.

*Moore, G. T., & Golledge, R. G. (Eds.). *Environmental knowing*. Stroudsburg, PA: Dowden, Hutchinson & Ross, 1976.

Morrill, R. L. The development of spatial distributions of towns in Sweden: An historical predictive approach. *Annals, Association of American Geographers*, 1963, *53*, 1-14.

Muehrcke, P. *Thematic cartography*. Resource Paper No. 19, Commission on College Geography. Washington, DC: Association of American Geographers, 1972.

Parlett, M., & Hamilton, D. Evaluation as illumination. In Gene V Glass (Ed.) *Evaluation studies review annual, vol. 1*. Beverly Hills, CA: Sage, 1976, pp. 140-157.

Pattison, W. D. The four traditions of geography. *Journal of Geography*, 1964, *63*, 211-216.

Rippey, R. (Ed.). *Studies in transactional evaluation*. Berkeley, CA: McCutchan, 1973.

Robinson, A. *Elements of cartography* (2nd ed.). New York: John Wiley, 1960.

*Robinson, A., Sale, R., & Morrison, J. *Elements of cartography* (4th ed.). New York: John Wiley, 1978.

Roseman, C. C. *Changing migration patterns within the United States*. Resource Paper for College Geography No. 77-2. Washington, DC: Association of American Geographers, 1977.

Rowles, G. D. Reflections on experiential field work. In D. Ley & M. Samuels (Eds.), *Humanistic geography: Prospects and problems*. Chicago: Maaroufa Press, 1978, pp. 173-193.

Saarinen, T. F. *Perception of environment*. Resource Paper No. 5, Commission on College Geography, Washington, DC: Association of American Geographers, 1969.

Saarinen, T. F. The use of projective tests in geography research. In W. H. Ittelson (Ed.), *Environment and cognition*. New York: Seminar Press, 1973, pp. 29-52.

Sauer, C. O. Homestead and community on the Middle Border. In H. W. Ottoson (Ed.), *Land use policy & problems in the United States*. Lincoln: University of Nebraska Press, 1963. Reprinted in P. W. English & R. C. Mayfield (Eds.), *Man, space, & environment*. New York: Oxford University Press, 1972, pp. 15-28.

Smith, D. M. *Human geography, a welfare approach.* New York: St. Martin's Press, 1977.

Smith, L. M., & Pohland, P. A. Education, technology, and the rural highlands. *AERA Monograph Series on Curriculum Evaluation* (No. 7), Chicago: Rand McNally, 1974.

Smith, N. L. Techniques for the analysis of geographic data in evaluation. *Evaluation and Program Planning.* 1979, *2*, 119-126.

Smith, N. L. Sources of values influencing educational evaluation. *Studies in Educational Evaluation,* 1980, *6*, 101-118.

Stake, R. E. *Evaluating the arts in education.* Columbus, OH: Charles E. Merrill, 1975.

Stake, R. E., & Easley, J., et al. *Case studies in science education.* Urbana: Center for Instructional Research and Curriculum Evaluation, College of Education, University of Illinois, 1978.

Stake, R. E., & Gjerde, C. *An evaluation of the Twin City Institute for Talented Youth,* 1971. (Reprinted in *Evaluation Report Series,* No. 1. Kalamazoo: Evaluation Center, College of Education, Western Michigan University, 1975.)

Stea, D. (Ed.), *Working papers in place perception.* Place Perception Research Report No. 2. Worcester, MA: Graduate School of Geography, Clark University, 1969.

Stea, D., & Blaut, J. M. Some preliminary observations on spatial learning in school children. In R. M. Downs & D. Stea (Eds.), *Image and environment: Cognitive mapping and spatial behavior.* Chicago: AVC, 1973, pp. 226-234.

Templin, P. S. Still photography: Can it provide program portrayal? Paper presented at the American Educational Research Association annual meeting, Toronto, March 1978.

Tuan, Yi-Fu. Space and place: A humanistic perspective. *Progress in Geography,* 1974, *6,* 211-252.

Tuan, Yi-Fu. Humanistic geography. *Annals, Association of American Geography,* 1976, *66,* 266-276.

Williams, W., & Evans, J. W. The politics of evaluation: The case of Head Start. *The Annals,* 1969, 385, 118-132.

*Wolpert, J. The decision process in a spatial context. *Annals, Association of American Geographers,* 1964, *54,* 537-558.

Wolpert, J. Behavioral aspects of the decision to migrate. *Papers and Proceedings of Regional Science Association,* 1965, *15,* 159-169.

Wolpert, J. Directional and distance bias in interurban migratory streams. *Annals, Association of American Geographers,* 1967, 57, 605-616.

Wolpert, J. Departures from the usual environment in locational analysis. *Annals, Association of American Geographers,* 1970, *60,* 220-229.

Wolpert, J., Mumphrey, A., & Seley, J. *Metropolitan neighborhoods: Participation and conflict over change.* Resource Paper No. 16, Washington, DC: Association of American Geographers, 1972.

Zannaras, G. The relation between cognitive structure and urban form. In G. T. Moore & R. G. Golledge (Eds.), *Environmental knowing.* Stroudsburg, PA: Dowden, Hutchinson & Ross, 1976, pp. 336-350.

Case Study Bibliography

Theory and Conceptualization of the Study

Adelman, C., Jenkins, D., & Kemmis, S. *Rethinking case study: Notes from the second Cambridge conference.* Cambridge: Nuffield Foundation, Churchill College, 1975.

Becker, H.S. et al. Design of the study. *Boys in white.* Chicago: University of Chicago Press, 1961, Pp. 17-32.

Blumer, H. *Symbolic interactionism: perspective and method.* New York: Prentice-Hall, 1969.

Bogdan, R., & Taylor, S.J. *Introduction to qualitative research methods: A phenomenological approach to the social sciences.* New York: John Wiley, 1975.

Bruyn, S.T. *The human perspective in sociology: The methodology of participant observation.* Englewood Cliffs, NJ: Prentice-Hall, 1966.

Cusick, P.A. *Inside high school: The student's world.* New York: Holt, Rinehart & Winston, 1973.

Denzin, N.K. The logic of naturalistic inquiry. *Social Forces.* 1971, 50, 166-182.

Denzin, N. *The research act.* Chicago: AVC, 1970.

Glaser, B.G., & Strauss, A. *The discovery of grounded theory.* Chicago: AVC, 1967.

Hamilton, D. *A science of the singular?* Urbana: Center for Instructional Research and Curriculum Evaluation, University of Illinois, 1976. (mimeo)

Hammond, P.E. (Ed.). *Sociologists at work.* New York: Basic Books, 1964.

Johnson, J.M. *Doing field research.* New York: Free Press, 1975.

Rist, R.C. Ethnographic techniques and the study of an urban school. *Urban Education,* 1975, 10.

Schatzman, L., & Strauss, A. *Field research: Strategies for a natural sociology.* Englewood Cliffs, NJ: Prentice-Hall, 1973.

Smith, L.M. An aesthetic education workshop for administrators: Some implications for a theory of case studies. Paper presented at the American Educational Research Association annual meeting, Chicago, 1974.

Smith. L., & Geoffrey, W. *The complexities of the urban classroom.* New York: Holt, Rinehart & Winston, 1969.

Stake, R.E. *The case study method in social inquiry.* Urbana: Center for Instructional Research and Curriculum Evaluation, University of Illinois, 1975. (mimeo)

Tittle, C.K. The case study: A possible paradigm for evaluation. Paper presented at the American Educational Research Association annual meeting, New Orleans, February 1973.

Walker, R. The conduct of educational case study: Ethics, theory and procedures. In B. McDonald (Ed.), *SAFARI: Innovation, evaluation, research and the problem of control.* Norwich, England: Centre for Applied Research in Education, University of East Anglia, 1974.

Wolcott, H. Criteria for an ethnographic approach to research in schools. In J.T. Roberts & S.K. Akinsanya (Eds.), *Schooling in the cultural context.* New York: David McKay, 1976.

Yin, R. K., & Heald, K. P. Using the case survey method to analyze policy studies. *Administrative Science Quarterly*, 1975, 20.

Zelditch, M. Some methodological problems of field studies. In G. J. McCall & J. F. Simmons, *Issues in participant observation*. Reading, MA: Addison-Wesley, 1969.

Confidentiality, Anonymity, and the Rights of Data

Macdonald, B. Evaluation and the control of education. In *SAFARI: Innovation, evaluation, research and the problem of control*. Norwich, England: Centre for Applied Research in Education, University of East Anglia, 1974.

Macdonald, B. The portrayal of persons as evaluation data. Paper presented at the American Educational Research Association annual meeting, San Francisco, 1976.

Rainwater, L., & Pittman, D. Ethical problems in studying a politically sensitive and deviant community. In G. J. McCall & J. L. Simmons (Eds.), *Issues in participant observation*. Reading, MA: Addison-Wesley, 1969.

Sjoberg, G. (Ed.). *Ethics, politics, and social research*. Cambridge, MA: Schenkman, 1967.

Access and Entry

Broadhead, R. S., & Rist, R. C. Gatekeepers and the social control of social research. *Social Problems*, 1976, 23.

Geer, B. First days in the field. In P. Hammond (Eds.), *Sociologists at work*. New York: Doubleday, 1967.

Henderson, R. D. Denial of research privileges in a black school: Implications for researchers. *Educational Leadership Research Supplement*, 1974, 333-337.

Kahn, R., & Mann, F. Developing research partnerships. In G. J. McCall & J. F. Simmons (Eds.), *Issues in participant observation*. Reading, MA: Addison-Wesley, 1969.

Wax, R. The first and most uncomfortable stage of fieldwork. In *Doing fieldwork: Warnings and advice*. Chicago: University of Chicago Press, 1974.

Data Collection

Burnett, J. H. Event description and analysis in the microethnography of urban classrooms. In F. A. Ianni & E. Storey (Eds.), *Cultural relevance and educational issues: Readings in anthropology and education*. Boston: Little, Brown, 1973.

Leacock, E. *Teaching and learning in city schools*. New York: Basic Books, 1969. Pp. 9-20.

Ogbu, J. *The next generation: An ethnography of education in an urban neighborhood*. New York: Academic Press, 1974. pp. 11-20.

Scott, W. R. Field work in a formal organization: Some dilemmas in the role of observer. *Human Organization*, 1963, 22, 162-168.

Vaughn, W., & Faber, E. Field methods and techniques: The systematic observation of kindergarten children. *Human Organization*, 1952, 11, 33-36.

Data Analysis

Becker, H. S. Problems of proof and inference in participant observation. In G. J. McCall & J. L. Simmons. *Issues in participant observation*. Reading, MA: Addison-Wesley, 1969.

Becker, H. S. Fieldwork evidence. In *Sociological work: Method and substance*. Chicago: AVC, 1970.

Becker, H. S., & Geer, B. Participant observation: The analysis of qualitative field data. In R. N. Adams & J. C. Preiss (Eds.), *Human organization research*. Homewood, IL: Dorsey Press, 1960.

Everhart, R. Problems of doing field work in educational evaluation. *Human Organization*, 1975, *34*, 205-215.

Lazarsfeld, P. F., & Menzel, H. On the relation between individual and collective properties. In A. Etzioni (Ed.), *A sociological reader on complex organizations*. New York: Holt, Rinehart & Winston, 1969.

Lebar, F. M. Coding ethnographic materials. In R. Naroll & R. Cohen (Eds.), *Method in cultural anthropology*. Garden City, NY: Natural History Press, 1970.

Lofland, J. *Analyzing social settings*. Belmont, CA: Wadsworth, 1971. pp. 117-118.

Mulhauser, F. Ethnography and policymaking: The case of education. *Human Organization*, 1875, *34*, 311-314.

Smith, L. & Geoffery, W. *The complexities of the urban classroom*. New York: Hold, Rinehart & Winston, 1969. Pp. 228-250.

Vidich, A. Participant observation and the collection and interpretation of data. *American Journal of Sociology*, 1955, *60*, 354-360.

Exemplary Studies and Reports

Barker, R. G., & Wright, H. F. *Midwest and its children*. Evanston, IL: Row, Peterson, 1956.

Brauner, C. The first probe. *AERA Monograph Series on Curriculum Evaluation* No. 7. Chicago: Rand McNally, 1974.

Coles, R. *Children of crisis*. New York: Dell, 1967.

Davies, H. *The Creighton report*. London: Trinity Press, 1976.

Elofson, T. *Open education in the elementary school: Six teachers who were expected to change*. Unpublished Ph. D. dissertation, University of Illinois, 1973.

Hamilton, D. *Big science, small school*. Edinburgh: Scottish Council for Research in Education, 1975.

Hamilton, D. The case of the missing chairs. In D. Hamilton, *In search of structure: Essays from an open plan school*. Edinburgh: Scottish Council for Research in Education, 1976.

Jackson, P. *Life in classrooms*. New York: Holt, Rinehart & Winston, 1968.

Lacey, C. *Hightown grammar – The school as a social system*. Manchester, England: University Press, 1970.

Lewis, O. *The children of Sanchez*. New York: Random House, 1961.

Shipman, M. D., Bolam, D., & Jenkins, D. Inside a curriculum project: A case study in the process of curriculum change. London: Methuen, 1974.

Smith, L., & Pohland, P. Education, technology, and the rural highlands. *AERA Monograph Series on Curriculum Evaluation*, No. 7, Chicago: Rand McNally, 1974.

Stake, R. E. et al. *Case studies in the evaluation of educational programs*. Paris: OECD, 1976.

Tikunoff, W., Berliner, D. C., & Rist, R. C. *An ethnographic study of the forty classrooms of the beginning teachers evaluation study: A known sample*. Technical Report No. 75-10-10-5. San Francisco: Far West Regional Laboratory, 1975. (October)

West, F. E. A case study of Hogtown Creek: Justification for field observations. Gainesville: P. K. Yonge Laboratory School, University of Florida, 1973.

D. Bob Gowin
Professor, Department of Education, Cornell University

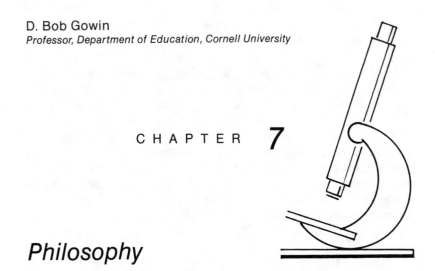

CHAPTER **7**

Philosophy

Bob Gowin, a philosopher, has long been interested in the philosophy of science as applied to research and evaluation. Claiming that facts and values ride in the same epistemological boat, he has developed arguments about the concept of value in evaluation, the philosophical structure of evaluation documents, and the differences in claims produced by evaluation, research, policy, and management studies. He published (with Jason Millman) Appraising Educational Research, *and helped edit the National Society for the Study of Education (NSSE) yearbook,* Philosophical Redirections for Educational Research. *He was president of the Philosophy of Education Society in 1969 and won the President's Prize of the Evaluation Network in 1979.*

CAN THE METHODOLOGIES available to contemporary evaluators be augmented by ideas from philosophy? If one were to make a raid on the storehouse of philosophy, how would one go about it? Is it plausible to think metaphorically about the relations between philosophy and evaluation? A metaphor establishes isomorphic structures between its primary and secondary parts, according to the view of philosopher Max Black (1962a, 1962b, 1977). Can we construe philosophy as the secondary part and evaluation as the primary part of some as yet unstruck metaphor?

The answer to the first question is, in general, yes. Beyond a general answer, there are special features of philosophy which can be (indeed have been) used in evaluation. Specific techniques of concept analysis seem readily transferable to conceptual problems of evaluation. As to the second question, making a raid on philosophy is not so easy to do, but it can be tried, and I will try it; but it will be a raid and not an inventory of the storehouse. The last question about metaphor is even more difficult to answer without a specific metaphor to analyze. In the phrase "philosophy as a metaphor for evaluation," the meaning of metaphor must be a broad one, asking us to consider how the concepts and methods of philosophy might be carried over into evaluation. The name for such a study is "conceptual research," a form of research basic to philosophy. The broad answer, then, to the third question construes *philosophical analysis* as the metaphor for evaluation.

This chapter has four sections. The first section contains a brief description of philosophical analysis, including its history, and an orienting metaphor for philosophy. The second section focuses on the application in philosophy of philosophical analysis. This application takes the form of philosophic work on the concept of metaphor itself. The third section includes a description of the techniques of concept analysis. The fourth section takes up some aspects of the problem of adaptation to evaluation of the concepts, methods, and techniques of philosophical analysis. A discussion of caveats and an estimation of limitations completes this chapter. An annotated bibliography is included at the end of the chapter.

Philosophy

Brief History of Philosophical Analysis

Philosophical analysis is the name given to the clarification of meaning of terms basic to philosophical inquiries. Socrates is called the patron saint of analysts for his persistent seeking of definitions. Modern work dates from the early thirties of the twentieth century, chiefly located in England, and following the lead of such thinkers as Bertrand Russell (mathematics), Rudolph Carnap (logical empiricism), G.E. Moore (ordinary language), and Ludwig Wittgenstein (language games, logical grammar). Arthur Pap (*Elements of Analytic Philosophy*) and Max Black were leaders in American universities. While topics and methods vary among these philosophers, a common thread is the focus on conceptual studies of language. The general aim is to make logical constructions of the immediately given. This approach began to take hold in the United States after World War II and some products appeared in philosophy of education in the late fifties and early sixties.

Philosophy and Philosophizing

I have already used metaphor fragments: "Philosophy is a storehouse," . . . "Make a raid," . . . "inventory the storehouse." I will be "drawing a picture" of philosophy as a "field," and so forth. It is as difficult to avoid metaphors as it is to construct inventive and evocative metaphors.

[I am putting these sentences in brackets because throughout this paper I will be commenting in brackets on what has just been said. It is a feature of philosophy to work at different levels of meaning, and to call attention to this fact.]

First, some terminological points. The term "philosophy" may be taken to refer to the products of the works of philosophers in the domain or field of philosophy. The discipline of philosophy, taken in an active sense, is that set of virtues accruing to those persons who follow its commandments. The term "philosophizing" may be taken to refer to the active working of philosophers as they try to answer questions in a characteristic way.

In this section I invite you to watch for three levels of meaning. One level is straightforward discourse, describing, naming, and exhibiting parts of philosophy. The second level of meaning invites the reader to engage in certain tasks: to think in certain ways, to find examples and clear cases in each person's experience, in such a way that the point of the philosophizing is directly experienced (insofar as that activity is possible through written discourse). The third level of meaning is about the first two levels of meaning, reflecting back on what has been exhibited and achieved. I am attempting to give the reader a chance to understand philosophy by seeing its products and by actively engaging in its process.

The term "philosophy" is ambiguous. Does it refer to the procedure or substance? We may claim that philosophizing is the process and philosophy is the product; in so doing we call attention to the process-product distinction, which is itself a product of the process of philosophizing. In calling attention to this distinction, we can also note a characteristic of philosophical works — namely, that they are *reflexive*. They turn back upon themselves, not only making distinctions but looking at the distinctions made in a critical fashion. Thinking about thinking is how William James characterized philosophical work. It is rather easy to become confused as we move up and down between layers of meaning, commenting on comments, and adding another layer of meaning to those already unclear. Yet the persistent thrust of philosophizing is to make distinctions which will clarify confusions about things, events, and persons in the world in which we live so that we can have judgment and knowledge about the life good to lead. Philosophy is the love of wisdom [dormant metaphor].

"Philosophy is the love of wisdom." One of the reasons for saying that the "love of wisdom" is a dormant metaphor is that in this culture the notion of "wisdom" is not very important. For any metaphor to work there must be in the speech community competent individuals to interpret both the literal and metaphoric meanings of a statement. Further, the antecedent conditions for philosophy have been only infrequently satisfied. (For example, the philosophy of science that should attend the making of scientific knowledge has been largely divorced from the activities of scientists. Most scientists work in a standard paradigm. They seldom have need for philosophy. The philosophic argument between a Carnap and a Popper (verifiability vs. falsifiability) is not a discussion shared by the speech community of modern scientists to any great extent.) The notion of "love" in ordinary language is so commonly associated with "romantic love" of sentiment, immediate passion, and nonintellectuality that "love of wisdom" strikes most as a peculiar and misleading metaphor. To say "I'm (romantically) in love with wisdom," would be a gaffe. The tradition in philosophy, moreover, with respect to the concept of love, is to avoid giving it explicit treatment. Philosophical thought is only confused by passion (eros); thought should be dispassionate to be clear; thought is cold, not hot. All of these considerations have exceptions, of course, but I believe the general tenor of the interpretation is appropriate. The main point is about metaphor. For a metaphor to work, both the speaker and hearer, writer and reader, must share a framework of experience and meaning such that both the literal and metaphoric meanings can trade on each other. (How metaphors appear to present something new and unfamiliar will be discussed later.) These comments anticipate a caveat: To the extent that evaluators are quite unfamiliar with modern philosophy, the striking force of metaphors relating the two fields will be blunted.

Philosophy, in a large sense, is a moral enterprise, stimulated by human problems and directed toward furthering human enlightenment in thinking, feeling, and acting. Concept clarification, the work-horse of philosophy, aids the moral undertaking by helping us to be responsible for clear thinking and to avoid the oppressions of muddled language. Like human life itself, the conditions for philosophy are both precarious and stable, changing and unchanging. The philosophic task, to use knowledge and go beyond it to wisdom, is never ultimately completed, but the possibilities for a genuinely shared set of illuminating beliefs and values is never beyond the potential of human beings. We build with what we have. We project idealizations that lead us beyond the ordinary present so that we may better see what we have and what we may become. Philosophy, the love of wisdom, is an achievement, like anything that is loved well; and it is a task, like anything that is loved well. Love requires knowledge, interest, effort, caring, training, and experience. To say "Philosophy is the love of wisdom," is to speak both literally and metaphorically. And it is to say, like so many other things philosophy works with, that the claim itself is a problem for philosophy, requiring sustained analysis and producing compelling but competing answers.

"Educational evaluation is the pursuit of practical wisdom." This metaphor has some appeal, and it needs to be briefly analyzed. What might "practical wisdom" mean? If wisdom refers to the use of facts and reason to reach balanced judgments about what to think and feel, and how to act, then practical wisdom would focus on the practical activities of thinking, feeling, and acting. The metaphor would enjoin us to pursue balanced judgments. We should apply a test of coherence in the relations among thinking, feeling, and acting.

The notion of the practical has many different meanings. Aristotle, for example, distinguished practical knowledge from theoretical (for example, physics) and productive (for example, art) knowledge. Practical knowledge is generated by reflective scrutiny of choices we make in ethics and politics. Practical knowledge begins with a local context, with particular problems; any choice or decision that leads to an action is always particular, not universal. We do not act at large or in general. Practical knowledge may be conceptually complex, containing a variety of elements: concepts, rules, reasons, principles. The practical syllogism (such as "Black houses are ugly; your house is black; therefore your house is ugly.") is a logical device that brings together a principle, a factual claim, and a rating. This argument form can be directly useful in evaluation studies.

The combination of "practical" and "wisdom" as philosophic concepts does point us toward activities found in the practice of evaluation. Indeed, the pursuit of practical wisdom gives an orienting point to evaluation.

Facts, Concepts, and Events

Let us try another metaphor. "Facts without concepts are blind and concepts without facts empty." This assertion, attributed to Immanuel Kant, is a philosophic metaphor. It calls our attention to the interaction between two systems, the systems of concepts and facts. Concepts keep us from being blind because they enhance our vision, our viewpoint, our insights, our perspective. [Notice the metaphors of vision.] Thinking and seeing are brought together metaphorically in much of our ordinary and technical discourse. Thinking is not literally seeing with the eyes. Metaphorically, though, thinking develops perspectives of the mind.

If facts need perspective, concepts need content. Some concepts are empty;[1] they carry nothing; they are forms which are not formative. So the metaphor would lead us. What is it that "fills" an empty concept? Is a concept a vessel? A vehicle? Can a concept carry water? On both shoulders? Is a concept a ferryboat, carrying passengers from place to place? What is a concept?

Events and objects. The relation between concepts and facts is important, but it needs the addition of one more element: What are the concepts or facts *about*? I choose the terms "events and objects" to stand for particulars of experience and nature that we would inquire into and try to come to understand. Our language is full of verbs calling attention to events and nouns naming objects.

Take events. Suppose someone asks, "What is the boiling point of water?" If we are careful, we can give a three-part answer by saying that "boiling point" is a concept, the event and a fact. We could boil some water and make an event of boiling happen. We could name what counts as an instance of boiling, and what does not. We could show the regularities in liquid events which we think of as "boiling" and that is the concept of boiling. The fact of boiling is arrived at by the ways we make records of the event. Perhaps we use a thermometer (an object), take a reading or sets of readings, and record them on a chart or other record-making device. Facts are records of events. More precisely, facts require three things in relation: the event, the record, and the judgment that this record is indeed the record of the event it purports to be. We can now answer the question about boiling point. We have constructed a piece of knowledge by bringing into relation an event, its record, and its conceptualization.

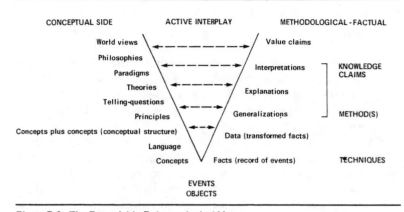

Figure 7.1   The Extendable Epistemological Vee
SOURCE: Gowin (1977, p. 8). Reproduced by permission of the author.

The Vee: A heuristic for knowledge structures. I have found it useful to draw a vee (see Figure 7.1) to show the relations found in knowledge structures. The vee helps us to locate the place of philosophic studies as distinguished from other studies primarily concerned with establishing facts. The vee may also help in the problem of the adaptation to evaluation of the various contributions of other disciplines.

Conceptual structures. As we move up the conceptual side of the vee we begin to note conceptual structures. These conceptual structures take many forms and become complex patterns of relations of concepts. We have many names for different kinds of conceptual structures: theories, models, metaphors, principles, telling questions, schemata, paradigms, philosophies, world views. The work of philosophy is mainly conceptual, using conceptual methods.

Factual structures. As we move up the factual side of the vee we note familiar epistemological elements. We transform facts into data. We make this transformation by various devices which help us find patterns of relation in the records of events. We measure, judge, chart, graph, and analyze statistically, grouping and regrouping data. Then, we generate knowledge claims, typically generalizations that show correlation and causation. Next, we go beyond descriptive generalizations to explanations. Finally, at the top of the vee, we find value claims, typically estimations of the significance of the knowledge claims we have constructed.

When most people in research and evaluation use the term "methodologies," they refer to the factual side of the vee. A method, in general, is a procedural commitment (a case study method or an experimental method), a way to study events and objects by getting facts, ordering them, and making a general claim of knowledge or value. Philosophy has its methods, but they are conceptual methods. These methods are ways we have of transforming concepts into conceptual structures, generalized ways we have of thinking about events and objects.

At this point I will resist the temptation to invent more telling metaphors. The search for such metaphors is also the task of others in this book. Guba's metaphor, "Evaluation is reform journalism," is an example. It is tempting to analyze it immediately. Before we can analyze it, however, we need to pay attention to the concept of metaphor itself. Metaphor is a feature of language well worth our attention because of its powerful function in language. After we have given an analysis of metaphor, then we can use that analysis to elucidate other metaphors that might be invented to show relations between evaluation and other fields.

In the next section of this chapter I lay out in some detail the concept of metaphor, discuss the methods philosophers use in analyzing the structure and function of concepts, and describe techniques of philosophical analysis. Because this approach to philosophy begins with clear cases, I will present such a case of a philosopher working. The case is Black's analysis of metaphor.

The Concept of Metaphor

The sorts of judgments evaluators make must be clear and intelligible to clients. They must be statements that will be easily grasped by the members of the speech community to whom they are addressed. For some writers of evaluation reports, this means statements must be literal. To construct a metaphor is to make an assertion that is not literally true. The ancient formula for a metaphor is to say something and mean something else. Is there some sort of odd perversity in asserting a thing to be what it is not?

What is Metaphor?

What is metaphor? What is *a* metaphor? Faced with a choice between these two questions, modern philosophizing begins with the second. The first question could be taken to mean an invitation to inquire into the *nature* of metaphor, a search for its essence. This search for essences is largely eschewed by modern philosophy but not by traditional (classical) philosophy. For classical philosophy questions about the nature of an object or event were appropriate, but today philosophers leave to science the task of finding out the facts about things. Modern philosophy is more concerned with *questions of meaning* than with questions of fact.

Of the three major domains of philosophy — metaphysics, axiology and epistemology — the discussion of metaphor belongs most appropriately in that of epistemology. Within that domain, it belongs with discussion of philosophy of language, a dominant part of modern philosophy. In that tradition are Max Black's two seminal papers on metaphor which will be used to explain the interaction view of metaphor. That explanation is a case in point of what philosophers do. Techniques that might be exploited in the field of evaluation are discussed along the way. The attempt is to explain philosophy, to exhibit philosophy at work, and to provide evaluators who are not philosophers with a guided tour through one of the tunnels of philosophic enlightenment.

Black's View of Metaphor

In two papers, separated by fifteen years (1962a, 1977), philosopher Black has given us a philosophical analysis of the notion of metaphor. Black calls this view the "interaction view," a development and modification of I. A. Richard's work (1936), contrasted with the "comparison" and "substitution" views of metaphor. The substitution view (briefly) avers the metaphor to be a substitute for some set of literal sentences. The comparison view (which is what most teachers of English use in saying a metaphor is "an implied comparison") makes a metaphor a condensed simile, seeing in it some similarity or analogy. Black argues against the reduction of metaphor to anything else, whether a literal paraphrase, analogy, or a similarity statement. (For example, notice that something is lost in reducing "The ship plows the sea." to "The ship is like a plow in the sea.") For Black, metaphors are not expendable or optional or decorative or ornamental. Instead, metaphors are *emphatic* in the focus of the salient words or expressions because they require in the hearer or reader an active working out of the implications that lie behind the literal meaning. And metaphors that yield a high degree of elaboration of the many implications are *resonant* (Black's implicative complex). Both emphasis and resonance are matters of degree, and they are not independent of each other; a metaphor markedly emphatic and resonant Black calls a *strong* metaphor. The strong, active metaphors are the ones he is most interested in analyzing is these two papers.

The literal and the metaphorical. When a poet writes "A poem is a walk," he does not mean it literally. Why does he not say what he means? The metaphor user may reply that he did say what he meant and what he meant was not a literal claim. Metaphors are a claim to a clear meaning, and the claim is not simply an odd way of making a literal claim. Indeed, if we analyze a collection of so-called literal statements, we may find in them many hidden metaphors. The literal is not the standard for what is unproblematic in discourse. As Black notes, to reduce metaphor to literal assertion leads us into "the blind alley taken by those innumerable followers of Aristotle who have supposed metaphors to be replaceable by literal translation" (1977, p. 435). So, I suggest in advance of further analysis that metaphors are meaningful assertions; they cannot simply be reduced to literal assertions. Evaluators do use metaphors in report-writing. The study of metaphors may, in fact, improve the intelligibility of evaluation reports as evaluators learn to use, and not ignore, constructive metaphors.

Clear cases of metaphor. An example has already been given in "A poem is a walk." Wallace Stevens wrote "A poem is a pheasant." and "Society is a sea" (Stevens, 1957, p. 21). Most people are familiar with "Man is a thinking reed," and "Man is a wolf," and "The Lord is my Shepherd." These are classic cases. Can we make up examples of our own?

The metaphorical statements seem to draw attention to a pair of things. Suppose we pair any two nouns at random and see what we get. Around my office now are chairs, paintings, typewriters, a telephone, a candy jar, a wastebasket, syllogisms, briefcases. If I assert "A chair is a painting," then I suspect you would not think it much of a metaphor. If I say "A chair is a syllogism," you might, as Black does, claim that to be a *failed* metaphor. It seems nonsense to me. If I say "A telephone is a candy jar," I might be understood by those who observe the incessant adolescent use of the telephone. To say "A telephone is NOT a candy jar" might get approval from harried adults. If I say "A briefcase is a temporary wastebasket," you recognize we carry home materials at night that go in the trash the next day. From these examples of metaphor one can see a *range* from nonsense to failed to slightly evocative to interesting to those classics that invite a sustained reflection on the multiple meanings stimulated by the metaphor. There should be no important difficulty in recognizing the prevalence and versatility of metaphors in our language. [Part of the clear case technique of philosophers is to invite the reader or hearer to perform certain acts, the upshot of which should be an example of the sort of thing we are studying.]

Black makes five points about metaphorical statements. (1) The statement has two distinct subjects, the primary and secondary. (2) The secondary subject is to be regarded as a system rather than an individual thing (both parts may be a system). (3) The metaphorical statement works by projection upon the primary subject a set of associated implications (comprised in the implicative complex) predicable of the secondary subject. As I understand the example, in the metaphor "Society is a sea," the primary subject is "Society"; when we think of the "sea" we generate a number of associations and implications that we in turn project back on "Society." One might think they are drowning in an oppressive society. Further, there are changes in the meaning of the secondary subject. For example, one might think the sea is a class structure, the strong dominating the weak. This back-and-forth shift of meaning is an interaction. (I. A. Richards [1936] refers to an "interanimation of words.") (4) The primary subject is illuminated by statements from the secondary subject which are *isomorphic* with it. (The two systems have, as mathematicians say, the same "structure.") Thus, the detailed analysis of a metaphor would consist of a set of statements about the primary subject, each of which would be paralleled by a similar set of statements about the secondary subject. Black writes: "Every 'implicative complex' supported by a metaphor's secondary subject . . . is a *model* of the ascriptions imputed to the primary subject: every metaphor is the tip of a submerged model" (1977, p. 445). (5) In the context of a particular metaphorical statement, the two subjects interact in the mind of the reader so that (a) the primary subject incites the reader to select properties of the secondary subject, which (b) invites the reader to construct the implicative complex to fit the secondary subject. Black uses the terms "focus," "frame," and "metaphor-theme" in addition to "emphasis" and "resonance." Perhaps a metaphor about metaphor may be illuminating.

A metaphor is a ping-pong game. The ball is the focus, the players are the primary and secondary subjects, and the table and court area may be taken as the frame. The ball is driven from court to court by the players; each action receives the prior action and induces a subsequent action. There is an active interplay between the parts of the metaphor. A strong, active metaphor with emphasis and resonance is a rally with many volleys, the extent being a function of the many talents of the players. As additional players work the game, perhaps change the rules (doubles instead of merely singles, for example), the metaphor accrues a metaphor theme. (If we think of education metaphorically as growth, then the "growth" theme is easily one of the most popular in thinking about education.)

[*Reflective comment on Black's analysis of metaphor. This section is in brackets.*]

[Black's analysis of how a metaphor works gives us a way to analyze any given metaphor. Such an analysis would presuppose that we have a context, can recognize a clear case, and understand the questions we think relevant. Each of these three presuppositions can be satisfied in different ways. A choice of how to proceed at this juncture is a choice in philosophic method. Since I am in sympathy with Black's approach, I will discuss each of these choices as a "move" a philosopher makes in doing the work of philosophizing.

First, we must assume a context for language use which includes a speech community, competent speakers-hearers, or writers-readers, the act or acts of communicating, familiarity with the language in use, and a number of other facts about language. The point initially is to call attention to the need for *stipulating a context*. We need not become explicit at this turn, for such an ordinary and common event as "language-use" is not problematic. If, however, stipulating the context did become problematic, then we would have to move again to call attention to our basic assumptions about communicating. (The terms "common," "communicating," and the terms "communal," "community," signify shared meaning and suggest shared experience as the basis for shared meaning.)

The second move many contemporary philosophers make is to present *a clear case* as an instance of what is to be discussed. We may want several examples of what we are talking about to ensure communication. Sometimes this move to find a clear case is called the "paradigm case argument." The clear case is a paradigm case, as "Boiling an egg for three minutes" might be taken as a paradigm case of "cooking."

In starting with clear cases, philosophers often appear to be trying to answer the questions "What is the nature of X?" "What is X?" "Is X real?" We can easily recognize that such questions might be, or might become, metaphysical questions. Other philosophers, not wishing to plumb fundamental realities at this stage of an argument, could rephrase the questions by asking: "What is the analysis of the notion of metaphor?" "What is the 'logical grammar' of 'metaphor'?" "How do we become clearer about the use of the word 'metaphor'?"

The overlap between these two sets of questions might seem to be a preference for metaphysics rather than semantics. A philosopher might say, "I'm doing semantics, not metaphysics now." and be perfectly well understood by other philosophers. Nevertheless, there is a major point to be made about the difference in the two types of questions. To ask "What is the nature of X?" is to ask a question that historically belongs to traditional philosophy. It is often thought to institute the search for the *essence* of an object, and the name given such effort is "essentialism." To find the essence of metaphor would be to be able to state the necessary and sufficient conditions for the correct application of the term to the object. (To understand the logic of necessary and sufficient conditions is basic to the study of philosophy. Most logic texts will explicate the meaning of this powerful tool in philosophic thinking.)

Now, most modern philosophers find the search for an essence to be misleading. For one thing, it is the province of science to make knowledge claims about objects. For another, it seems futile, especially in creative domains such as language or art or education, because "things" keep changing. For another, not everything is profoundly blessed with a "nature" such that its characteristics, if known, would inform and improve the human community to any great extent. There is, then, more than a mere preference for the second set of key philosophic questions. In general, the modern philosophers ask: "What is the meaning of X?" "What is the function of X?" "What is the role of X?" "How does X work?" These semantic and pragmatic questions may supply us with just the sort of answers we actually need in any given context. One avoids the speciously profound in favor of the luminously practical.]

Contrary cases and counterexamples. Any universal claim can be refuted logically simply by comparing it to a clear counterexample. To refute the statement "All crows are black," one need only show the existence of one legitimate white crow. This move with respect to truth-making and falsification has been generalized as a technique useful in etching the boundaries of concepts. It is a move to help clarify the meaning of concepts. Let us take an example of the contrary case *move* from Black's paper.

Monroe Beardsley is a philosopher who has contributed much to contemporary philosophy and to the discussion of metaphor specifically. In his 1962 article he searches for a criterion by which to identify a metaphor. He notes the peculiar feature of metaphors which appear to be saying one thing while meaning another. Thus, they may be literally false (controversion thesis: Beardsley's mark of a metaphor is that taken literally it would have to count as a logical contradiction or an absurdity, in either case something patently false.) Perhaps this oddity is the mark of a metaphor. Is it the *necessary* condition for the correct application of the term to the object?

Black finds a counterexample in hyperbole ("I've told you a thousand times!") as a piece of language that expresses absurdity and falsehood. The simple device of negation within a metaphor itself takes care of the notion of logical contradiction. ("Man is NOT a wolf" is just as metaphorical as "Man is a wolf.") From these contrary cases and additional arguments Black constructs a generalization he thinks applies to all metaphors. This generalization is an important one, for Black claims we cannot find any single criterion that will satisfy the necessary condition for an expression to count as a metaphor. (The search for essence is defeated again.) "Every criterion for a metaphor's presence, however plausible, is defeasible in special circumstances" (Black, 1977, p. 450).

Part of Black's reasoning turns on the problem of ambiguity. Much of language is ambiguous, because it has more than one legitimate meaning. Indeed, some modern philosophers claim that all language is always both illuminating and misleading. Every statement says both more and less than is intended by the speaker and is interpreted by the hearer. Where statements are problematic with respect to their meaning, we must engage in semantic analysis to pluck out the meanings intended and to be sure our audience agrees with us. Black claims that "there is no infallible test for resolving ambiguity, so there is none to be expected in discriminating the metaphorical from the literal" (1977, p. 450). Hence, Black contends that it is an important mistake in (philosophic) method to seek an infallible mark of the presence of metaphors. The search for a necessary condition is abandoned.

How do we recognize metaphors? First, we must know what it is for a statement to be metaphorical. This knowledge comes from the examination of cases so clear to members of the speech community there is no disagreement. Second, we must use judgment to decide if a metaphorical reading of a given statement is here preferable to a literal one. There may be a number of different reasons to support our judgment, including reasons such as the patent falsity of the literal claim, its lack of point if taken literally, its banality. A metaphor is a rule violation, and there are no rules for "creatively" violating a rule. Metaphors invite different, even partially conflicting, readings; ambiguity, even indeterminacy, accompany them.

Major values of metaphor. Some metaphors, Black contends, can be considered "cognitive instruments." These metaphors can sometimes *"generate new knowledge* and insight by changing relationships between the things designated (the principal and subsidiary subjects)" (1977, p. 451). The point here is that we could view some metaphors as *creating* a similarity (rather than merely formulating some similarity which already exists). An example Black gives is the slow-motion appearance of a galloping horse which is created by the man-made intervention of cinematography. What is seen in the slow motion film becomes a new part of the world once it is seen. Black contends that a metaphor, "Nixon is an image surrounding a vacuum," was the verbal formulation necessary to his seeing Nixon that way. The constructive metaphor enables us to see aspects of reality. It is an instrument in our epistemology. The reality or world we do see, however, is always necessarily a world under a certain description; that is, a world seen from a certain perspective. Metaphors can create such perspectives.

Do metaphorical statements ever reveal "how things are?" Yes, according to Black, if we disengage the verification or confirmation test of statements from other useful statements. For Black it is a misguided strategy of philosophic analysis to try to answer the question "Can metaphorical statements be 'true'?" We become almost obsessed with the question of "truth" when discussing statements; we fail, therefore, to see other uses of language. Metaphors can represent the way things are, much as charts, maps and photographs are representational. The test of these cognitive devices is a test of significance rather than truth-falsity. When a strong metaphor is analyzed, we can determine whether the isomorphic structures are appropriate, partial, superficial, faithful, and so forth. Those metaphors that survive the analysis provide genuine insight into the systems to which they refer. Thus, they can tell us "how things are" in reality.

The two judgments Black makes about the worth of metaphors point to epistemology (cognitive instruments) and metaphysics (how things are). In making these moves Black is not merely engaging in semantic analysis. It is one of the techniques of philosophy as Black practices it to connect the methods and results of philosophy to wider human concerns. Unfortunately, in my view, many technically trained philosophers only take in each other's wash; they do not work on problems of general human concern, and it is difficult for the outsider to see why they should be doing what they are doing at all. I fear that a little knowledge about philosophy may be a dangerous thing for evaluators to acquire because they may not be able to stick with philosophical analysis long enough to see its value; and they may also get side-tracked from their wider human concerns.

Additional Techniques of Metaphor Analysis

I now wish to leave Black's paper to make a few other comments about metaphor.

Some metaphors are so embedded in ordinary language that we often fail to notice them. Instead of encouraging active thinking, they actually obscure the need for thought. Metaphors that are too familiar to us encourage us to think of the two things compared as the *same* thing. We stop thinking. For example, we often think of thinking itself as a form of vision: we "see" the point, or we "see" the light, or we "see" clearly. A thinker is called a person of vision. But thinking is not merely viewing. If we are stuck with the metaphor, then we are disinclined to ask other leading questions about thinking.

The technique of multiple metaphors. How do we break the hold of thought-controlling metaphors? One technique I use with some success in my classes is "The Technique of Multiple Metaphors." When a student gets stuck on a metaphor ("Education is growth"), I suggest we try to invent a number of other metaphors. One class developed these examples.

Education is: a ladder
a factory
a processing facility
sheepherding
pouring in the cream
mining
shaping and molding clay
cultivating
drawing out what is inside
a system
a mistake
a care package
a human emergency

Each of these examples can be analyzed according to Black's five points. The shock that comes from recognizing (actually *re*cognizing) alternative formulations breaks the numbing hold of conventional language. Stretching language until it seems to "break" is a recommended technique of modern language philosophers. It relieves mental cramps.

Constructive metaphors. We already know that metaphors have a way of leading us from the familiar to the unfamiliar. In developing perspective, metaphors seem to explain things; that is, to express important ideas the truth of which we assume already has been established. We explain to others that the flow of electricity is the flow of water in a garden hose. The "current" has a pressure (voltage), a volume (amperage), and so forth. The truth about electrical currents is not being tested by the metaphorical elaboration; rather, electric phenomena are being explained by reference to what is already familiar to students. A strong, emphatic metaphor delights a teacher.

Constructive metaphors can be instruments of invention. We formulate relations with their help. These formulated relations we next wish to test, or confirm, to make the connection between the imagined relations and actual relations. Suppose I invent the metaphor "A bureaucracy is a social habit." Immediately I can think of some propositions to test. For example, if habits are unthinking responses, then what quality of thinking do I find in bureaucracies? Do workers in a bureaucracy become demented? Is repetition of actions the desired conditions for such workers?

Metaphor and imagination. Metaphor requires imagination in both maker and receiver. Saying one thing and meaning another, thinking of A as B, tracing out the implications, expressing what is difficult to express literally — all of these acts require imagination. Normal science and routine evaluation require us to collect facts, sort information, assemble claims carefully (even assiduously), and express them clearly with little apparent need of imaginative statements. Indeed, we are surprised if an author tucks in a metaphor here or there.

Useful imagination (the two words clash, like "speculative instruments") requires us to set assiduity aside. In a strong metaphor we should find ourselves responding immediately, as we do to a novel event. The metaphor must move us with its sudden salience. It must jiggle our customary patterns of expectation. It should evoke wonder, a glance both introspective and prospective. A reverberating metaphor brings about an altered state of conscious rationality. The metaphor is the hunting horn of inquiry.

Metaphor: Combining thinking and feeling. Some metaphors have a more powerful and immediate appeal to us than do others. Thought by itself moves nothing, claims Artistotle. Since metaphors are important ways of thinking, those metaphors which move us are those which get at thinking and at our depth of feeling. The language of feeling and the language of thought are combined in a well-struck metaphor ("Society is a sea"). In modern philosophy the distinction between informative language (cognitive) and expressive language (noncognitive) has been well worked. The issues are relevant to evaluating because buried there are all the conflicts over whether value judgments are grounded in facts and reasons or whether they are merely expressions of approval ("I like X.") and direction ("And you should like it too."). Insofar as value *judgments* are *judgments,* they are grounded in facts and reasons. Value claims parallel the status of knowledge claims. Insofar as they are claims of value, however, they parallel expressions of liking, approving, prizing, which carry feeling with them. If we want value judgments to move others to decision, to action, to conviction, to commitment, then we would do well to select language which combines the rational and the emotive. (A well-wrought slogan works this way.)

A combination of the rational and the emotive occurs in some metaphors. "By its novelty, a poetic image *sets in motion* the entire linguistic mechanism" (Gaston Bachelard, *The Poetics of Space,* 1964, p. 19). Philosopher Bachelard gives the following analysis. Readers of poetry feel the grip of a line of poetry that resonates and reverberates within. We feel a poetic power rising naively within us. The image touches depths before it stirs the surface. We are moved before we think. We begin to have the notion that we have created it, that we should have created it, because it expresses us so well. As the expression holds us, so it becomes a part of our being, and we begin to express it. The poetic image comes from language (and is, logos, cognitive) and moves to person. (This is why, perhaps, some people are so loath to have poems analyzed; it is soul surgery.)

Imagined cases. Researchers and evaluators are familiar with establishing matters of fact. Such claims are called empirical claims by philosophers in contrast with a priori claims. These a priori claims ("Every effect has a cause.") are thought to be true, not simply in this world but in all imaginable worlds. The truths a posteriori are contingent. It is possible that they would not be true. We can make the contingent claim that "The sun rises" just as easily as "The sun does not rise." The matters of fact will settle it. But a priori claims require the test of invention and imagination. Is it possible to imagine a world in which effects are not linked to causes? Whatever you answer to that question will be part of what is required for a complete analysis of the concept of causality.

Unless we are trying to reduce all conceptual arguments to matters of fact, the distinction between the conceptual and the factual would seem unproblematic. Perhaps a major contribution analytic philosophy could make to evaluation is to show the value of conceptual techniques, methods, and distinctions in contrast with the methodologies required to produce and test empirical matters.

Conceptual Analysis

The Techniques

The foregoing discussion of the concept of metaphor exhibits some of the techniques of concept analysis. Black's work was presented as a clear case of philosophy (as product) and philosophizing (as an analysis taking place). It is an example of modern linguistic analysis combining good features of the English philosophical tradition and the American pragmatic tradition. (Bachelard's phenomenological analysis is a brief example of continental European tradition.)

Philosophy, in the eyes of many philosophers, is more of an activity than it is a textbook subject to study. Since we want to assess philosophy as a potential source of methods for evaluators, we are concerned with explicit techniques of philosophic work. I am tempted to say that the best test of philosophy would be the use of its distinctions in the context of evaluating. This test waits for another study in which the two activities of evaluating and philosophizing are combined. I can, however, list and discuss several techniques of analysis and suggest how they might become part of some evaluation study.

The purpose of concept analysis. The analysis of concepts is a philosophic technique readily transferable to nonphilosophic fields. As a technique, it can be taught to nonspecialists (John Wilson's book *Thinking with Concepts* (1963) was written for and used in secondary schools in England). Learning the techniques is like learning any technical skill (translating Spanish, solving quadratic equations). The chief purpose is to clarify abstract general concepts, to determine what meaning or different meanings such concepts have, and to see how such concepts work when we are seriously and deliberately thinking (for example, about evaluating). The techniques I describe are not the same thing as logic, which deals in the forms of arguments. Rather, the techniques are an informal logic, dealing with questions of meaning and the role and function of concepts. The techniques can also be contrasted with other techniques used in research to establish matters of fact. While the techniques of concept analysis require us to work with concrete cases (and thus appear to have a factual quality about them), they are not ways to make records of events (which is part of my working definition of fact). The techniques can also be contrasted to other techniques used in dealing with questions of value (see Gowin & Millman, 1978). To the extent that evaluation is the assessment of value, the whole of evaluation is often seen as the use of facts in judgments of value. Concept analysis can be added to evaluation studies and should make space for itself in relation to questions of fact and value.

Suppose a project comes about requiring the evaluation of science teaching in secondary schools. The project is stimulated by the recent scattered evidence that science teaching has deteriorated in the past several years. The general question "Is science teaching worse in 1978 compared to what it was in 1968?" needs analysis. It can be asked as a series of other questions: (a) What are the facts about science teaching? (b) What criteria do we need to judge whether it is better or worse (a *value* question)? (c) What concept of teaching, of science, and of science teaching are we using?

It is the third kind of question for which the techniques of concept analysis are appropriate. Sorting out the types of questions is itself a piece of philosophic analysis. Distinguishing conceptual questions from other kinds is recommended as a good first move in an evaluation. There is no point in gathering facts and shaping data until you are sure what sort of event counts as science teaching and what does not. Isolating and identifying the conceptual questions first also helps because we set the context and the conditions which would make some answers relevant and others irrelevant and because we begin to make explicit our criteria or reasons for judging instances.

Where do we begin the concept analysis? We begin in midstream. We begin in the middle of things rather than with what subsequent analysis will show to be logical starting points. We begin by looking for clear cases, exemplary cases, model cases of "science teaching." We observe; make records; describe activities. But this starting point is in the middle because we *already* have some concept of "science teaching" even if it is a rough idea. We already have some notion of how teaching science is different from teaching poetry or training video technicians or milking cows. It is as if we are in a dialogue with ourselves: "Do I mean this by science teaching (explaining the second law of thermodynamics) or that (dissecting a porpoise to show that it stores oxygen in muscle tissue)?" The objective of concept analysis at this early stage is to clarify what, in some sense, we already know. It is, in part, to try to answer a question like "What does 'science teaching' *mean*?"

Our aim. Concept analysis, however, is different from simply giving definitions of the meaning of terms. We would not complete an analysis by looking in dictionaries for meanings of words. Instead, we are seeking a reason or *explanation for why we use* the terms in particular ways when we talk about science teaching. Why do we think about it first one way (explanation) and then another (description)? How does the concept give structure to our thought? How does the concept work in our thinking and acting? Some philosophers claim that the analysis of a concept is the description of its use. Complete descriptions specify the context or contexts of usage, different meanings in different contexts, different thoughts which are possible with different uses, and exhibits of different applications of the concept.

Concepts have different uses and permit different inferences. There is no single answer to the question "What is *the* concept of science teaching?" or similar questions. Most of the concepts we use in such practical activities as educating, teaching, and evaluating are open, not closed, concepts.

How do we conceive of objects and events? How do we think about activities, such as teaching or evaluating or playing a game? To have a concept of, for example, teaching is to be able to talk about the regular features of the activities of teaching. It is to know what counts as an instance of the activity and what does not count. It is to be able to cite clear cases, contrary cases, borderline cases; and in a full analysis of a concept like teaching, it is to be able to invent new cases, even contrary-to-fact cases. From these cases we extract commonalities, regularities. When we give these regularities a name (a term, word, sign, symbol), we have conceptualized the events. When we are additionally aware of the reason we sort out the cases in the way we do, then we can speak of the rule which governs the cases or the principle which regulates the activities. Concepts, rules, reasons, and principles, represent an increasing order of conceptual complexity.

What is a concept? This question has many answers. I have worked out a definition of concept as "a sign-symbol pointing to regularities in events or records of events." This definition has limitations, as do other definitions. Some define concept as a rule — a rule of human behavior in the use of language (Green, 1971, p. 15). Others think of concepts as a category, a class, or a statement of what is common among instances. Like many other key elements in modern philosophy, the definition of concept is itself a philosophic problem with different solutions. Doing a conceptual analysis of the concept of concept is very difficult, but some have attempted it (see Weitz, 1977).

One philosopher, in some exasperation, said: "A concept is a cluster concept." This remark was intended to convey the point that a concept like "teaching" has a variety of related meanings. Teaching is closely related to training, to giving instruction, to explaining, to indoctrinating, and so forth. One way to analyze a concept is to examine the ways it is closely related to other concepts.

The A-without-B procedure. Conceptual complexity can arise when we simply want to distinguish between two related concepts. How do we proceed? Green (1971) recommends and uses the procedure of asking "Can we have A without B?" "Is it possible to have B without A?" We assume we have before us sufficient examples of the language illustrating the uses of the specific concepts. Can we have evaluation without judging? Probably not. Can we have judging without evaluation? Probably so. The procedure would call for presenting clear cases of judging requiring no evaluation. This technique is a simple line of questioning and using examples which results in a reason or set of reasons (arguments) for etching the boundaries of the two related concepts. We come to understand the characteristics of some concepts by establishing the nature of their relations to others.

Review of Techniques of Concept Analysis: The Steps

(1) Purpose. The aims of concept analysis are to clarify abstract general concepts, to assess the meanings of such concepts, to see how such concepts work (their function in our language and thought).

(2) Context. All the steps presuppose the context is clear (mutually accepted) in which the distinctions of logic and language appear.

(3) Starting points. We begin in midstream. We collect examples of language which describe the event or object; we make lists of activities; in so doing we must already have a rough idea of the concept we want to analyze.

(4) Focus on language. The logical aspects of concepts can be analyzed linguistically — that is, we use language as the way into conceptual structures. Language is the stalking horse of conceptual analysis.

(5) Questions. Distinguish conceptual questions from questions of fact and value. Sorting out questions is a purpose and result of concept analysis.

(6) Cases. Make a list of cases: model, contrary, borderline, imagined. While we start with clear cases which are particular instances, we do not remain there. The effect of concept analysis is to begin with the particular but to serve the interest of the general. Making distinctions multiplies questions rather than answering simple questions. Concept analysis increases the precision of questions while decreasing the certainty of answers, chiefly due to the ambiguity of ordinary language.

Adaptation to Evaluation

The simplest way to adapt these procedures to evaluation would be to try them out. Like any new technique, it will take practice to learn how to use them. Experienced evaluators already know how to assemble facts and to make value judgments, both of which require concepts of methods and techniques of work. Having the sense to recognize conceptual problems as different from problems of fact or value is a result of practicing conceptual analysis. Evaluators could begin to look for conceptual problems in their practice. Insofar as the practice does have conceptual components, these techniques can become useful.

How do evaluators find conceptual problems? Suppose one undertakes to evaluate student loan programs in higher education. We find such programs employ the idea of a "needy person." Can we clarify this concept? It is a concept because the terms signify regularities in certain events. We already know, roughly, what "needy person" means. We do not know how the evaluation staff, the funders, the students, and interested others use the term. So we collect examples of language using the words "needy person." Following our techniques we could ask the evaluation staff to construct a sentence identifying four kinds of cases: clear, counter, borderline, and imagined. Thus, we might come up with the following:

(1) Clear case: "A needy person has a financial need." (ability to pay)

(2) Counter case: "A needy person has emotional needs." (ability to feel)

(3) Borderline: "A needy person has a 'favored' ethnic background." (ability to contribute to society)

(4) Imagined case: "Needs of persons are randomly distributed." (unrelated to ability)

From these uses of the concept, we look for the reason we think one case counts and others do not. Why we do not accept emotional needs as a basis for granting student loans? If, for example, we say our concept of a needy person is related only to intellectual ability, then, if we accept this notion, we have a rule of the evaluation practice that helps us to sort our cases. If we do not accept this notion, then we must expand the concept of need admitting other cases. We repeat this process until the concept is clarified. Sorting cases helps us to assess the worth of the loan program and to see if it is aiding the people who need it.

With any concept important to your practice, the search for clear and counter examples helps determine what counts and what does not count as a case. This move alone is immensely clarifying. If you can continue and can find the key *reason* the cases are different, then you can likely construct *rules* of practice that sort out cases. And, beyond rules, you can look for explanations of what governs the practice. These consequences should make evaluation work more intellectually satisfying.

If you wish to continue in concept analysis, you might ask, and try to answer, the four key questions modern philosophers ask of abstract general concepts.

What is the meaning of X?   (e.g., "needs")

What is the function of X?   "

What is the role of X?   "

How does the concept of X work?   "

Making work more intellectually satisfying is one of the positive values of the potential contributions of philosophy to evaluation. If you accept my view that philosophy, in a large sense, is a moral enterprise, then you may be able to identify more clearly the moral qualities of educational evaluation — and that, I think, would be a gain.

Another application of adaptation for evaluation from this chapter is the suggestion that we apply the techniques of concept analysis to the key concepts of evaluation. Such concepts as "value," "valuing," and "value judgment" are especially in need of explicit attention. If you modify the multiple-metaphor technique a bit, you might develop an exercise for the staff of any evaluation group. Ask these people to develop a list of the four cases, beginning with (1) "This evaluation is about _____" citing the event/object being evaluated, and (2) "A case of evaluation is _____" and then citing a clear case, a contrary case, a borderline case, and imagined case of evaluation. This exercise should begin to clarify how individuals are using the concept of "evaluation." The listing of claims about the events/objects to be evaluated would help to clarify the multiple perspectives of the participants. The second list of cases of evaluation (what evaluation is and is not) should uncover the variety of biases, perceptions, and points of view of what evaluators think about their work.

Concepts are what we think with. This psychological claim may not be true, but I believe it is without being able to prove it true. We think with concepts (at least), though we may also think with other things: images, qualities, sentiments of rationality. Supposing that we think with concepts, however, helps make a direct connection between concept analysis and the work of evaluation. It bears on clear thinking. The main reason for concept analysis is clarity of thought. And the techniques of concept analysis help to reveal the structure of thought (conceptual linkages) and the function of thought (activities we engage in directly).

From this chapter you should understand how a metaphor works. You can obtain that understanding by (a) composing your own metaphors and (b) by analyzing important metaphors in your field. Black's five points about metaphors should be clear. Deliberately searching for apt metaphors to include in evaluation reports could improve communication with the audience.

The Vee

This heuristic is a simplifying way to think about complex issues of knowledge and value, method and product, concepts and facts, the events and objects of our interest, levels of meaning, the different focuses of philosophy and science, and the virtue of any work to come down to a *point*! Practically, the vee can be used as a device for the analysis of the structure of claims in any evaluation study. You can learn to "lay the vee" on documents. While it spreads apart the theoretical-conceptual domain from the methodological-factual domain, it also shows that they interact and are not totally independent of each other. As a device of criticism, the vee reveals in any particular evaluation study where the weighting is heaviest — whether on facts and method, on value claims, or on concepts and theories. Most studies are overweighted and unbalanced on the right side of the vee. (An example is worked out in Gowin, 1979.)

Finally, I want to make a few specific suggestions for evaluators becoming acquainted with both philosophy and philosophers. In addition to undertaking philosophical training (for example, at the level of a doctoral minor), we could invite philosophers to become members of evaluation teams. We could commission them to produce concept analyses on contemporary issues. It would be interesting, for example, to have a philosopher do a conceptual analysis of the concept of science teaching found in Stake and Easely's *Case Studies in Science Education* project (1978); the National Science Foundation could fund it. Most philosophers would be happy to receive commissions (!), but, more important for them, the expansion of philosophical concerns into evaluation areas would open up new problems and should be intrinsically stimulating. Additionally, philosophers can help evaluators in constructing value claims. The use of normative concepts in ethics and social philosophy is "bread and butter" work for philosophers. Also, evaluators might seriously consider taking enough work in philosophy so they can at least read with understanding the products of contemporary philosophy. These are simple suggestions; once the bridge between the two areas is built, I feel sure the traffic will be there.

Caveats

Concept analysis will increase the precision of questions while decreasing the certainty of answers. Is this a good thing for evaluation? Should we not simply realize the protective coloration that vagueness and ambiguity in our main ideas provide us? Maybe we need the ecology of concepts rather than the logic or geography of concepts. Maybe we need shadows of nuance and difference to soften hard ideas. One more technique (like multivariate analysis) that is unexplainable and unacceptable to a public is unneeded. (Anyone who thinks he can get a single precise answer to an ambiguous question is not thinking clearly: ask him if he has stopped beating his wife yet.) Yes, there is a question here. I believe that there is a penalty: Illumination casts a shadow. Any time we become clear, illuminating, and clarifying, we can cast a shadow. Still, I cannot help but think that intelligence in the modern world becomes valued as we experience its benefits in practical activities. Until we can educate them, we can expect resentment of consumers, clients, funders, and even other evaluators about evaluation outcomes which are complex, contextual, and apparently less certain than hoped for. The evaluative intelligence is wonderful when it appears, because it pushes us toward wisdom by using knowledge and by thinking that our humanness, rough though it is, is always a value.

My experience with evaluators and other professional practitioners in education makes me aware that many people fear philosophy. Some people give it exaggerated respect, and in the main they fail to use it. Some people think they know philosophy already; they have made up their minds about the important things in life, and they see little relation of philosophical studies to improvement in day-to-day practical matters. They fail to study philosophy. Other people have no knowledge of philosophy; they are ignorant. They can be taught, but first they will have to realize that they do not know what they do not know. To say of a person "He's ignorant" is not to demean him; it is to congratulate him for his capacity to know something new. These caveats apply mostly to questions of temperament and training. Both can be shaped by proper instruction, which is the most direct way to adapt to evaluation the concepts and skills of conceptual analysis.

Without a clear concept of education, the products of educational evaluation studies will show enormous variation, which is the fact at the present time. Hundreds of research and evaluation papers have been published on such topics as teaching, "good teaching," teachers, and teacher preparation without any significant prior clarification of the concept of education or of teaching. This deplorable state of affairs will continue until we realize that we need to pay attention to philosophies, theories, and concepts of *education*. Facts without concepts *are* blind. Simple improvement in factual methodologies will not help. Improvement can come if we understand the crucial relations among facts, events, and concepts, and especially if we clearly work with educative events.

If we assume that evaluation has social utility, then a whole set of other philosophical questions become relevant. We should turn to social philosophy. We would turn from epistemology, with its concepts for meaning and knowledge, to axiology (the name for philosophical theories of value). Value theory would have a prima facie claim on evaluation as a consequence of a definition of evaluation as the assessment of value. Another time, another philosopher, and the goods of that storehouse should be raided. The problems (concepts, methods, analyses) of social philosophy are most difficult (in my judgment) and they may just be more important to the disciplined study of education. I agree with Green: "Linguistic analysis is not the most profound view to take on philosophy; it is simply the easiest; and therefore it represents a useful starting place" (1971, p. xi).

Note

¹A concept may be called "empty" when it does not refer to any regularities in nature or experience.

References and Annotated Bibliography

Bachelard, G. *The poetics of space.* Boston: Beacon, 1964.
  Phenomenological analysis of poetic-linguistic imagination reverberating with metaphors.
Beardsley, M. C. The metaphorical twist. *Philosophy and Phenomenological Research,* 1962, 22, 293-307.
  The controversion thesis well stated.
Beardsley, M. C. Metaphor. In P. Edwards (Ed.), *Encyclopedia of philosophy.* New York: Macmillan, 1967, pp. 284-89.
  Useful references, especially for metaphor in different parts of philosophy.
Black, M. Metaphor. In *Models and metaphors.* Ithaca, NY: Cornell University Press, 1962. (a)
Black, M. Models and archetypes. In *Models and metaphors.* Ithaca, NY: Cornell University Press, 1962. (b)
Black, M. More about metaphor. *Dialectica,* 1977, 31, 432-457.
  Source most relied on in the second section of this chapter.
Ennis, R. *Logic in teaching.* Englewood Cliffs, NJ: Prentice-Hall, Inc., 1969.
  Good discussions of the logic of definition, explanation, and justification in the company of clear cases and uses in teaching.
Gowin, D. B. *Educating.* Ithaca, NY: Cornell University Press, 1981.
Gowin, D. B. Quemac value. Paper presented at the American Educational Research Association annual meeting, April, 1979.
Gowin, D. B. & Millman, J. Meta-evaluation and a direction for research on evaluation. *CEDR Quarterly,* 1978, 11, 3-6.
Green, T. *The activities of teaching.* New York: McGraw-Hill, 1971.
  The best introduction to philosophic analysis in the substantive study of education. Each of nine chapters provides (a) an analysis and (b) an explication of the philosophic technique used in the analysis, including its data and limits. This is the most substantive and methodologically sound book and is recommended as the best starting point for those unfamiliar with philosophical analysis.

Pap, A. *Elements of analytic philosophy.* New York: Macmillan, 1949.
Written for American college undergraduates; a classic use of analytic techniques with concepts from science.

Richards, I. A. Metaphor. Lecture V of *The philosophy of rhetoric.* Oxford: Oxford University Press, 1936, pp. 89-138.
The interaction view of metaphor.

Scheffler, I. *The language of education.* Springfield, IL: Charles C. Thomas, 1960.
Israel Scheffler was an early leader with this book which contains readable chapters on definition, slogans, educational metaphors, and the "good reasons" concept of teaching.

Shibles, W. A. *Metaphor: An annotated bibliography and history.* Whitewater, WI: Language Press, 1971.
Four thousand titles on metaphor! A useful bibliography.

Smith, B. O., & Ennis, R. (Eds.). *Language and concepts in education.* Chicago: Rand McNally, 1961.

Soltis, J. *An introduction to the analysis of educational concepts* (2nd ed.). Reading, MA: Addison-Wesley, 1978.
Schematic, introductory primer; includes a chapter on the pedagogy of analytic skills development and a useful bibliography for analytic works in education.

Stake, R. E., & Easely, J. *Case studies in science education,* vol. I & II. Urbana: Center for Instructional Research and Curriculum Evaluation, University of Illinois at Urbana-Champaign, January 1978.

Stevens, W. *Opus posthumous.* New York: Knopf, 1957.

Studies in Philosophy and Education, Edwardsville, IL: Studies in Philosophy and Education Incorporated.
Published early essays and debates, the products of the methods and techniques of concept analysis.

Weitz, M. *The opening mind.* Chicago: University of Chicago Press, 1977.
Advanced philosophical reading, especially significant for the basic distinction favoring open over closed concepts in philosophic studies of humanistic concepts. Continues his classic analysis of "What is art?"

Wilson, J. B. *Thinking with concepts.* Cambridge: Cambridge University Press, 1963.
Written for and used in secondary schools in England; pages of actual examples of analysis, plus commentary on teaching and learning the techniques.

Gabriel M. Della-Piana
*Director, Bureau of Educational Research, Professor of
Educational Psychology, University of Utah*

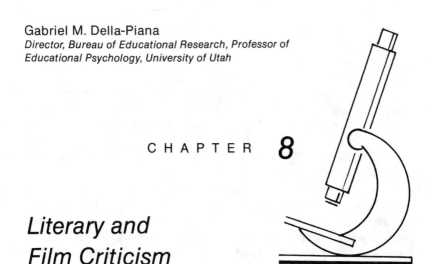

CHAPTER **8**

Literary and
Film Criticism

*Gabriel Della-Piana has worked for the past several
years in instructional technology in connection with
writing skills and revision processes in the writing of
poetry. Currently he is applying the perspective of
this chapter to the evaluation of CAI courseware and
directing a four-year project on a synthesis of code-
oriented and language-oriented instruction in reading funded under the National Basic Skills Improvement Program of the Department of
Education.*

*I'd rather learn from one bird how to sing,
than teach ten thousand stars how not to
dance.*

> E.E. Cummings

Suppose one were to look at the methodology of program evaluation from the perspective of *some* tools or techniques of literary
criticism. That is what I have attempted here.

The perspective I have chosen for my focus is "literary criticism
as the illumination of form and style in a text or performance of a
text." This perspective is taken primarily from the work of Sontag
(1966). I shall use the term "form" to refer to any perceptible characteristic of a work — its sound, thematic units, symmetry, how it
represents objective reality, its discontinuities in word and image.

"Style" shall be taken mainly as the repetition and variation of form and the repetition of relations between forms. From this perspective, considerations of content are dissolved into considerations of form and style. Style and form focus our attention and thus emphasize some things and not others. Critical techniques for the illumination of such emphases may prove provocative for the analysis of program evaluation methodology. There is, however, a major and divergent view of the nature and function of literary criticism (most clearly stated by Hyman 1952): "criticism as interpretation and evaluation."

I shall proceed by describing these two views as presented in the writing of Hyman (1952) and Sontag (1966). Then I shall present the perspective of this chapter, followed by some rather detailed illustrations of the chosen critical perspective in actual analyses of sample texts (poems, stories, and film[1]). Accompanying the illustrative analyses will be explorations of possible parallels between the methods of literary criticism and the reporting and criticism of evaluation. The concluding sections of the paper sketch out the sources of other perspectives from literary and film criticism and a "perhaps strategy" for finding one's own perspective.

Two Divergent Views of the Nature and Function of Literary Criticism

Criticism as Interpretation and Evaluation (Hyman, 1952)

Literary criticism *is* what literary critics *do*. According to S.E. Hyman (1952), the "ideal" critic would

> investigate the whole problem of what the poem communicates, how, and to whom, using every available source of information to find out what it was meant to communicate; and then use every technique, from introspection to the most objective laboratory testing, to find out what it actually does communicate, to differing individuals and groups at different times and under different circumstances, . . . investigate the whole problem of symbolic action in the poem, . . . place the poem in the development of the author's writing from every angle, . . . and finally . . . subjectively evaluate the poem and its parts aesthetically in relation to aim, scope and

validity of aim, and degree of accomplishment, place its value in terms of comparable works by the same poet and others, estimate its present and future significance and popularity, assign praise or blame, and . . . advise the reader or writer or both about it (pp. 400-401).

Hyman's statement is presented here because it encompasses most of the traditions of literary criticism[2] and because it serves to clarify my own focus by contrast. But let us go on with Hyman's position and the realistic modifications he makes to bring the "ideal" critic down to the "best" critic.

What modern criticism is, could be defined crudely, and somewhat inaccurately, as the *organized use of non-literary techniques and bodies of knowledge to obtain insights into literature.* . . . The key word of this definition is "organized." Traditional criticism used most of these techniques and disciplines, but in a spasmodic and haphazard fashion. . . . Modern criticism (also) does a number of things that criticism has always done: interpreting the work, relating it to a literary tradition, evaluating it, and so on. . . . Modern criticism asks a number of questions that have, for the most part, not been asked of literature before. What is the significance of the work in relation to the artist's life, his childhood, his family, his deepest needs and desires? What is its relation to his social group, his class, his economic livelihood, the larger pattern of his society? What precisely does it do for him, and how? What does it do for the reader, and how? What is the connection between those two functions? What is the relation of the work to the archetypal primitive patterns of ritual, to the inherited corpus of literature, to the philosophic world views of its time and of all time? What is the organization of its images, its diction, its larger formal pattern? What are the ambiguous possibilities of its key words, and how much of its content consists of meaningful and provable statements? Finally, then, modern criticism can get to the older questions: What are the works' intentions, how valid are they, and how completely are they fulfilled; what are its meanings (plural rather than singular); and how good or bad is it and why? . . . Each critic tends to have a master metaphor or series of metaphors in terms of which he sees the critical function, and . . . this metaphor then shapes, informs, and sometimes limits his work. . . . Modern criticism is developing in the direction of a democratic criticism . . . "every man his own critic." . . . By extending method, *more* men can be capable critics in most cases not professionally, but in their private reading and their lives. And the vested interests *that* possibly menaces are much bigger game than the priesthood of literary criticism (Hyman, 1952, pp. 3, 4, 6, 8, 9).

Hyman points up the impossibility of anyone achieving the ideal he posits as the task of the critic, and finally suggests that the *best* critics are rare masters who pick and choose whatever seems fruitful for the work under discussion (pp. 401-402). Thus, Hyman's position appears to be that the *best* critics draw on a variety of perspectives (every available source of information, non-literary technique, or body of knowledge) and subjectively select whatever methods appear appropriate to the task of obtaining insights into the literature and judging the work. The approach Hyman recommends is heavily focused on *interpretation* and *judgment* of the work. Sontag presents a very different view of the critic's task.

Criticism as Sensitization Through the Illumination of Form and Style in a Work (Sontag, 1966)

Sontag argues that "the function of criticism should be to show *how* [*a work*] *is what it is,* even *that it is what it is,* rather than to *show what it means*" (Sontag, 1966, p. 14). For Sontag, interpreting a work of art impoverishes the world. Interpretation by others limits, even possibly "kills," one's own response to a work. At the least, interpretation becomes an obstacle to discovering one's own response to a work. What is needed is for us to see more. Thus, the kind of criticism that is most needed is that which illuminates form or helps us to see *how* things are what they are.

Criticism as Sensitization Through the Illumination of Form and Style in a Work

The perspective on criticism taken in this chapter is closer to the quotation from Sontag than to the one from Hyman. Interpretation leads to mystification; it does our feeling for us, and thereby may make us lazy, dependent, and ultimately helpless. *What is really needed* is to demystify it, to increase our sensibility and our confidence in making judgments.

Thus, the focus here is on criticism that is "against" interpretation (in the sense of giving us *the* meaning of a text and ignoring its form or how it means). It is "against" judgment (in the sense of stating for us *the* value of a work). It favors an illumination of forms that will enhance our sense of how a work is what it is, how it means or comes alive. Such criticism, it is hoped, will at the same time make the work itself come alive and lend it more meaning for the reader. I do not say that other kinds of criticism are unnecessary, nor do I say that the approach to artistic statements suggested here is completely absent from current evaluation.[3] This chapter is an investigation and exploration of a general perspective and of techniques of criticism that I believe are both stimulating and needful for program evaluation in our time.

Illustrations of Method in Literary Criticism as Sensitization through the Illumination of Form and Style in a Work

There are innumerable techniques of analysis of literature, poetry, film, and the performance of literary works (or scripts) on stage or film. Most of the "best" critics do not limit themselves to one technique and what they do accomplish is difficult to portray, except in a holistic analysis of a poem or other work of writing or performance. Thus, in this section I present in considerable detail six pieces of criticism on fiction, poetry, and film in order to illustrate vantage points and specific techniques which might be used to approach program evaluation and the criticism of program evaluation. The first is an application of a matrix analysis of themes in a short story by Isaac Babel; the second is an "accurate, sharp, loving description" of a poem by Robert Frost; the third is a formal analysis of the representation of reality in a story by Virginia Woolf; the fourth is deep focus and lateral tracking cinematography; the fifth is symmetry and repetition in Keaton's silent comedies; and the sixth is the discontinuity of word and image in film, especially in Godard's "My Life to Live." After each portrayal of method, I attempt to note parallels of program evaluation. The parallels are primarily to evaluation reports and criticism of evaluation, although obviously these applications have implications for design. If the selection of these six above all other methods seems a presumptuous act, the statement of parallels is a preposterous one for reasons I present in the final section of the paper. I consider the statement of the perspective (the preceding two sections) as the most valuable part of this chapter, the methods parts of this section as the next most valuable, and the evaluation parallels parts of this section as the least valuable because they are simply examples of possible parallels and not generalizable principles. I suggest looking at the "parallels" as "thought exercises" and enjoying them for their intent more than for their substance, or for your thought more than mine.

Criticism by Thematic Matric Analysis of a Story

The method presented here is an intuitive application of a small part of Pike's work (Pike, 1967; Brend & Pike, 1976; Pike, 1964b; Brend, 1972; Pike, 1964a). The application I attempt is an analysis of Isaac Babel's "Crossing into Poland."

For the general approach and analytic scheme in this analysis of Babel's story, I am indebted to Richard Young (University of Michigan), although I take responsibility for the details of the application. Here are the four steps involved in the method.

1. *Read the piece of work and chunk the plot sequence into arbitrary thematic units (1), (2), (3), . . . etc.* This very short story has nine paragraphs which seem to sort into thematic chunks as follows: (1) Novograd taken by Cossacks — notice to move out with baggage to there, (2) description of nature's beauty and the blood and smell of war mingled together, (3) description of house where speaker is billeted in Novograd — one pregnant Jewish woman, two "red-haired, scraggy-necked Jews," and a third huddled up asleep. A mess of room, human filth, coats, and other stuff all over the floor, (4) the speaker commands the woman to clean things up, and she and the others do and put a bed (that had been "disemboweled") for him beside the one asleep, (5) silence and the moon, (6) the speaker dreams of the battle and screams and the woman gropes over his face waking him up, (7) the woman tells the speaker his tossing around is pushing her father and that she will make a bed in another corner for the speaker, (8) she gets up to make the bed and removes the blanket from the sleeper; the speaker sees the sleeper; an old man, dead, throat torn out, face cleft in two, etc., (9) the woman explains that "the Poles cut his throat," and that the old man had asked them to do it in the yard so his daughter wouldn't see and that "where in the whole world . . . could you find another father like my father?"

2. *Reread the story several times to find the semantic categories that have some repetition or parallels. Identify each of the plot units or chunks in those terms.* My choice is to stick mainly with thematic (semantic) categories in this case, although the method may be used with grammatical or phonological categories. What seems to be dominant is courage vs. cowardliness — the heroic and the nonheroic. There is a repetition of the heroic and the nonheroic that is worth analysis.

3. Set up a matrix. In this case the subjective choice of dimensions is heroic/nonheroic *scenes* on one axis and heroic/nonheroic *actions within scenes* on the other axis. Scene (5) is pivotal. It is simply a quiet scene in nature (the moon, etc.) and for people (sleeping); thus, it is not in the matrix. The action moves from dominance by the Cossacks in Scenes 1 to 4, to dominance by the Jews (woman) in scenes 6 to 9.

4. *The final step of the method is to say what you see.* If there is "interpretation" here, it is not *the* interpretation. But more important, the method shows us *how* the story is what it is in a way that perhaps makes the experience of it happen more powerfully. Thus we see the *repetition* of a confirmation of the stereotype of the Jew in Russia of this time (nonheroic, messy, cowardly) and of the Cossacks (independent, free-spirited, courageous). But the matrix also reveals the repetition of *contradictions* of the stereotype (courageous Jews and cowardly Cossacks). And there is a movement from Cossack dominance in the first four scenes to scene five as pivotal (a quiet scene in nature) and Jewish dominance in the last four scenes.

Parallels between thematic matrix analysis and program evaluation. I have taken the Stebbins et al. report (1977) on the evaluation of Follow Through and the House et al. critique (1978) of the evaluation and have applied the technique of thematic matrix analysis. Thus, this is an example of criticism of criticism. The semantic categories I fixed upon for the matrix were statements concerning method and conclusions of the study on one axis and agreement and disagreement with the statements on the other. The summary below shows how these categories evolved out of an analysis of the reports.

House and Stebbins disagree on the proper unit of analysis and on the appropriateness of the presentation of data allowing comparisons among models, but agree on certain weaknesses in method (the omission of measures relevant to different models and the lack of program implementation data). And there is an apparent lack of consistency in the digest and body of the Stebbins report on the conclusion concern-

TABLE 8.1   Thematic Matrix Analysis for "Crossing Into Poland"

Acts Within Scenes	"Scenes" or Arbitrary Thematic Units in the Plot Sequence	
	Heroic	Nonheroic
Heroic	(1) Cossacks are victorious and "move on" (7) The woman is courageous in a heroic scene — tells off the Cossack	(6a) Woman acts courageously in a cowardly (the dream) scene (8) The death scene and the woman acts heroically, beautifully (do what one must do)
Nonheroic	(2) Nature (beautiful) but blood and bodies strewn about (4) Conquering Cossacks (heroic) — billeted with Jews and order them to "clean up," Jews behave submissively in their shabby quarters	(6b) Cossack (speaker) is cowardly in dream and upon awakening (3) Messy, filthy quarters of Jews submitting to "quartering" Cossacks

ing the superiority of "basic skills models." But three persistent repetitions stand out: the tremendous agreement between House and Stebbins on both methods and conclusions, some disagreements between the House and Stebbins reports, and the qualifying remarks within Stebbins' report with respect to both methods and conclusions. In the next section I will examine the repetitions in qualifying remarks by Stebbins et al. with a different method.

Criticism as Accurate, Sharp, Loving Description

Randall Jarrell (1965, pp. 191-231) brings a variety of techniques to bear upon an explication of Robert Frost's dramatic poem, "Home Burial."

Jarrell's method in this case is to begin with a line-by-line close reading or paraphrasing of the poem, although that is too modest a statement for what he accomplishes. Here are some examples. Rather than summarize or quote in the form Jarrell puts it, I shall record some of this very long poem and leave spaces between the lines for Jarrell's comments. The poem is in quotes; Jarrell's comments, in parentheses. The four asterisks indicate some lines omitted in the

TABLE 8.2   Thematic Matrix Analysis For Follow Through Evaluation
Reports

Thematic Unit	*Semantic Category Analysis**
1. Measures lack sensitivity to unique outcomes of the different models.	Statement of method: H *agrees* and S *agrees*.
2. The proper unit of analysis is the classroom rather than the child.	Statement of *method*: H *agrees* and S *disagrees*.
3. Models emphasizing basic skills succeeded better than other models in helping children gain these skills.	Statement of *conclusion*: H *disagrees*, S *disagrees* (or qualifies) in body of text but *agrees* and does not qualify in the "digest" of the study
4. Program implementation was not assessed.	Statement of *method*: H *agrees* and S *agrees*.
5. Summary charts allowing comparisons among models are misleading because of the intersite variation in effects within models being greater than variations between models.	Statement of *conclusion*: H *agrees* and S (implicitly) *disagrees*.

*H stands for the House et al. critique (1978); S stands for the Stebbins et al. report (1977).

poem. I have taken the liberty of combining Jarrell's comments under
several lines of the poem where he made them after only a phrase or
line. The following material is excerpted from pages 191-231.

"He saw her from the bottom of the stairs
Before she saw him"
(implies . . . that, knowing herself seen, she would have acted
differently)

"She was starting down
Looking back over her shoulder at some fear."
(at *some fear* . . . not a specific feared object. . . . Normally, we do
not look back over our shoulder at what we leave, unless we feel for
it something more than fear)

"She took a doubtful step
and then undid it

To raise herself and look again."
(A vertical ballet of indecision toward and away from a fearful but
mesmerically attractive object, something hard to decide to leave
and easy to decide to return to . . . the surprising use of *undid* gives
her withdrawal of the tentative step a surprising reality.)

* * * *

"He said to gain time: 'What is it you see,'
Mounting until she cowered under him.
'I will find out now — you must tell me, dear' "
(to "gain time" in which to think of the next thing to say, to gain time
in which to get close to her and gain the advantage of . . . his
physical bulk. His next 'What is it you see' is the first of his many
repetitions; if one knew only this man one would say, 'Man is the
animal that repeats.' . . . The identity of the vowels in 'mounting'
and 'cowered' physically connects the two, makes his mounting the
plain immediate cause of her cowering. 'I will find out now' is
another of his rhetorical announcements of what he is going to do
[implying] 'this time you're going to tell me, I'm going to make you.'
But this heavy-willed compulsion changes into sheer appeal, into
reasonable beseeching, in his next phrase: 'You must tell me, dear!'
The 'dear' is affectionate intimacy, the 'must' is the 'must' of
rational necessity yet the underlying form of the sentence is that of
compulsion.)

This brief sample does not do justice to Jarrell's technique. But
clearly one thing he does well is "paraphrase" or "elaborate" to make
clear how the work means and the mood of the work. There is no
intent to say that the paraphrase is *the* meaning. The emphasis is more
on *how* the work means.

Now Jarrell moves to analysis of form and style where content
dissolves into form. He does not neglect form or style in the first part
of his analysis: note the "repetitions" and the vowel identities referred to above. But here we have more attention to form and style.
The man in the poem has just said,

"A man can't speak of his own child that's dead."

(Earlier the woman had given two entirely different specific and
unexpected answers to this rhetorical question of his; this time she
has a third specific answer, which she makes with monosyllabic
precision and finality.)

"You can't because you don't know how to speak"

(He has said that it is an awful thing not to be permitted to speak of his own dead child; she implies that it is not a question of permission but of ability, that he is too ignorant and insensitive to be *able* to speak of his child. Her sentence is one line long, and it is only the second sentence of hers that has been that long. He has talked at length during the first two-thirds of the poem, she in three- or four-word phrases or in motions without words; for the rest of the poem she talks at length, as everything that has been shut up inside her begins to pour out. She opens herself up . . . striking at him with her words . . . the first sentence has indicted him; now she brings in the specific evidence for the indictment. She says)

"If you had any feelings, you that dug
with your own hand"

(but after the three stabbing, indicting stresses of

your   own   hand

she breaks off the sentence . . . but the fact of things continues)

"I saw you from that very window there"

(the same stabbing stresses, the same emphasis of a specific damning actuality, that 'your own hand' had and that soon)

"my own eyes"

"Your own baby's grave"

(and other such phrases will have).

(Then there is the re-creation of sustained hysteria she felt as she first watched him digging the grave. The sounds of)

"leap and leap in air,
leap up like that, like that, and
land so lightly"

(are Le! le! le! li! li! la! li!)

(So the stones leap and leap and land so lightly but the animate being, her dead child, does not move. After landing so lightly, the stones)

". . . *roll* back *down* the *mount* beside the *hole*"

(The repeated o's say "oh! ow! ow! oh!"
In an extraordinarily conclusive condemnation of him she says)

"You could *s*it there with the *s*tain*s* on your shoe*s*
of the fresh earth from your own baby'*s* grave.
And talk about your everyday con*c*ern*s*"

(The hissing or splitting s's together with the damning stresses and the judge's summing up give an awful finality to this condemnation. Later she says that he lives by proverbs and he'll die by them. Now — she turns them on him and in breathless outrage.)

"Think of it, talk like that at such a time!"

(The repeated sounds of th, t, t, th, t, t, are thoroughly expressive.)

Certainly this approach does not have the clarity of rules that was in the method of thematic matrix analysis. Jarrell gets into the work and follows his own hunches. He stays close to what is there. He deals with simple meaning, searches for forms (repetitions, sounds, intonation), and their repetitions and relations to meaning and to each other.

Parallels between Jarrell's "accurate, sharp, loving description" and program evaluation. Suppose that in place of, or in addition to, negative evaluation reports or criticisms of evaluation reports there were more "sharp, accurate, loving descriptions." This would suggest that one find "excellent studies" to treat in this way. One is not likely to do such descriptions of studies that are not in some way meritorious. Thus, Glass and Smith (1978; Smith and Glass, 1978) might well have conducted such a description for the "best experiment" (Sloane et al., 1975) they identified on a comparison of psychodynamic therapy and behavioral therapy. House et al. (1978) did focus effectively on how the Follow-Through evaluation means (statistically and logically) more than on what it means. And in the above section on "thematic matrix analysis" I noted the repetitions in qualifying remarks concerning method and conclusions in the Stebbins et al. report (1977).

But I have wondered whether I could convey some of the same messages that we obtained from the House et al. critique of the Stebbins' report by using an accurate, sharp, and loving description that makes the study come alive for the audience House et al. intended to reach (partly the "general public"). I will attempt here a sharp, accurate, and loving description of *the repetitions in the tortured qualifying treatment by Stebbins et al. of the measures of effects on children.* The Stebbins' report is truly a poem. It made me weep and sense the complexity of the situation. Their sense of what is of worth is certainly apt. Let me give you a hint of the poetry. Notice as you read the shift from the impersonal and institutional *it* and the assumed *they,* to the responsible *we,* and notice what is pivotal or discriminative for the shift. The italics and the parenthetical statements are mine.

"*It* was soon realized that no common battery . . . would encompass all the various sponsors' goals and objectives" [p. 10].

(A truly uncommon one would be needed.)

"*OE . . . requested . . .* sponsors . . . devise evaluation . . . for those objectives not covered in the national evaluation . . . with . . . memorandum . . . November 1972" [p. 10].

(These are official decisions and the authority and rationale lie in their officialness as indicated by the memorandum date and reference to the higher authority.)

"*The national follow through* evaluation does not include in its scope the individual sponsor's evaluations" [p. 11].

(The form is still impersonal — the "we" comes later.)

"This *battery was selected as a 'best compromise'* between the need for accountability and the difficulty of measuring sponsors' diverse goals and objectives" [p. 35].

(Up to here the situation is relentlessly and clearly one beyond the control of the writers. It is all "it" and "they" and not a matter they particularly want to take responsibility for until the pivotal "this battery was selected as a best compromise." After the compromise it is *we*. We agree with those who urge caution be exercised in drawing conclusions. We describe the measures thoroughly so the reader may judge their adequacy. We caution the reader that outcome measures other than the ones available might have been able to demonstrate effectiveness in the domains which go untapped in this evaluation [p. 35].

The critique by House et al. (1978) on this same issue has a different tone. The House et al. report does a great service in documenting "cognitive-conceptual" and "affective" goals not tapped by the measures used in the study. But a thematic matrix analysis and "loving description" might do as well and leave judgment to the reader without the judgmental implications of terms such as "the evaluator's admission," "poorly defined," "to their credit," "in spite of sensitivity," "admit as much."

Criticism as Formal Analysis of the Representation of Reality

Auerbach (1953) is one of those choice critics who is able to effectively dissolve considerations of content into those of form and yet look at literature from the vantage point of how text (literary representation or imitation) leads one to interpret reality. And he applies the hunches he picks up in an analysis of Homer, the Bible, Dante, Boccaccio, Goethe, Flaubert, Virginia Woolf, and Proust.

Auerbach approaches analysis of text "without" a specific purpose. He takes a few motifs from the history of the representation of reality and tries them on a series of texts, ancient and modern. What he sees developing gives him some satisfaction. "It is still a long way to a common life of mankind on earth, but the goal begins to be visible. And it is most concretely visible now in the unprejudiced, precise, interior and exterior representation of the random moment in the lives of different people" (Auerbach, 1953, p. 552). His analysis is focused on the representation of reality as form (content dissolved into it), and the effect (for me) is to make the experience of the text "happen" more powerfully than the text alone.

Auerbach's method is illustrated in his analysis of a piece of prose from Virginia Woolf's novel, *To the Lighthouse,* first published in 1927. The approach I take here is to state some of his generalizations and then illustrate them.

"The writer as a narrator of objective facts has almost completely vanished; almost everything stated appears by way of reflection in the consciousness of the [characters]" (Auerbach, 1953, p. 534). Thus, we get what Mrs. Ramsay thinks or feels about the house rather than objective information the author possesses.

> She looked up . . . and saw the room, saw the chairs, thought them fearfully shabby. Their entrails as Andrew said the other day, were all over the floor; but then what was the point, she asked herself, of buying good chairs to let them spoil up here all through the winter when the house, with only one old woman to see it, positively dripped with wet? Never mind: the rent was precisely two pence half penny; the children loved it; it did her husband good to be three thousand, or if she must be accurate, three hundred miles from his library and his lectures and his disciples; and there was room for visitors [Auerbach, 1953, p. 525].

We are given Mrs. Ramsay's character as it is reflected in and as it affects various figures in the novel. The device is "stream of consciousness" or "interior monologue." The impression of an objective reality completely known to the author is obliterated. The author represents herself at times as "someone who doubts, wonders, hesitates, as though the truth about her characters were not better known to her than it is to them or to the reader" (Auerbach, 1953, p. 535]. We are given not just one person whose consciousness is rendered but many, with frequent shifts from one to the other. We are confronted with an endeavor to *investigate* objective reality — the "real" Mrs. Ramsay.

> The treatment of time. . . . These are the characteristic and distinctively new features of the technique: a chance occasion releasing processes of consciousness; a natural . . . rendering of those processes in their peculiar freedom, which is neither restrained by a purpose nor directed by a specific subject of thought, elaboration of the contrast between "exterior" and "interior" time. . . . Exterior events have actually lost their hegemony, they serve to release and interpret inner events rather than to prepare and motivate significant exterior happenings [1953, pp. 537, 538].

Mrs. Ramsay is going to make stockings for the lighthouse keeper's boy and is measuring the length of the stocking against her boy's legs. There are a number of interludes (the passage above beginning "she looked up" is one of them). *The time the narration takes is devoted not to the occurrence itself (it is terse –the measuring of the stocking) but to the interludes. Yet the time it took for such interior monologues is certainly in reality not as long as the time it takes to read or hear them.* The reason is that to make ourselves intelligible to others takes more language. *Thus, reality (time passed) is violated to get at reality (the conscious wanderings of the mind).*

In another interlude we suddenly have a flashback, a new speaker, new scene, new time, and the time is not stated ("once"). Its content: the things people think about Mrs. Ramsay, a telephone conversation with Mr. Bankes. The continuity of the scene with what comes before is not an objective one but an impression of Mr. Bankes that sums up the sadness of Mrs. Ramsay's beautiful face. The interludes are not filled with tension to get back to the story line or release of the tension of the story, and the indication of time is inexact — in contrast to the story of Odysseus' youth in Homer. *The exterior reality of the moment is nothing but an occasion to release things seen only by reflection in consciousness and not tied to the present or the occurrence which releases them.*

> He who represents the course of human life, or a sequence of events extending over a prolonged period of time and represents it from beginning to end, must prune and isolate arbitrarily. . . . But the things that happen to a few individuals in the course of a few

minutes, hours, or possibly even days — this one can hope to report with reasonable completeness. . . . It is precisely the random moment. . . . The more it is exploited, the more the elementary things which our lives have in common come to light [Auerbach, 1953, pp. 548, 549, 552].

Thus, *To the Lighthouse* describes portions of two days in widely separated time. The multipersonal representation of consciousness, time strata, disintegration of the continuity of exterior events, and shifting of the narrative viewpoint are all most possible in the random moment and represent a transfer of confidence away from the power of great exterior turning points and blows of fate and toward any random fragment plucked from the course of a life at any time as a way of portraying the totality of its fate. *Auerbach's method of formal analysis of the representation of reality illuminates three characteristics of form and style:*

(1) Most objective facts appear as reflections in the consciousness of several characters; this engages us in the *investigation* of objective reality.

(2) The reality of *time passed* in exterior events is violated to get at the reality of conscious wanderings of the mind, by devoting more space (time) to the latter; that is, to the conscious wanderings of the mind.

(3) The things that happen to a few individuals in a random moment (minutes, hours, a day or two) represented in completeness, exploited fully, is favored because it reveals more of the elementary things our lives have in common than the course of a human life over a prolonged time, arbitrarily pruned and isolated.

Parallels between Auerbach's "representation of reality" and program evaluation. The parallels here are primarily with respect to reporting strategy, although being able to report in this way would require some attention to evaluation design and implementation stages.

Public Law 94-142 has created significant changes in the operation of special education programs. In many programs, teachers are spending four weeks or more testing children and having conferences with parents to place children in the least restrictive environment consistent with effective educational programming. That *"objective fact"* about the program (the four weeks of testing while waiting for instruction) may well be represented through, or *reflected in,* the continuing consciousness of several characters such as the special education teacher, the classroom teacher, or the child, reflecting on the current instruction and other elements in the situation and out of it. But the portrayal could reverse the time (space) devoted to "testing" and "consciousness of the characters"; brief mention of events in four weeks of testing and longer portrayals of momentary consciousness of children waiting . . . not being taught by the presumably carefully designed programs (the IEPs).

The Follow Through evaluation by Stebbins et al. (1977) has been criticized by evaluators themselves for not designing instruments that represent the divergent goals of different programs. It would be instructive to portray a teacher, parent, or child in one of the models (for example, the responsive education model) with conscious wanderings of her/his mind on parents and children while reading through the instrumentation section of the evaluation report in preparation for reporting to parents on the results of the national evaluation.

It is not difficult to imagine a teacher reading the instrumentation section description of the Metropolitan Achievement Test — Primary I subtests on word knowledge, word analysis, and reading (Stebbins et al., 1977, p. 40) and the earlier conclusion that "the basic skills measures are probably a reasonable battery for . . . achievement" (1977, p. 35). Probably, indeed! The teacher and child can think of a broader range of skills they have been practicing. Picture the teacher reading and writing and reflecting on one child (Adam, who, in the first month of school, wept at the slightest provocation, threatened to leave school, left the room to look for his sister, screamed if touched, looked and listened elsewhere during instructions on the activities of each "center"). Picture the reflection of the child in the consciousness of the teacher during the crises and the reflection of the changing child in the consciousness of the parents. Then imagine these reflections around the broad range of mastery models for reading comprehension characteristic of such a program (Della-Piana, 1978b); the child reading a rehearsed text as a performance for other children, the child recalling studied text material (stories, songs) to tell others, the child reading underlined discussion points previously discussed orally as reminders during a group discussion of a defense of or modification of the maxim "anything worth doing is worth doing well" (and later reading a transcription of the discussion), the child participating in a reader's theater presentation with script in hand previously transcribed from an improvisational dramatic presentation growing out of a minimal situation set up by the teachers, and the child trying to follow instructions written by another child on how to tie the High- wayman's Hitch. The objective facts are thus represented in the consciousness of several characters, and what happens to them in a few moments is exploited fully. Such subjective reporting would require validation (confirming data from multiple sources) in any reasonable evaluation. But attention to this perspective might well change the evaluation design, and this form of reporting or criticism of reports may add another dimension of understanding.

Criticism as Analysis of "Deep Focus" and "Lateral Tracking" Cinematography[4]

" Deep focus" is a camera technique in which the middle range and background of an individual shot are as clear as the foreground. Its most noticeable quality is "the cultivation of crisp focus throughout an unprecedented depth of field in the scene photographed" (Agee, 1971, p. 19). Deep focus tends toward long duration takes and the use of a carefully placed camera that moves only when necessary. It is more cameraman-oriented than editor-oriented. Scenes which typi- cally call for a shift from close-up to full shot are planned so that the action takes place simultaneously in extreme foreground and extreme background. This kind of cinematography is in sharp contrast to the more editor-oriented approach in which the content of a given shot is subordinated to the effect (feeling, meaning) generated by its coming between two other shots in a sequence. Deep focus has been used with "natural" light to get a more realistic scene in which the drama is something you "discover" rather than something that is forced on you by studio lighting and camera focus. Orson Welles used deep focus in *Citizen Kane* in a more extreme way. He (together with cameraman Gregg Toland) developed the style for dramatic rather than naturalis- tic effect. Lighting was used to black out the irrelevant and spotlight the crucial action, such as one might do on stage. It allowed Welles to get the effect of crowds without a crowd, to highlight movement of someone in the background while focusing on foreground, instead of cross-cutting or shifting from full shot to close-up; and it allowed the appearance of a great room on a simple stage. This composition-in- depth has been said to correlate with Welles' centering on impenetra- ble mystery (the scene is complex and, though spotlighting may focus attention on some things more than others, there is much to "dis- cover" and there are a multiplicity of viewpoints). Though there is a mulitplicity of viewpoints and perspectives creating the inexhaustible mystery, there is nevertheless a certainty concerning the underlying theme. One scene illustrating the complexity of this composition in depth is the shot in which Mrs. Kane learns of her son's inheritance. The shot is narrow and deep. In the cabin room we see mother large in the foreground, the banker from the East behind her, the window in the wall of the cabin behind them and then in the far distance, young Kane playing with his sled outside. Composition, dialogue, and action force one to look back and forth in that scene.

There are, of course, an infinite number of ways to use deep focus and there are innumerable contrasts to deep focus cinematography. One interesting contrast was developed by Godard in his later period; it is the "lateral tracking" shot. As Godard used it, this is a camera style in which the prime element is a long, slow tracking shot that moves laterally only, in one direction only (though occasionally doubling back), over a scene that does not move in relation to the camera's movement. The shot moves neither backward nor forward, and the track is exactly on the 0° to 180° line, with the scenes or subjects shot on a parallel line. Occasionally there is a slight "angling" left or right by the camera as it moves laterally. This camera style (in Godard's work) is correlated with the context in which it appears. For example, as a character

> describes her awakening to social contradictions . . . the camera tracks slowly (from right to left) across the shabby, overcrowded dwellings of Algerian workers who live near the university, coming to rest at last on the modern efficient buildings of the university complex. The worker's shacks are flat and horizontal, the university buildings high and vertical, but the . . . camera does not have to move back to take in the tall commanding structures. . . . Godard observes the time and space relations and lets the viewer make the social relation [Henderson, 1976, p. 426].

The shot thus has its own internal relations and logic. It never follows a subject. It never prefers one subject over another — all receive equal attention. All are seen from the same perspective and time. (See Ogle (1971), and Kael (1974) for more depth on the above discussion of deep focus and Henderson (1976) for the contrast between deep focus and lateral tracking.)

Parallels between deep focus and lateral tracking cinematography and program evaluation. There is a direct parallel between cinematography technique and program evaluation. Whether with camera or pen, one can describe a program in process. And the different camera techniques suggest different ways of getting perspective on a program or different ways of analyzing the program. Consider a comparison of deep focus and lateral tracking cinematography as ways of representing models for assessing reading comprehension. The reading comprehension models are taken from Della-Piana (1978b).

Model one in Table 8.2 would, I believe, be more effectively represented by the *lateral tracking* shot since it shows the redundancy of task monotony and relevance.

Lateral tracking would again seem a priori to be more effective, this time for showing the repetition of pairings of good reading and attentive listening, in the model two situation.

Deep focus would seem more effective for representing model three in order to illuminate the complexity of small group discussion.

Deep focus would also appear to be the more effective technique for representing model four. Lateral tracking would miss the complexity of the classroom with its various centers of activity and would miss the nonverbal behaviors of the reader's theater group without picking up anything unique. However, an even better approach to cinematography for model four might well be the "word-image dissociation" of Godard discussed below.

One can readily see here the possibilities of representing a classroom or therapeutic situation or treatment program of some kind. If one has first observed the situation and then written a script, the proper cinematographic technique may be selected to portray whatever seems appropriate.

Criticism as the Illumination of Symmetry and Repetition in Comedic Style

The greatest comedy era was the one dominated by Chaplin, Keaton, Lloyd, and Langdon. James Agee (1969) captured this era in a statement that is still the best in "criticism as the illumination of form and style in silent comedy." Agee's description of the cadenza-like movement the silent comedian goes into when hit upon the head makes that sequence come alive again as if it were visually presented. He does a masterful job of treating all four of the great comedians of this period in a way that illuminates their individual styles and captures the uniqueness and beauty of each. For Agee, Chaplin had the

TABLE 8.3 Cinematographic Procedures in Program Evaluation

Reading Comprehension Assessment Model	Deep Focus Shot	Lateral Tracking Shot
1. Child reads text and fills in blanks in paraphrases of the text.	Jim in foreground filling in answers. Other children are doing the same work in middle and background. All heads down working.	Camera tracks across one row of children from same distance, including Jim, equal time and attention to all doing the same work, quiet, heads down.
2. Child performs for a large group of the class by reading a self-selected story already rehearsed.	Jim reading aloud already rehearsed story in foreground. Most of the group listening, some with full attention all the way to background, one looking elsewhere.	Jim reading aloud rehearsed story, voice heard but camera tracks along one row of students, each attending until last one looking elsewhere.
3. Child in small group discusses proverb "the squeaky wheel gets the grease" using printed prompt sheet listing the proverb and questions suggesting defense of proverb or modification of it to make it more acceptable or accurate.	Jim in foreground in small group discussion of the proverb adds a comment "it gets the grease but it may need new ball bearings." In the background teacher is moving a noisy child to a seat to "watch others and see how one might behave so others can work too."	One hears Jim's voice and at first he is seen but with no more time and distance than others on the same parallel across room. Each child doing own work until one gets to the "noisy child" and hears superimposed on Jim's voice the teacher's voice in moving the child.
4. Child performs in a reader's theater situation, dramatizing with text already rehearsed but in hand.	Jim reads in reader's theater with two other students in foreground. In middle and background are children doing other tasks representing models one, two, and three. One hears the voice of Jim in his reader's theater presentation.	One hears Jim in the reader's theater presentation of a small group (3 children) while camera tracks slowly across the three sitting in a row and across the rest of the room to all on an even parallel but still hearing the voice of Jim in reader's theater.

broadest range, "the finest pantomime, the deepest emotion, the richest and most poignant poetry" (1969, p. 10). In my judgment, among modern creators of comedy, Woody Allen has come closest to approaching some of Chaplin's "soul and comedy." But if Chaplin was the first comedian to give the silent language a soul and to influence others to do likewise, it was Buster Keaton who brought pure physical comedy to its greatest heights. Keaton is our major focus for illuminating three ways in which sheer symmetry and repetition serve for a laugh a minute. Our chief source is the volume by Daniel Moews (1977) which presents Keaton's best nine features released between 1923 and 1928. These nine features were rapidly made but with sustained excellence. The symmetry is most pronounced in *The Navigator* — particularly the symmetry of motion. The story is simple. A roomful of spies plot to unmoor and set adrift a supply ship just purchased by the rival country. Keaton and a girl (the daughter of the wealthy shipowner and the girl who refused Keaton's proposal of marriage) accidentally end up on the ship and are set adrift.

One of the structures central to the features is the Keaton hero falling asleep halfway through his adventures. Sleep is always pivotal to the action — an abbreviated sleep of a few camera shots and title which signals a decisive turning point. When the hero wakes he has undergone a change. In six of the films, he bumbles and fails as the typical comic underdog in the first half and astonishingly succeeds in the second. In *The Navigator,* the hero and the girl, both rich and foolish and unused to waiting on themselves, display a comedy of bumbling efforts to get food and shelter. After a brief sleep (sitting side by side at a table), they wake to the title "weeks later" in comfortable staterooms and with incredible competence manage all tasks, engage in chase and battle, meet real dangers, and end happily.

Keaton is master of the classic "gag." The Keaton hero must do everything at least three times. That is the minimum number required to get a laugh. The first occasion introduces the action (for example, the girl throws overboard a picture of a scowling seaman and it catches and swings back and forth in front of Keaton's cabin porthole — the hero blinks as if something is wrong), the second establishes the action (the face swings again and the hero is restless, stirs), and the third is the capping event (the face swings by again and the hero is satisfactorily frightened). Then there is another triad: the hero is frightened and lies trembling in the bunk, more frightened he hides under the sheet, and finally leaps out of bed covered by the sheet and runs through the cabin door. This of course begins another sequence — the ghost. And the laughs build along a gagchain. The gagchains make the Keaton hero a "comic Sisyphus" — pushing a stone to the top of a hill only to have it roll down again, but with a comic release and variation that creates not a repetition of the same act but a leap to a variation of the theme in some new trials.

Keaton's use of pure symmetry of motion dominates the entire film in *The Navigator*. In the first major example of symmetry in this film, our hero goes out of his home with hat, cane, and orchid, climbs into a Rolls Royce open limousine, is chauffeured down the street a half block to an abrupt U-turn, and parks directly across the street. The hero goes in, proposes, gets turned down, pauses (for the first time in this sequence, but not with all motion stopped), and with a look of blank stupefaction, retraces his course back home. The most highly developed and prolonged symmetry of mirror reversals in *The Navigator* is "the search." Keaton, adrift on the ship he believes is empty, drops a cigarette and the girl finds it and cries out. He hears her. They each try to find one another. First they walk purposefully and turn corners, just in time not to see each other. Then they trot, each at the same pace and miss one another again. Then they go like bats out of hell. Again they miss. Then the camera moves to the stern and watches the whole superstructure of the ship and the search from level to level with the characters always missing each other by a hair but with movements choreographed and shot in a way that restricts them to horizontal and perpendicular mechanical runs, where each runs to and away from the camera, alternately changing from miniature figures in the distance to giant closeups as they run forward and then reverse again.

Parallels between illumination of symmetry in silent comedy and program evaluation. The three comic structures in Keaton may be used in program evaluation reporting or in criticism of program evaluation. Who has not experienced program development in which the first half is a series of goofs and bumbles and after "one fine night's sleep" there is a change and astonishing success with incredible competency not to be accounted for in any way? If it is to be humorous it must be incredible.

The "gag formula" may be used also — doing everything at least three times. Picture an evaluator administering the Stanford Achievement Test to some first-grade student who has been in a classroom organized around learning centers for the whole year with rather free movement from center to center. Allen (during the vocabulary test) says, "This is hard." After going back to his paper for a few seconds, he says, "This is really hard." And in a few more seconds, he says, "This is too hard," folds up the test booklet, walks over to the bookrack, picks up a book, sits down in the reading area, and begins reading.

Pure symmetry of motion is illuminated in a speeded-up film showing a highly teacher-scripted, tightly sequenced, direct instruction program. Picture a film of five children going through a 45-minute reading instruction sequence with three phases. In Phase One, the teacher gives direct instruction on sounds and on blending sounds into words, first demonstrating, then giving prompted practice, and then calling for unprompted responses. In Phase Two, the children get their workbooks, sit down, read the workbook lessons, and write their responses. They then get up to get self-instructional tapes which introduce new sounds and words, use the tapes, and put the tapes and workbooks back when they are finished. In Phase Three the children get "storybooks" and read them to each other in pairs. Now speed up the film and play it forward, then backward. The pace of the three phases will be different. Phase Two, the speeded-up version, depicts some symmetry similar to Keaton's "search" sequences on the deck of the ship as children get their self-instructional tapes and return them. Both Phases One and Two, when speeded up, show the form of text- and teacher-controlled instruction in a frantic and humorous way. And Phase Three is a change of pace — speeded up, it is still a slower pace, and child-on-child has a more relaxed mood and is beautifully pivotal to the reverse of the sequence. Most important, the form and style of instruction is depicted in a memorable way that allows us to see what we have not seen before, or to see it in new and more profound ways.

Poking fun at programs in this way is not intended as a negative evaluation of a program. It illuminates form and style and increases our sensibilities — helps us to see what we have not seen or to see it more profoundly or to see it with humor. The facts are slightly distorted in such portrayals, but they are distorted in the interest of portrayal of some aspect of reality. Reality as faithful reproduction is violated in order to get at reality as recognition of forms and repetition of forms that we might not otherwise see.

The three major techniques of Keaton are a good beginning point for making use of this relatively unexploited parallel. Beyond this beginning, one may take on the more poignant poetry of Chaplin. Or, one may work with other visual displays which help illuminate what data are available. Perhaps someone will take the work on exploratory and confirmatory data analysis (see Tukey, 1977; Erickson & Nosanchuk, 1977), especially the graphic representation in that work, and with the insights of a Keaton or a Chaplin find new ways of representing data to illuminate form.

Criticism as the Illumination of Word and Image Dissociation in Film

If you have seen foreign films with subtitles, you may have noticed that most of them attempt to include *all* the dialogue, and some have brief subtitles to suggest the essence of the dialogue. The experience of the viewer is very different under these two conditions. The latter (brief subtitles) are more like many of the early silent comedies which combined in the subtitles very little dialogue and very little documentary narrative. The effect of the more minimal subtitles and the combination of dialogue and narrative is to involve the viewer more, to allow the image to dominate, and to put the viewer in a position of drawing on his/her own experience to make sense of the film.

For the early statements on the issues surrounding word and image relationships in cinema, see Eisenstein's 1928 manifesto (Eisenstein, *Film Form,* 1957, pp. 257-260) and Arnheim's 1938 inquiry (Arnheim, 1957, pp. 199-230). For more comprehensive outlines of the problematic and successful possibilities of joining sound and image in the cinema, see Bordwell and Thompson (1979, pp. 189-220) and Kracauer (1960, pp. 102-132); for a contrary position, see Mast (1977, pp. 225-234). I am concerned here less with the debate than with the possibilities. One must agree there are limitless possibilities in joining film, sound, and image in ways that clarify images, contradict them, or render them ambiguous. The effect on the audience can be comic or serious, keep one curious, create discomfort, cause one to draw on one's own experience to make sense of what is seen/heard, and even leave one with a need to complete what has been left unfinished. Let me illustrate some of the possibilities using materials from the above sources.

Consider the comic effect of sounds not faithful to the source as we conceive it or anticipate it: a cat barking, a young child with a deep bass voice, a swinging door that sounds like a plucked cello string, or a dropped plate with the sound of a clash of cymbals. Or consider the serious effect of the sounds of raindrops falling and a clock ticking in a highly magnified volume as might be heard by a confused, fearful person alone in a room on a rainy night.

The same sequence of images (shot of a bus passing a car on a city street and several shots of workers paving the street) may be repeated with a different sound track on each of three repetitions — the documentary narrative that is first critical, then laudatory, then objective.

Roving circus people in their pitiful physical existence and indifference are shown camping on the bleak outskirts of a city and one of them says something to the effect that they have now reached Rome.

A woman is shown in a wedding ceremony and the sound is of her internal speech in which she shifts between reacting to immediate situations and to past events.

Images of Britain today are seen, while on the sound track we hear two voices alternating — one a narrator of a documentary at the time of World War II and the other a Winston Churchill speech.

A woman, told by her boss to deposit a large sum of money, decides to steal it. We see her driving away while on the sound track we hear an exact replication of the lines spoken by her boss telling her to deposit it. We see her again (still driving) and on the sound track hear her premonition concerning what the boss *will* say on Monday when he discovers the theft. Or, we see the woman and hear her narrating earlier events which we see in image flashbacks.

We see a retired cavalry officer standing motionless and silent, wanting to go out with a patrol leaving for a mission, and we hear the sound of departing riders singing, and quick hoofbeats — with only occasional shots of horses and singers.

The above examples of experimentation with word-image dissociation give a sense of the "audience involvement" that can result. But let us look briefly at one work of a director who has been a persistent experimenter in this area. Godard is perhaps one of the most effective investigators of word-image dissociation as a device for getting audience involvement and making artistic statements in uniquely cinematic ways. In Godard's *Vivre Sa Vie* (My Life to Live) there is much novel use of word and image that has powerful effects. The analyses of this film by two women (Beh, 1977; Sontag, 1966, 1977), though reaching different conclusions, point up how Godard's use of word and image creates spaces for the participation of one's imagination, for discomfort, and for involving the audience in completing the action.

The film uses prostitution as a metaphor for the study of a woman, or, more generally, the study of the elements of a life — the testing ground for sorting out the essential from the superfluous. The story is of Nana, whose last days are told in 12 parts (stations of the cross). There is the end of her marriage to Paul and his refusal to lend her money, the refusal of her landlady to give her the apartment key because of unpaid rent, and Nana's trying to break into movies through a phony press agent. She is arrested for pocketing 1000 francs and accidental propositioning in the street. She is seduced into professional prostitution by Raoul, her pimp. She meets Luigi and falls in love when he wards off a confrontation between Raoul and Nana when Raoul becomes hostile at Nana's trying to enter into the conversation. She decides to leave prostitution for Luigi. Raoul sells her to another syndicate of pimps and Nana is inadvertently killed in the final tradeoff scene. So much for the story. In Episode VIII we get the documentary style — one sees a "car ride" through Paris and then a rapid montage of fast cuts, shots of a dozen clients, the routines of the prostitutes' vocation in hotel rooms and on sidewalks, the handling of money in exchange for sex. At the same time one hears a dry flat voice rapidly detailing the routine, hazards, and appalling arduousness of the prostitutes' vocation and the laws and rules regulating prostitution in Paris. *The viewer is involved – has to put it together.* In Episode XII the happy banalities exchanged between Nana and her young lover are projected on the screen in the form of subtitles. The speech of love is not heard at all. *One draws on one's own experience and imagination.* In the opening credit sequence, the credits occur over a left profile view of Nana (dark, almost in silhouette), then full face, then right side, occasionally blinking and shifting her head or wetting her lips, posing uncomfortably. She is being seen. *We too are uncomfortable.* Episodes are titled. The first is "Episode I: Nana and Paul. Nana Feels Like Giving Up." The opening shot is a conversation between Nana and a man. Their backs are to us. We learn that the man (Paul) is her husband, that they have a child, that she left both of them to try to become an actress. Paul wants her back. She is revolted by him. *The sparing conversation keeps us curious, while the setting creates some discomfort.* Godard systematically deprives the viewer who is not allowed to see (backs to us, faces blurred reflections in a mirror) but only to hear. *We become involved.*

In the next-to-final episode ("The Young Man Again . . . The Oval Portrait"), Luigi reads a story from Poe ("The Oval Portrait") about an artist striving for a perfect likeness in a portrait of his wife and finally achieving it at the moment his wife dies. There is a fade out on these words to show the image sequence of Raoul forcing Nana through the courtyard of her apartment house and pushing her into a car. The transition from words (about the death of the artist's wife) to action (forcing Nana into a car) prepares us formally for Nana's death. *We are involved, curious due to the ambiguity, and must complete the scene ourselves.*

But back now to the "Oval Portrait" scene. Nana is trapped by words of the story at the same time that the camera tightens to a long take, in a close-up framing her like a painted picture. At the beginning of this episode, the scene is silent and the dialogue (Shall we go out? Why don't you move in with me?) is presented in subtitles. Then Luigi, lying on the bed, begins reading aloud from Poe's "The Oval Portrait."

In Godard's work, the function of art is sensory and conceptual dislocation. the image is emotional, immediate, and invites the spectator to identify with what is seen. The words (both heard and seen on the screen), the dialogues, signs, texts, stories, sayings, recitations, and interviews function to emotionally distance the spectator from the action and to make the spectator into a critic. This developing style, this concern with the problem of language, is a matter of form in the service of insisting on something. Language is not used by Godard for "greater realism" on the screen (which only serves for escape into the unreality of the story), but to a greater realism of involvement. Godard's experimental use of word and image forces us to see what happens in a multiplicity of ways to increase our sensibilities.[5]

Parallels between word and image relations in film and program evaluation. In all these techniques of Godard and others, one sees how discontinuities in word and image involve the audience more and get the audience to draw upon its own experience in making sense out of what is seen and/or heard — completing it in some way.

Consider the following excerpt from Stake and Easley (1978) *Case Studies in Science Education.* The excerpt is from a section of the findings with the heading "Teacher is Key."

A child learns a great deal about science out of school . . . sometimes finding surrogate teachers . . . Most children are unable to do that . . . As the student body grows smaller, the faculty grows older. Old solutions seldom fit new problems. Most teachers have trouble teaching at least a few children. (There was a strong tendency to categorize these children as Learning Disability children.) Teachers needed assistance of one kind or another. In most of our sites the inservice program was providing little aid, partly because it was anemic and aimed elsewhere, partly because the teachers paid little heed to it. Like professors in charge of preservice education, the inservice personnel we saw were seldom oriented to helping teachers solve such difficult problems as keeping the lesson going or adapting subject matter to objectives for which it was not originally prepared. The teachers were apparently sometimes more "on their own" than they wanted to be [1978, Chapter 19, p. 1, 2].

Now here is one possible use of word-image discontinuities applied to the Stake and Easley excerpt in a way to suggest different techniques for data portrayal.

1. Take some analytic scheme such as that in Gilbert's (1978) performance analysis or Brofenbrenner's (1976) experimental ecology of education and identify the key deficiencies in programs. Some structure is necessary here to identify forms that will have some redundancy and will illuminate what is happening. For example:

   • Inservice trainers get a negative *balance of consequences* from teachers.

   • Inservice training *goals* are not directed toward teacher needs.

   • Teachers want *"guidance"* or "modeling" or support systems.

   • Student understanding of science is influenced by a nested arrangement of *environmental structures* at successive levels from the immediate setting containing the learner (classroom) to family, community, and overarching institutions of the culture (macro-systems).

2. Collect the data *across sites* that support the statement, "In most of our sites the inservice program was providing little aid." (This gets at the redundancies of the forms identified.)

3. Summarize the variety of situations (sites, teachers, subjects) in which teachers "look for" help and get something unrelated.

4. Portray the data as follows. Film teachers looking for help and getting inservice unrelated. Along with visual display of film, use minimal subtitles or a documentary low key rapid voice detailing the problem, but not describing the specific thing

being seen. The same thing could be done in print (summary of data — a few words telling about it). Occasionally, make a fast cut to another situation which by association is related to this portrayal (e.g., a gardener clears rocks from an area and comes back to find them replaced).

This kind of presentation will not only show how the situation is what it is but will stimulate viewer (reader) involvement because the text is not directing every thought or everything to look at or to conclude. The case study approach used by Stake and Easley yields rich material, but reader involvement must be aided by some such device as suggested here.

Other Perspectives

There is no way I can cover the infinite number of perspectives on program evaluation one might gain from literary criticism.[6] The *Princeton Encyclopedia of Poetry and Poetics* provides a convenient source for other perspectives. Similar works in literature, film, and drama could provide additional ones. There are a few perspectives, however, that I would like to highlight as worth exploration. The work on genres (Frye, 1957; Van Ghent, 1953) gives one a sense of structures that need not be used as guides to writing but provide discriminations for analysis. The literature on negative influence of audience from the poet's perspective (Dickey, 1964, p. 10; 1970; Shapiro, 1953, pp. 71-72) suggests obstacles for any writer, even the program evaluator. The work of poets on the purpose of poems (Eliot, 1950, pp. 12-14; Shapiro, 1953, pp. 43, 64, 65; Dickey, 1964, pp. 9, 10; Thomas, 1961, p. 3; and Ciardi, 1963) suggests what may well be the purpose of any writer (scientist, technologist, news reporter) — to make writing an art (that is, moved from within by integrity and craftsmanship). The poets have also written on the positive influences of the audience (Dickey, 1970). Studies of criticism by one's audience, in the sense of reader response to a work, are increasing and provide highly useful perspectives for the program evaluator (Richards, 1929; Squire, 1964; Purves & Beach, 1972; Terry, 1974; Odell & Cooper, 1976). They have implications for the question "Who is the audience?" as well as for revision of a work. As for revision itself, see Della-Piana (1978a). Finally, the work on criticism in theater and film is rich with perspectives. A performer interprets and illuminates a text and is thus a "literary critic." The work of the director of theater or film provides probably the most useful perspective. The style of a work comes, finally, from the director. Since the cinema provides a permanent record of the work of the director and the greatest possibilities for experimentation, it is here that I would go for the most thorough immersion, in works such as Arnheim (1957), Bazin (1967), Braudy & Dickstein (1978), Eisenstein (1957), Kracauer (1960), Mast (1977), Metz (1944), Monaco (1977), and Nichols (1976).

Starting Points

What would be the best starting point for obtaining perspectives and techniques of literary criticism from which to approach the tasks of program evaluation and the criticism of program evaluation? For me, the answer at this time is *immersion* in the criticism of fiction, film, and poetry by someone experienced in the theory, method, and practice of program evaluation. By immersion, I mean doing this kind of criticism for a significant period of time — at the minimum, two years. And by doing it I mean performing literary, poetic, and film criticism from the major perspective of this chapter (criticism as sensitization through the illumination of form and style) and perhaps using one or more of the methods illustrating this perspective. If I were to pick one medium I would pick the criticism of film for the reasons hinted at in this chapter. That's all there is to it, except to return from poetic heights to the wordless world and make things happen — learn how to sing. For, like e.e. cummings, "I'd rather learn from one bird how to sing, than teach ten thousand stars how not to dance."

Notes

[1] Film is often the performance of a text, although some films are made from minimal scripts and are worthy of analysis as "texts" in themselves. See E. Panofsky (1947) for a discussion of how early films were made (with minimal scripts) as well as for one of the earliest insightful pieces on the aesthetics of film. Elsewhere (and I cannot remember where) I have read that many of the early silent comedies were created using minimal scripts. For example, there is the classic cafeteria-restaurant scene in which the comic (was it Keaton?) walks past the hatrack and "bouncer" with hat on. The scene was set up with instructions for the hat to be taken off by the bouncer. The rest developed through improvisation. The comic walks by, the bouncer takes the hat off him and puts it on the rack. The comic circles and picks up his hat, repeating the same thing a couple more times. Finally, the comic walks by the hat rack, takes off his own, puts on someone else's hat, and when the bouncer takes the hat off, the comic puts on his own hat and proceeds down the line.

[2] For a sense of historical context, I have examined the work of Hall (1963), Hyman (1952), Preminger (1974), Wellek and Warren(1956) and Wimsatt and Brooks (1957). It would be impossible here to do justice to a review of the history of literary criticism, even in the western hemisphere. One also wonders what different perspectives would have been sifted out with a broader cultural look. Thus, how would we deal with the song in honor of a Chippewa brave (Preminger, 1974, p. 20), consisting of only two words — one meaning warrior and the other the name of the hero? Since people knew of the valiant deeds, it was not necessary to mention one of them. What I have done is obtain some sense of history and select two divergent perspectives which in my judgment are the key polarities in the business of literary criticism. I choose my own perspective because it is more manageable and because it is what I feel is most needed today.

[3] The perspective of this chapter is related to the approach to evaluation which Eisner (1977) calls "evaluation as connoisseurship and criticism." For Eisner *connoisseurship is the art of appreciation and criticism is the art of disclosure*. More specifically, connoisseurship is the art of discerning the characteristics and qualities of whatever work (object, event) one has encountered. This discernment, says Eisner, requires an understanding of past forms, attention to the formal qualities of the work, understanding of ideas that gave rise to the work, understanding of the sociocultural context in which the artist worked and the sources from which the artist drew, and the influence of the work upon the work of others. Criticism is the art of rendering in linguistic terms (or, I presume, film, visual displays, and the like) what it is that one has encountered so that others not possessing the same level of connoisseurship can also experience the characteristics and quality of the work. *Applied to the classroom,* criticism is the art of saying what is going on. The task is to provide a vivid rendering replete with metaphor, contrast, redundancy, and emphases so that others may see what transpires and experience the quality and character of the educational life so represented.

At the level of general perspective, the present work has much in common with Eisner's approach. However, where I speak of criticism as the illumination of form and style in a work, Eisner would say "recognition and disclosure," and that is, of course, what I intend. Also, my limited focus is no doubt only an instance of the general perspective taken by Eisner — an instance which I argue is the most fruitful perspective to be taken from literary criticism and perhaps the most needful for our time. Finally, the detailed methods (or strategies and techniques) illustrated here for making use of the perspective are, I believe, largely unexploited in the evaluation literature.

[4] For an excellent introduction to film technique, see Bordwell and Thompson (1979). Here you will find illustrations, descriptions, and functional analyses of the shot or mise-en-scene (what is "put into the scene" of one frame), cinematography (the speed, perspective, framing, or duration of the shot), editing (the coordination of one shot with the next in ways that are spatially, rhythmically, meaningfully, or otherwise continuous or discontinuous), and sound (speech, music, sound effects and how they are related to the image, how faithful to the perceived source, whether off screen or on, and whether occurring simultaneously with story action or not). Excellent references for further study are included.

[5] It was after final typing of this chapter that I came across Susan Sontag's *On Photography* (1977). I had been searching for material on word-image dissociation that was not tied to *moving* pictures, and there was Sontag on photography. She refers

(1977, p. 72) to Michael Lesy's *Wisconsin Death Trip* (New York: Pantheon Books, 1973). Lesy's book is a portrait of a rural county in Wisconsin between 1890 and 1910. He juxtaposes photographs of the time with quotations from newspapers, medical records from the state mental institution, words from a novelist, and two mythical voices (a local historian and a local gossip). The method, as Sontag notes, is that of "quotations which have nothing to do with the photographs but are correlated with them in an aleatoric intuitive way, as words and sounds are matched at the time of performance with the dance movements already choreographed by Merce Cunningham" (1977, p. 73). Actually, I believe Cunningham's method is more of chance juxtaposition, except that his selection of composers was not accident. The photographs by Charles Van Schaick (a commercial photographer in the county) had been preserved by the State Historical Society of Wisconsin stored as glass negatives. The effect is certainly to involve the reader-viewer much as Godard's method does. As Warren Susman notes in his preface to Lesy's work, it

> has shaped the structure of those aspects of the Wisconsin experience of the 1890s that he has selected in such a way that we can never look at our past as before, but rather are now forced to raise questions: about the fascination with death and the morbid, with suicide and murder, about consciousness of decline and degeneracy, about attitudes toward sex and family [Lesy, 1973, preface].

I recommend reading Sontag with Lesy — especially her sensitive discussion of the power of images with respect to our sense of reality and the possibilities of social change being replaced by a change in images (pp. 68-82 and 153-180). For what is easy to forget is that the illumination gained by representations of reality can influence us to attribute to real things the qualities of an image. In a restaurant a few days ago, champagne popping and foaming over the guests brought a loud response from an adjacent table, "just like the movies!" Thus the representation of reality can become the perspective by which we see reality. This is not all bad (see Moffet & Wagner, 1976, p. 461, 462). Using methods of juxtaposing images and images or images and words in ways that draw out and direct our subjective responses does not lead to the highest level of experiencing or the highest stage of growth, but it is a necessary stage. Discouraging the subjectivity, forcing it out too soon or too far only sets us up for finding an outlet for subjective responses some other time and some other way, sometimes not so felicitous. It is being able to have the best of both worlds that should guide and moderate our investigations into the subjective experiencing enhanced by methods investigated by Lesy and Godard. It is being able to do logical, analytic investigations of reality as well as intuitive subjective ones and being able to fuse in a moment "self with world, one thing with another" and to come back into the nonverbal world of here, me, and you that should be our guiding image.

    [6] For a different treatment of evaluation from the perspective of literary criticism, see Kelly (1975). Kelly deals well with a problem I have dealt with only lightly — the problem of making judgments of worth. My position is that literature (and program evaluation) is of worth if it meets the criterion Dickey states:

> One thing is certain, if the reader does not, through the writing, gain a new, intimate, and vital perspective on his own life as a human being, there is no poem

at all, or only a poem written by a collective entity called Modern Poetry, Period 1945-1960. . . . What matters is that there be some real response to poems [Dickey, 1964, pp. 9-10].

I put it a bit differently. For me, one decides if a piece of literature (or a program evaluation) is of worth using Dickey's criterion, or at least my own version of it. Then, if it is of worth (my subjective judgment), it is worth criticism. And the criticism I recommend is to illuminate the *forms* of the work so others can see *how* it is what it is, and perhaps even so it will come alive for them more and have more meaning than it otherwise would. Again, I do not argue for this as the only useful perspective from literary criticism nor as the only kind of evaluation criticism I would recommend. It is simply a much-needed kind of evaluation criticism and a much-needed guide to evaluation itself. Kelly provides an excellent illustration of the impossibility of describing or explicating without interpretation and judgment. And he also discusses "the range and number of problems involved in making judgments of worth and . . . some practical guides for the curriculum evaluator to use when he encounters them" (1975, p. 98). He treats problems of description, the justification of judgments (do they meet a particular norm and are the norms appropriate?), and credibility. These are valuable contributions that go beyond what I have attempted but which are complementary to the work presented here.

References

Agee, J. *Agee on film, Vol. 1: Criticism.* New York: Grosset, 1969.

Arnheim, R. *Film as art.* Berkeley: University of California Press, 1957.

Auerbach, E. *Mimesis: The representation of reality in western literature.* Princeton: Princeton University Press, 1953.

Bazin, A. *What is cinema?* Berkeley: University of California Press, 1967.

Beh, S. H. Vivre sa vie. In B. Nichols (Ed.), *Movies and methods.* Berkeley: University of California Press, 1977, Pp. 180-185.

Bordwell, D., & Thompson, K. *Film art: An introduction.* Reading, MA: Addison-Wesley, 1979.

Braudy. L., & Dickstein, M. *Great film directors: A critical anthology.* New York: Oxford University Press, 1978.

Brend, R. (Ed.) *Kenneth L. Pike, selected writings.* The Hague: Mouton, 1972.

Brend, R., & Pike, K.L. (Eds.). *Tagmemics: Aspects of the field, vol. 1.* The Hague: Mouton, 1976.

Bronfenbrenner, U. The experimental ecology of education. *Teacher's College Record,* 1976, 78, 157-204.

Burke, K. A grammar of motives. Berkeley: University of California Press, 1962.

Ciardi, J. *Dialogue with an audience.* New York: Lippincott, 1963.

Davison, N. *Sound patterns in a poem of Jòsé Marti.* Salt Lake City, UT: Damuir Press, 1975.

Della-Piana, G. Research strategies for the study of revision process in writing poetry. In C. R. Cooper & L. Odell (Eds.), *Research on composing: Points of departure.* Urbana, IL: National Council of Teachers of English, 1978. (a)

Della-Piana, G. Comprehension of written text: Alternative mastery models. Unpublished manuscript. Salt Lake City, Utah: Bureau of Educational Research, University of Utah, 1978. (b)

Della-Piana, G. & Endo, G. T. *Toward third stream evaluation.* Paper presented at the meeting of the American Educational Research Association annual meeting, New York 1977. (Available from the Bureau of Educational Research, University of Utah, Salt Lake City, UT 84112.)

Dickey, J. *The suspect in poetry.* Madison, MN: Odin House, 1964.

Dickey, J. *Self interviews.* New York: Dell, 1970.

Eisenstein, S. *Film form and the film sense.* Cleveland, OH: World, 1957.

Eisner, E. W. On the uses of educational connoisseurship and criticism for evaluating classroom life. *Teacher's College Record,* 1977, 78, 345-358.

Eliot, T. S. *Selected essays.* New York: Harcourt Brace, Jovanovich, 1950.

Empson, W. *Seven types of ambiguity.* New York: New Directions, 1966.

Erickson, B. H., & Nosanchuk, T. A. *Understanding data.* Toronto: McGraw-Hill Ryerson Limited, 1977.

Frye, N. *Anatomy of criticism: Four essays.* Princeton: Princeton University Press, 1957.

Gilbert, T. F. *Human competence: Engineering worthy performance.* New York: McGraw-Hill, 1978.

Glass, G. V & Smith, M. L. Reply to Eysenck. In T. D. Cook et al. (Eds.), *Evaluation studies review annual, vol. 3.* Beverly Hills, CA: Sage, 1978. Pp. 698-699.

Hall, V. H., Jr. *A short history of literary criticism.* New York: New York University Press, 1963.

Henderson. B. Toward a non-bourgeois camera style. In B. Nichols (Ed.), *Movies and methods.* Berkeley: University of California Press, 1976. Pp. 422-438.

House, E. R., Glass, G. V, McLean, L. D., & Walker, D. F. No simple answer: Critique of the Follow Through evaluation. *Harvard Educational Review,* 1978, 48, 128-160.

Hyman, S. E. *The armed vision.* New York: Alfred A. Knopf, 1952.

Illich, I. *Tools for conviviality.* New York: Harper & Row, 1973.

Jarrell, R. *The third book of criticism.* New York: Farrar, Straus and Giroux, 1965.

Kael, P. *The Citizen Kane book.* New York: Bantam, 1974.

Kelly, E. F. Curriculum evaluation and literary criticism: comments on the analogy. *Curriculum Theory Network,* 1975, 5, 87-106.

Kracauer, S. *Theory of film: The redemption of physical reality.* New York: Oxford University Press, 1960.

Mast, G. *Film/cinema/movie: A theory of experience.* New York: Harper & Row, 1977.

Metz, C. *Film language: A semiotics of the cinema.* New York: Oxford University Press, 1974.

Moews, D. *Keaton: The silent features close up.* Berkeley: University of California Press, 1977.

Moffett, J., & Wagner, B. J. *Student-centered language arts and reading, K-13: A handbook for teachers.* Boston: Houghton Mifflin, 1976.

Monaco, J. *How to read a film.* New York: Oxford University Press, 1977.

Nichols, B. (Ed.). *Movies and methods.* Berkeley: University of California Press, 1977.

Odell, L., & Cooper, C. R. Describing responses to works of fiction. *Research in the teaching of English*, 1976, 10, 203-225.

Ogle, P. Deep-focus cinematography: A technological/aesthetic history. *Filmmaker's Newsletter*, May 1971, 19-33.

Panofsky, E. Style and medium in the motion pictures. *Critique: A Review of Contemporary Art*, 1947, 1, 5-28.

Pike, K. L. Discourse analysis and Tagmeme metrices. *Oceania Linguistics*, 1964, 3.1, 5-25. (a)

Pike, K. L. Beyond the sentence. *College Composition and Communication*, 1964, 15, 129-135. (b)

Pike, K. L. *Language in relation to a unified theory of the structure of human behavior*. The Hague: Mouton, 1967.

Preminger, A. (Ed.). *Princeton encyclopedia of poetry and poetics*. Princeton: Princeton University Press, 1974.

Prickard, A. O. (trans.). *Longinus on the sublime*. Oxford: Oxford University Press, 1926.

Purves, A. C., & Beach, R. *Literature and the reader*. Urbana, IL: National Council of Teachers of English, 1972.

Richards, I. A. *Practical criticism*. New York: Harcourt Brace Jovanovich, 1929.

Richards, I. A. (Ed.). *The portable Coleridge*. New York: Viking Press, 1969.

Shapiro, K. *A primer for poets*. Lincoln: University of Nebraska Press, 1953.

Sloane, R. B., Staples, R. F., Cristol, A. H., Yorkston, N. J., & Whipple, K. *Psychotherapy versus behavior therapy*. Cambridge, MA: Harvard University Press, 1975.

Smith, M. L., & Glass, G. V Meta-analysis of psychotherapy outcome studies. In T. D. Cook et al. (Eds.), *Evaluation studies review annual, vol. 3*, Beverly Hills, CA: Sage. Pp. 684-692.

Sontag, S. Godard. In B. Nichols (Ed.), *Movies and methods*. Berkeley: University of California Press, 1977. Pp. 370-389.

Sontag, S. *Against interpretation*. New York: Delta, 1966.

Squire, J. F. *The responses of adolescents while reading four short stories*. Urbana, IL: National Council of Teachers of English, 1964.

Stake, R., & Easley, J. A., Jr. *Case studies in science education*. Champaign, IL: Center for Instructional Research and Curriculum Evaluation, January 1978.

Stebbins, L. B., St. Pierre, R. G., Proper, E. C., Anderson, R. B., & Cerva, T. R. *Education as experimentation: A planned variation model, Volume IV-A, an evaluation of Follow Through*. Cambridge, MA: Abt Associates, 1977.

Terry, A. *Children's poetry preferences*. Urbana, IL: National Council of Teachers of English, 1974.

Thomas, D. Poetic manifesto. *The Texas Quarterly*, 1961, 4, 45-53.

Tukey, J. W. *Exploratory data analysis*. New York: Addison-Wesley, 1977.

Van Ghent, D. *The English novel*. New York: Holt, Rinehart & Winston, 1953.

Welleck, R., & Warren, A. *A theory of literature*. New York: Harcourt Brace Jovanovich, 1956.

Wimsatt, W. K., Jr., & Brooks, C. *Literary criticism*. New York: Alfred A. Knopf, 1957.

William J. Gephart
Independent Consultant, Bloomington, Indiana

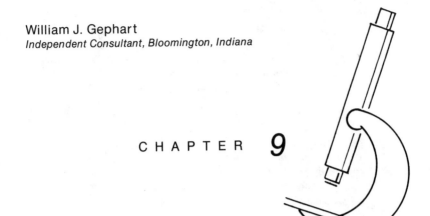

CHAPTER 9

Watercolor Painting

William Gephart has invested 27 years in the study of painting. For the past 20 years he has worked almost exclusively with watercolors. His paintings are in public and private collections in seven countries. He has had several one-man shows and has participated in numerous group shows, his paintings having been displayed in galleries in Florida, South Carolina, Kentucky, Indiana, and Michigan. Dr. Gephart has been making contributions to the understanding of the evaluation process for 15 years through co-authorship with Daniel Stufflebeam and five others of Educational Evaluation and Decision Making *(F.E. Peacock, 1971); as editor of Phi Delta Kappa's CEDR* Quarterly; *as founder and co-director of the National Symposia for Professionals in Evaluation and Research (NSPER); and as founder and past-president of the Evaluation Network.*

CAREFUL EXAMINATION of what I do and what I need to know to paint a representational watercolor painting has pinpointed a number of ways in which painting, used metaphorically, leads me to insights about the evaluation process. I hope that in the discussion which follows I can share those insights with you, the reader.

(1) Both painting and evaluating are processes. That is, ideas, materials, and activities are brought together to paint a picture and to evaluate a program, product, or performance.

(2) Both painting and evaluation result in a product that is a representation of something. Painting (at least representational watercolor work) produces a two-dimensional representation of some object or objects. Evaluation produces a verbal representation of the worth of some program, product, or performance.

(3) Both painting and evaluation, if done well, involve the use of cognitive knowledge, affect, and psychomotor skills.

(4) Both painting and evaluating frequently require knowledge about and use of problem-solving techniques. Painters frequently have to engage in exploration in order to produce a desired visual effect necessary for accurate two-dimensional representation of some subject matter. Evaluators often encounter situations in which procedures for determining some facet of the worth of a program, product, or performance do not exist. Such instances require the evaluator to employ problem-solving procedures.

(5) Both painting and evaluating are purposive activities. That is, they are engaged in deliberately.

(6) Both painting and evaluating can serve many purposes. Paintings have been done to record the image of something or someone (portrait painting, a painting of the crucifixion of Christ, and a picture of the assault of the Normandy beaches on D-Day are illustrative), to entertain (a Norman Rockwell view of the old swimmin' hole), to decorate, to communicate a message. Painting sometimes serves recreational and/or therapeutic purposes. The purposes served by evaluation are sometimes proactive, sometimes post hoc, and sometimes pro forma. That is, we sometimes want to know the relative worth of each of the options being considered in a decision to be made at some particular time in the future (e.g., Which reading series shall we purchase for next year? Should we build more buildings or move to a year-around program?) At other times we want to know if we got full value for our investment (the accountability question), and sometimes we engage in evaluation because it is mandated by a funding agency.

(7) Both painting and evaluating can be (and are sometimes) done very unsystematically. Painters sometimes approach a surface to be painted with little or no idea as to the nature of the end product. At other times an end product is in mind, but the sequence of activities to be carried out, techniques to be employed, or materials to be used have not been thought through. Evaluators sometimes follow the same pattern; that is, their works are carried out with little thought about the product needed at the end of the evaluation. At other times the general character of the evaluation report is in

mind, but little or no advanced consideration is given to the activities and/or materials needed to get that report.

(8) Both paintings and evaluations can be critiqued. Criteria can be listed which can be used to determine the quality of a painting. This qualitative analysis can be performed from a chronological perspective or as a composition and rendering, irrespective of time and context. Criteria can be listed to determine the quality of an evaluation, meta-evaluation. Further, both evaluations and paintings can be critiqued by the person who did them and by others.

The material which follows is an effort to detail the process of doing a watercolor painting and to examine the elements of that process for insights into the nature of the evaluation process. My analysis of the painting process rests on 25 years of painting experience and extensive study of the approaches used by widely known watercolorists such as Kautsky (1963), Pike (1973, 1978), Whitney (1974), Pellew (1978), Barbour (1975), Szabo (1971, 1977), Croney (1973), and Schlemm (1978), and Schmalz's work (1978) on the art of critiquing one's own paintings. The often-stated caveat holds. The credit for the useful ideas in what follows should be given to those author-artists. I accept the responsibility for any confusion, illogic, or error. (For those interested, an extended bibliography appears at the end of this chapter.)

Watercolor Painting

Before describing the relationships between watercolor painting and evaluation, two ideas need to be discussed. First, as Pike (1978) so clearly says, there are many ways to paint a watercolor. What follows is not *the* way to paint with watercolors. Rather, it is *a* way and one that is generally effective for me. This does not mean that my approach lacks generalizability. It may be effective for others completely or partly. It does mean that what is described as my approach to watercolor is something I "found" through my 25 years of painting successes and failures. Sometimes those failures were due to the fact that I had not mastered certain skills and knowledge, items that are crucial if a person is going to make this approach work. For example, when a brush loaded with water and pigment is applied to a sheet of watercolor it will leave on the paper a brilliant area of the color deposited by that pigment. Ten to fifteen minutes later the water deposited with the pigment will have evaporated, and the color will be less intense — it will look lighter or fainter. All watercolor pigments do this, but they do not all do it to the same degree. "Okay," you say, "so you may have to go over a section until you get the intensity you want." Wrong! Part of the inherent beauty of a watercolor painting is the transparency of the medium. Unlike oil or acrylic paintings, light passes through watercolor and reflects from the paper on which the pigment is adhered by gum arabic. By contrast, light reflects off oil and acrylic paint. Going back over a segment of your painting until you get the intensity that you want risks coating the watercolor paper with so much pigment that it becomes opaque at that spot. Thus, at that spot you have caused a different type of light transmission that helps make the eye process that spot differently — a spot that visually is out of place with the rest of the picture. You don't correct for this. You learn to do it right through practice, practice, practice. Use a color and watch how much it will fade when it dries. Try it again and again, till you feel you are sensing the amount of compensation needed. Then on a practice sheet put down a swatch of color and let it dry. Then mix some more of the same color and brush the second batch right next to the first. Does it work? Does it match? Cheers. But, practice, practice, and practice more until it becomes a natural reflex. So, painting with watercolor requires a good deal of work with the medium before a person can feel that his or her approach works consistently.

Defining Evaluation

The second idea that seems needed before proceeding to a discussion of watercolor painting and evaluation is the meaning of the term "evaluation." It is easy to find what look like conflicting definitions of the term. If the reader does not understand the definition being used in this discussion, it will be easy to reject what may be very useful insights about evaluation from the metaphoric analysis of painting.

I choose the stance of Cady (1967) to structure a definition of evaluation. Cady indicates that the definition of a complex entity cannot be accomplished through a single phrase or sentence, or even through a brief paragraph. Such an effort to define loads so much meaning on a term that most of it is hidden.

A further roadblock, according to Cady, is the fact that we have a half-dozen different ways to define, and most of us fall into the habit of using only one of them. Some people prefer to define ostensibly. They will point to or show you an instance of the entity being defined and, having done so, assume that we mean the same thing when we refer to the entity in subsequent discourse. Another person may habitually use operational definitions. (Some of my most respected empiricist friends fall into this category, and I, too, often do likewise.) They want to know, "How does it work?" There is a good deal of Rube Goldberg in those of us who use operational definitions exclusively. Look at the battle shaping up. To the "operational definer," the "point-to-it" definition does not do much good at all, and vice versa.

To complicate things still further, enter another person into the discussion who has over the years adopted a what-is-it-made-of approach to defining. We can point to an automobile and describe how it works and still have arguments from this third party about our definition. The what-is-it-made-of definer's needs usually are not met by showing an instance of the thing we are interested in, nor by showing how it works.

Cady describes three more evaluation strategies: synonym and antonym usage, classificatory, and comparative. The first of these three definitional approaches appears easiest; the simple substitution of one word for another. Unfortunately, few words are exact representatives for other words. Their context and affective loading often contribute more confusion than illumination regarding the term being defined. Comparative evaluation involves (1) identifying terms closely related to the term being defined and (2) determining the ways the chosen terms are alike and different. An illustration of comparative definition can be seen in efforts to define the term "reading." Listening, speaking, and writing are related activities. They, along with reading, focus on the transmission of coded messages. Reading is like listening because they both involve receiving and decoding a message. They are different in that reading involves messages that are visually encoded, while in listening the messages are orally encoded. Reading is like writing because they both involve the transmission of visually encoded messages. Reading and writing differ in that reading is the decoding of such messages, while writing is the encoding of messages.

Classificatory definitions attempt to show where and how the thing being defined fits into the grand scheme of things. Again, an illustration is useful. We can define a city court by stating that it is a unit of our judicial system which deals with a prescribed type of legal case, and that its decisions can be appealed through a hierarchy of courts.

Cady is persuasive, at least to me. To define the term "evaluation" in a way that will help one apprehend its meaning requires the use of all six definitional approaches. The meaning of the term is incomplete otherwise. Cady also calls for the analysis of term use if we would apprehend all the meanings of the term. For example, sometimes evaluation is a noun and at other times evaluation is a verb. We refer to doing it as evaluating and to getting or having a product as "an evaluation." We may switch back and forth, often unconsciously, between these uses so that meaning is obfuscated.

Evaluation Defined

The use of Cady's definitional approaches leads to the following definition of evaluation.

Classificatory definition. Educational evaluation is a problem-solving strategy. It is employed when educators or education's policy makers have the responsibility for making a choice and when the relative or absolute worth of each of the options in that choice is not known by the choice maker(s). Educational evaluation fits in the education enterprise in several ways and places. It is an activity that can be used to make informed choices about (1) goals schools are to accomplish; (2) procedures to be used to achieve a selected goal; (3) options in the implementation of a selected procedure; and (4) steps to be taken given data on the results of such an implementation. In some cases, educational evaluation is carried out in a systematic manner. In other cases, evaluation is subjective. The concern here is for those instances in which evaluation is systematic and replicable.

Comparative definition. Educational evaluation is similar to, but at the same time different from, educational research, educational design and development, and educational administration. Each of these are systematic, problem-solving strategies. As such, they are variants of the scientific method. As such, each is a purposive activity organized in ways designed to reduce bias as much as possible. To do so, all of these purposive activities focus on the collection and use of objective data. These systematic problem-solving processes differ, first, in the nature of the problem for which they are the most efficient solution startegy. A problem, in the language of scientific method, is a combination of an intention and one or more barriers to the realization of that intent. Research problems are intentions to know in a generalizable or theoretical way, intentions that are blocked by either the fact that the item we intend to know has never been investigated systematically or the fact that those investigations that have been done are inconclusive. Evaluation problems exist when we intend to make a choice and we do not know the relative value of the competing options. Development problems exist when our intent is to carry out some activity and we do not have the tools or procedures that will do the amount or quality of work we intend. The operational systems for resolving these different intention-barrier combinations differ. A single process cannot be equally efficient for different purposes.

Operational definition. An evaluation starts with the definition of the decision — that is, the listing of the options to be considered and the variables that will be used to determine the value of those options. Next, the evaluator plans how the information which describes each of the options on each of the variables will be or might be collected. This plan should be approved by the individuals who will make the decision.

Once the evaluative plan is set, the evaluator carries it out so that the data needed to create the specified information are generated. Those data are analyzed and interpreted and a report is submitted to the evaluation client which attempts to describe the relative (and possibly the absolute) worth of each of the choices on each of the relevant variables. In some cases, the evaluator interprets that report and helps the decision maker use the information.

Componential evaluation. The evaluation process includes a problem, a situation in which there is a need to make a choice among several options that are deemed complex and important enough to merit the systematic collection of data on the relative or absolute worth of the options in that choice-making situation. Evaluation includes a setting in which a choice is going to be made, a setting which is structured by a set of values held by the people in that setting. It also includes a time frame within which the decision is to be made. And it includes a body of knowledge, some of which focuses on the options in the choice to be made and some of which focuses on ways of generating useful information about the worth of each of those options. An evaluation includes people — people who are going to make a choice and people who will generate worth descriptions of the options in those choices. Sometimes the same person plays both of these roles; sometimes the roles are played by different people. Evaluation has a technical component, the generating and interpreting of data. Included here are a wide range of measurement and analysis procedures for generating and/or aggregating data. The technical component also includes the procedures (statistical and others) for analyzing and interpreting the data. Finally, evaluation includes reporting, the transfer of the information developed by the evaluator to the people who will select one option or some combination of the options as the choice.

Ostensive definition. It is difficult to define ostensibly (to "point to" an instance of evaluation) in a written paper. In lieu of that, a couple of brief illustrations are presented.

A short while ago the dishwasher in my kitchen expired. After a brief period of mourning, my wife and I agreed we had a decision to make. What make and model of dishwasher should we purchase as a replacement? (Obviously there was a prior decision — should we or should we not replace it? And, just as obviously, we knew the relative worth of those two options beyond a shadow of doubt.) We used some readily available sources to obtain information about the brands of dishwashers available and the different models. We obtained information on price and on the operational specifications of the various models, their malfunction and repair data. We talked with friends about their experience and satisfaction with the different models. And we sat down with that information and made a choice of brand X and model Y. The delineation of our options and the collection and interpretation of the data on those options was evaluation.

A second illustration. When the "empty nest" syndrome encroached on our family, Mother began searching for ways of restructuring the use of her time. She learned of the range of options through reading, discussions with others, interviewing for specific positions, and through relatively short-term trials of some of the options. In that investigation, she gauged the pros and cons, the costs and benefits of the different possibilities. This analysis led to a decision to enter a master's degree program to prepare for work as a counselor. Again, what she did in determining the range of options and in collecting and weighing a variety of information about the value of those options to herself and others was an instance of evaluation.

Synonym and antonym definition. The dictionary lists judgment, appraisal, rating, and interpretation as synonyms of evaluation. These synonyms provide some general, but incomplete, idea of the meaning of evaluation, as indicated in the discussion below. In discussions of the nature of educational evaluation, some have argued that evaluation is not complete until a judgment has been reached. Others argue that evaluation is the activity that leads to, but stops short of, judgment. Appraisal is defined (*Webster's Third New International Dictionary,* 1969) as "an act of estimating or evaluating (as quality, status, or character) especially by one fitted to judge." The use of the word "evaluating" in the definition of appraisal reduces the utility of this synonym in understanding the meaning of evaluation. Among the definitions of rating is "a relative estimate or evaluation (as of status, achievement, or appeal)." Again, the presence of evaluation in the explanation of the synonym is troublesome. Definitions of interpretation include "activity directed toward the enlightenment of the public concerning the significance of the work or a public service or agency."

Legitimate antonyms for the term "evaluation" are elusive. In normal usage evaluation seems to be a positive term, a reference to something. As such, it has no natural opposite. Thus, a search for antonyms to aid in comprehending the nature of evaluation seems of little utility.

These definitions, taken together, form the concept of evaluation that guides the remainder of this presentation. This concept is not my creation. Rather, it is a synthesis of the ideas of many who have studied the evaluation process. They deserve the credit for its positive aspects. The writer accepts responsibility for its inadequacies and/or shortcomings.

Watercolor Painting and Educational Evaluation

The painting of a representational watercolor has six general phases: selecting a subject, creating a composition or design, preparing to paint, rendering, critiquing, and finishing. These phases to some extent overlap, and the decisions made and/or actions taken in one of them materially affects the product, the finished painting. Before describing these phases, it would be useful to discuss some of the characteristics or principles of watercolor painting.

Watercolor painting is usually done on paper. The medium is a mixture of particles of pigments and gum arabic, a mixture that is soluble in water. The paper that is used comes in various weights, surfaces, and materials. The lighter-weight papers cause problems. When lightweight paper gets wet, it usually ripples. And, since water easily flows downhill, trying to get color to stay on top of one of the ripples is virtually impossible, regardless of the painter's skill and experience. Most watercolor painters use heavy papers that do not ripple when wet.

Watercolor is a transparent medium. This means light passes through the pigment and is reflected by the paper. As it passes through the pigment deposited on the paper, many delightful visual effects can be obtained.

This transparency points to another unique characteristic of watercolor painting — there is no transparent white pigment. The white you see in a watercolor painting is the bare paper. This creates a planning and procedural constraint on the watercolor painter. It is difficult to remove pigment from a particular spot on a painting. Therefore, the watercolor painter *must* plan ahead and proceed in ways so that the white spaces in the finished painting are reserved from the outset. Some people use an opaque white paint to add white spots after other color has been put down. The true watercolorist eschews this approach. Opaque white adheres to the paper differently than does the transparent pigment. Thus, the opaque white additions all too often look like blobs added to the painting after the fact.

The painting of a watercolor involves the dilution of pigment with varying amounts of water and the application of that mixture in the appropriate places in the composition. The water then evaporates and the gum arabic adheres the pigment to the paper. But gum arabic is not a strong adhesive; the pigment can be scraped off, erased, moved by dragging a hand, brush, rag, or almost anything else over it. This is another of the watercolor medium's peculiarities that leads many would-be painters to conclude that it is too hard a medium to work with. This causes problems when a glaze of one color is put down and the artist wants to run another glaze over the same spot. If this is not done with care (light brush strokes), the second glazing will move the pigments of the first. Repeat this a couple of times, and a dull, muddy-looking spot will be created.

Watercolor can be applied to a paper when the paper is wet or dry. Most beginners assume that this is a dichotomy, that paper is wet *or* dry. But here is another of the peculiar characteristics of this medium that makes all but the very persistent give up early: paper can be bone dry, slightly damp, wet, running wet, or any stage in between. The importance of this concept is that the pigment does different things with differing wetnesses of the surface. For example, consider paper that is so wet that water is standing on the surface. If a brush full of pigment is dragged over this wet surface, the pigment will be affected by capillary action and/or gravity. The added pigment will spread, or if the surface is tipped the color will run downhill.

The same paper a few minutes later will appear dull, because some of the water has soaked into the fibers and the rest has evaporated. Now the surface looks dry, but it isn't. Try touching it with the back of your hand. It will feel cool. A brush full of pigment dragged over this still damp paper will spread some — not as much as when the paper is soaking wet, but some. And as the paper gets dryer there will be less and less spreading of the pigment of a brush stroke. This knowledge, cognitive knowledge, is an absolute necessity if a watercolorist wants to represent, for example, the subtle diffusion of color in a ripple of water approaching the shore of a lake or the gradual shading of color on the unlit side of a cloud.

These thoughts preface one of the rules that must be known thoroughly if a person wants to enjoy a modicum of success as a watercolor painter. If you want sharp demarcation between two colors, the paper must be dry. If you want gradual diffusion of one color into another, the paper needs to be wet. That is immutable; if you want sharp change from one color to another, the paper *cannot* be wet. You have to wait until the surface where that abrupt change is to be is completely dry.

Much more could and should be said about the principles and characteristics of watercolor painting. And there are numerous wellwritten, finely illustrated books on the topic (see the list of references). But what does this lengthy list have to do with educational evaluation? The need to know a vast amount of technical information and the knowledge of how that stuff fits together are common to both the evaluation process and the painting process. In both cases, a person can proceed without much knowledge of the basic principles and characteristics. People evaluate. Many times they do it without a fund of knowledge about the systematic evaluation process. People can paint with watercolors without knowledge of the medium. Most people who try to paint with watercolors without first developing that fund of knowledge do not do a painting that is worth saving. (There are few, very few, who are blessed with dumb luck.) In contrast, most of us who evaluate without a fund of knowledge about evaluative procedures and techniques are unaware of the subjective inaccuracies in our evaluation. If we want to be systematic, comprehensive, and consistent in the quality of our evaluations, we must master the meaning of and skill in using a sizable body of knowledge about the evaluation process itself and about its application.

Selecting a Subject for a Painting

I select a subject for a painting in one of two ways. Sometimes I see a scene that has an appeal that I feel a need to paint. There seem to be two types of appeal that work on me. Some places have a character that I want to record. That character may be a peacefulness, a torrent of action, or something else compatible with my mood at that moment. The other appeal is a scene that presents a challenge, a new problem in rendering. Sometimes it is the contrast of the texture of weathered wood and the metal of a sign, sometimes perhaps the force of waves on the immovable rocks of the shore. How can that texture, contrast, or whatever it is, be depicted on paper using colored water?

There does not seem to be major metaphoric value in this aspect of the painting process. There is perhaps a parallel in the selection of a subject by someone else. When someone comes to me and asks for a specific subject to be painted — a house, a building, a boat, a hot-air balloon, a specific covered bridge — the first consideration is, " Do I feel that it is a subject that does not present any new compositional or rendering problems?" When someone asks me to paint something, I want to feel confident that I can do the job. The same holds true in an evaluation. If someone wants to contract with me to do an evaluation, I want to feel confident that I can perform the tasks involved.

Creating a Composition or Design

There are several points in this facet of painting a watercolor that have parallels in the evaluation process. First, it should be noted that the selection of a scene to paint does not simultaneously set or finalize a composition. After an artist selects a scene, he constructs a composition, a design in which "the line (and value and color) arrangement leads the eye and holds it from escaping; . . . the values (and lines) are arranged to give the greatest contrast at the vital point as well as to balance each other and keep the center of gravity where it is wanted" (Kautzky, 1979, p. 52). Kautzky's words are clear; artists plan pictures.

In the discussion of picture planning, Kautzky and others use the idea "compelling the eye." A good composition has a major point of interest and some number of minor interest points. The task in planning the composition is to arrange this major interest point and the minor interest points so that the viewer's eye is compelled to move from point to point to stay within the rectangular boundary of the picture. The purpose of compelling the eye is obvious. If the major and minor points are so arranged that the viewer's eyes are directed out of the picture frame, the viewer's attention is lost. Conversely, if the elements of the composition are arranged so that the viewer's eye is led from the major interest point to a minor interest point to another minor interest point back to the major point of interest, the viewer's interest is prolonged. And given that, there is a greater likelihood that the viewer will get the artist's message and/or that the viewer will develop a desire to own the painting.

Kautzky discusses one of his compositions to illuminate the "compelling the eye" idea. He was interested in some sea gulls soaring along the New England coast and decided to capture the gracefulness of their flight. He drew a sea gull, wings spread wide, gliding a few feet above the water. To create maximum contrast (one way painters use to identify an object as a major point of interest), he drew a wharf in perspective as the background for this soaring gull. The white form of the gull against the dark shadows of the wharf provided a powerful attraction for the viewer's eye. But, there was a composition problem. The lines of the wharf provided strong diagonals that could direct the viewer's eye away from the gull in the lower right quadrant across and out of the picture on the left. These perspective lines acted almost as an arrow, saying, "Look this way quickly and be gone." (Straight lines in a picture tend to move the eye from point to point rapidly.)

To counter this movement out of the picture frame, Kautzky decided to put a minor interest point at the far end of the wharf. He drew "Motif Number One," a New England fishing shanty alleged to be the most frequently painted or photographed building (obviously a debatable allegation). To signal viewers that "Motif Number One" was a minor interest point, he used a reduced-value contrast in the drawing of the building (using grays rather than black and white).

In the developing composition, "Motif Number One" provides some entertainment for the viewer's eye as it moves from the soaring gull and speeds along the wharf perspective lines. The quick exit is slowed. But it does not take long for the viewer to note that the roof lines and the lines created by rows of lobster bouys hanging on the walls parallel the perspective of the wharf. "Motif Number One" becomes part of the arrow leading the eye to the left and out of the picture frame.

In an attempt to halt the eye's quick exit to the left, Kautzky drew in several sailboats moored out in the distance. Their masts provide lines perpendicular to the eye movement created by the wharf. It was hoped that those lines would stop the eye movement. But, to tell the viewer that the sailboats were in the distance, Kautzky used atmospheric perspective (objects in the distance are lighter in value and less distinct than those in the foreground). And in doing so, he created lines perpendicular to the dominant lines of the wharf that were not strong enough to stop the eye movement created by the wharf.

In his continuing effort with the composition, Kautzky returned to the gliding sea gull and the foreground of the picture. To try to reduce the pull of the wharf perspective lines, he expanded the foreground rocks, added some gulls on them and on the ground, and created some boards on the rocks and ground. These items added additional interest points to entertain the eye. But these shapes taken together direct the eye from the primary gull along the lower boundary of the picture and out of the picture frame at the lower left. Rather than resolving the composition, he now had two quick exit avenues.

After further thought, he invented a second wharf on the extreme left of the picture, a wharf that had long since decayed. Only two tall dark piles remain. When he drew them into the composition, the problem was solved. Now the viewer's eye could examine the graceful sea gull, follow the perspective lines of the wharf, examine the fishing shack, move past the masts of the sailboats in the distance, encounter the two dark foreground pilings, follow them to the rubble and rocks at the bottom of the painting, and be returned to the major point of interest — the gracefully gliding gull. The composition worked. It compelled the eye to move from the major interest point to one minor interest point after another and back to the major interest point, all the while encouraging the viewer's eye to remain within the picture.

The artist's concern for compelling the eye has a strong analogue in evaluation. A request for an evaluation is typically an indication that a major decision is to be made; at some point in the not-too-distant future someone has the responsibility for deciding to do A and not do B, C . . . N. Just as typically, a number of minor decisions must be made. This major and minor decision composite is analogous to the artist's major point of interest and minor interest points. As the artist is concerned with "compelling the eye," the evaluator is concerned with "compelling the mind." The evaluation needs to be composed (designed) so that the mind of the decision maker is compelled to deal with the minor decisions, but in a way that major attention is always turned back to the major decision. If the evaluation is designed so that it attends only to the major decision, the evaluator has created a quick exit avenue from the evaluation problem, an evaluation that is flawed by its failure to deal with all of the evaluation problem. If the evaluation is designed so that too much energy is expended on any or all of the minor decisions, or if it doesn't compel the decision maker to return to the major decision, it is again a flawed evaluation.

Edgar Whitney, an outstanding watercolor artist and teacher, makes another point related to the design of watercolor paintings: Subject matter exists in nature, but paintings seldom are the direct recording of nature. Whitney says that in creating a painting there are eight principles of artistic design and seven elements by which those principles are applied (Whitney, 1974, p. 96; italics added):

> Creative man strives for order, *unity*, everywhere. Nature's ecological law prevails from microcosm to macrocosm. Each unit, all organisms, all entities predisposed towards self-preservation and integrity, create *conflict* with competing units. This conflict can destroy unity, but *dominance* resolves conflict and regains unity. This cycle is endlessly *repeated* in all nature and in all creative endeavor. Conflict must be contrived for the sake of interest. No conflict, no plot. Unity must be achieved via dominance. A general character must be imposed upon parts by the whole. These principles must obtain, not only with the rectangle of your watercolor, but in subdivisions of the rectangle and in the use of tools employed in its production, namely, line, value, color, texture, shape, size, and direction.

Whitney clearly states that the understanding of these principles and elements ensures wiser solutions of every compositional problem.

Whitney's two chapters devoted to design principles and elements led me to construct a matrix, shown in Table 9.1, that has been very useful in designing a composition. Friends in the fields of music and photography have asked for copies of the matrix, and I have used it with watercolor students. Its use in design comes early in the process. Having selected a subject to be painted, I draw several small (about 1 × 1½ inch) rectangles within which I quickly rough in the general pattern of the scene. In these small rectangles I explore the positioning of the major point of interest in the scene — to the right? Left? High? Low? Up close? At a distance? These small rectangles present a general light-to-dark pattern which, if I squint at them, give a good enough representation for my planning of the composition.

TABLE 9.1
Design Principles and Elements

	Unity	Conflict	Dominance	Repetition	Alternation	Balance	Harmony	Gradation
Line								
Value								
Color								
Texture								
Shape								
Size								
Direction								

DESIGN PRINCIPLES

DESIGN ELEMENTS

SOURCE: From Gephart's adaptation of Whitney's chapters on design principles and elements (Whitney, 1977).

Whitney is saying that unity is a dimension of all compositions, that there is a oneness, a fit of the parts to a greater or lesser degree in all compositions. The purpose of the artist, the message she or he wants to communicate, determines whether that unity should be complete or partial; and if the latter, how partial? As the matrix suggests, unity can be achieved through the use of line, through the use of color, value, texture, shape, size and/or direction. Do the lines fit together, or do some of them not fit? If the latter, does that lack of fit accomplish the feeling that the artist wants to convey through the composition? The same goes for values, color, and so on.

Next, Whitney focuses on conflict as a dimension of a composition. Again, it is a variable. Again, it is accomplished to the desired degree by the way the artist uses line, value, color, and the rest. Then dominance is considered in the same way. And repetition.

I present Whitney's ideas about design principles and elements not because that is *the* way or *the* structure for designing or constructing a composition. There are others (see, for example, Schmalz, *Watercolor Your Way,* 1978). Whitney's, in my opinion, is simultaneously more useful and parsimonious. Whitney's ideas are presented here to emphasize that even in the creative arena of painting there are ways of systematically structuring the problem-solving process. To most people, the creation of a painting appears to be a highly subjective, intuitive activity. *It is not.* Certainly there are a few people who have developed artistic skill whose knowledge of how they compose is autistic — that is, it is in and of themselves and they lack the ability to make what they do public. But the vast majority of us do not operate that way. We need, want, and use heuristics, techniques that help us systematize our problem solving, *even in the area of aesthetics.*

This is an important point for would-be evaluators. Good evaluations don't happen — they are designed. And most of the time they are designed in advance. Furthermore, just as a composition is a single instance, so is an evaluation. An evaluation is situation-specific and to some extent unique. The evaluation we had done on our 1977 programs of the National Symposia for Professionals in Evaluation and Research (NSPER) could not be duplicated for our 1978 NSPER programs. At the same time, it is extremely valuable to have a general structure, a model or paradigm, to use when we plan a specific evaluation. It organizes our thinking so that we are less likely to miss activities or events that must occur if we are to do an adequate evaluation.

Evaluation and watercolor painting have another parallel here. The planning *must* be done in advance if we want consistently good results. Once I start rendering a watercolor painting I have a very difficult time changing the basic composition. That is, if I decide that the rocks in the lower right corner of my composition are so dark that they distract attention from the major point of interest, I will have a very difficult time changing that part of the watercolor painting. Corrections can be made. *But,* corrections on a watercolor usually wind up looking like corrections.

The same thing holds for an evaluation. If we realize after a project has started that we needed a measure of affect at the start of the project, we will have a very difficult time compensating for that oversight. Yes, corrections can be made. (We could ask people to recall how they felt at the beginning of the project.) But corrections in an evaluation design usually wind up looking like corrections.

There is another parallel between constructing a visual composition and planning an evaluation project, a parallel that is far more subtle. A good watercolor painting seldom presents all the details of the objects being rendered. Usually the watercolorist uses color, shape, texture, line, and value in a way that *suggests* the details in a way that leaves it up to the viewer to complete the picture. Pike (1978b), in a tape-slide presentation on watercolor painting, says to let the harness suggest the roundness of the horse's body, let the shadows of a tree that is out of the picture suggest the contours of the hillside or of the snow.

This requires that the painter identify *in advance* the basic essence of the thing to be suggested. And it requires that she or he determine the graphic elements that will *suggest* the thing being portrayed. There are a number of ideas hidden in this point. First, the thing to be represented is seen differently by different viewers. It is exceedingly difficult for most artists to be aware of the different ways viewers will see a specific barn. It is also difficult to portray the exact details of each of those views of that barn. So, as many watercolorists suggest, we present the essence of that barn (or rather, one of the essences) and let the mind of each viewer complete the picture.

The idea of presenting essences has important meaning for educational evaluators. The purpose of an evaluation is to determine the value, absolute or relative, of educational programs, products, or performances. Typically, in an evaluation there is a choice to be made among two or more items, and thus we want to know the value of each as the basis for the choice. There are ten or more goals school systems might try to accomplish. Which are the most important? When a goal has been selected there may be several ways of working toward achieving it. Which way is best for our school? In each of these cases the things to be evaluated are likely to be perceived differently by different individuals. The goal, to "Develop the desire to learn, now and in the future," will be perceived differently by different people, and it will be valued differently. Some will look at one composite of the attributes of that goal, others at another composite. One detailed description of the facets of that goal will be adequate for some and inadequate for others. To think that an evaluation report can present *the* universally applicable statement of *the* value of an educational program, product, or performance is a romantic myth. At best, it can present *a* description of one way of valuing the thing (or things) being evaluated. To be more than *a* description it would have to be the thing itself.

The realization that an evaluation produces *a* truth about an entity being evaluated is terribly defeating to many people. If we cannot produce an *objective* description, why do we waste our time trying to evaluate educational programs, products, or performances? This is the same as saying to the artist, if you cannot represent *the* realness of that barn, why try to paint it! There are perhaps two answers to this question: the comeback of the mountain climber, "it's there," and the statement Egon Guba encouraged us to use on the frontispiece of the book *Educational Evaluation and Decision Making* (Stufflebeam et al., 1971) —

The Purpose of Evaluation
Is not to Prove
But to Improve

By doing an evaluation we want to improve decision-making. If we can help people call up *their* version of the values of the entities considered in those decisions in ways that help them know more clearly what it is they are evaluating and how they are valuing those things, their decisions will be more informed. And we believe that more informed decisions are better decisions.

The suggestion from painting that we construct a design or composition has another subtle thought for the evaluator. Kautzsky's statement (cited earlier) says the artist arranges line, value, color, and so on to "give the greatest contrast at the vital point as well as to balance each other and keep the center of gravity where it is wanted" (p. 52). This is excellent advice in planning an evaluation. The evaluation design should ensure the greatest contrast at the vital decision point, and it should keep the center of gravity where it is wanted. Many evaluation studies ramble from point to point in such a way that the vital decision point is unidentifiable. Studies designed this way have no center of gravity and lead the people who have the responsibility for making the decision through value clarification in random or accidental ways.

If the advice of Kautsky, an accomplished watercolorist, is heeded, evaluation plans would identify the decision milieu, the decision options to be considered, and the people whose task it is to consider the value of each of the options. Then the plans would be used to explore the ways in which those people can be helped to clarify and use *their* perception of the items among which a choice is to be made. The evaluator would recognize that there is a high probability that the different people involved will perceive the options differently. The evaluator's task is to help inform the decision, not to make it, just as the artist's task is to help the viewer develop his picture of a barn, not to imprint the artist's image in the mind of the viewer.

Preparing to Paint

Before I start to paint, I have a number of preparations to make. The materials to be used have to be assembled, and the design has to be transferred to the paper. Watercolor is a quick medium; that is, a picture is painted in a relatively short period of time. As indicated earlier, different effects are accomplished as the water on a surface evaporates. Thus, the painter must plan a sequence of things to do in a two- to five-minute period. To accomplish that sequence of activities, paints, brushes, sponges, rags, blotters, and water must be readily available. I try to put my materials in the same place for each painting, and I set the materials in a way that minimizes error. For example, since I am right-handed, my water supply and pallette are on the right. That way, I do not carry a full brush across the painting and risk dropping an unwanted blob of water or paint on the picture. The good painter knows his or her tools and has them ready for use when needed. So does the good evaluator.

Transferring the composition to the painting surface is the second part of preparing to paint. The composition is usually a small pencil drawing. Drawing paper is much cheaper than painting paper, so the composition is done on paper where it costs less to make a mistake. But this means that the little drawing has to be enlarged and transferred to the watercolor sheet.

The transfer is made most easily be drawing a grid on the composition. This is done by drawing a vertical line that divides the composition in half, then two more lines that divide it into quarters. The same thing is done horizontally so that the composition has a 16-cell grid on it. The same grid is drawn (lightly) on the paper on which I am going to paint. Then the basic lines and shapes of the composition are drawn on the painting surface. This "squaring-up" helps maintain the proportions of the composition.

An evaluator should have an evaluation plan that specifies what is to be done. Care should be taken to see that the plan is implemented in a way that maintains the emphases designed in the plan.

Rendering the Painting

With a composition in hand, an outline of it on the painting surface, and the materials laid out in their regular places, I am ready to paint. In doing the composition I have made some general decisions about the sequence of activities. Because I want to be able to paint one element of the design on top of another, I have to be sure of the sequence. For example, a picture with some water in the middle distance and sand dunes with sea oats on them must be painted in that order. If the order were reversed, the sharp edges of the sea oats would smear when the water was painted.

I find the process used by high jumpers very helpful. They stand before the bar and *think* every muscle movement needed to make the jump. I select a segment of the composition on which to concentrate. I pick up the first brush or sponge to be used and think about the mixture of colors I will use. Then I put that brush down and decide what has to be done next and which brush to use for that. This is continued until I have *thought* through that wetting of the paper. That is, I have *thought* through each step, from wetting a section of the paper until that section is perfectly dry. Then I do those steps.

This thinking through and doing cycle is repeated over and over until the composition is finished. Sometimes a section of a composition will be wet, worked, and dried several times before the desired effect is accomplished. Two to three minutes of painting for ten minutes of thinking is a good ratio.

The message for evaluators here concerns administration. An evaluation project must be administered. A variety of people are involved in a variety of activities and a variety of materials are to be used. The person responsible for the evaluation should think through the next phase of the evaluation effort to be sure everyone involved knows what is to be done, by whom, and with what. This is an aspect of evaluation attended to by too few evaluation theorists.

There is another thing done in rendering a watercolor. From time to time I step back from the painting and look at it in another way. Sometimes I back away, sometimes I turn the paper upside down, sometimes I look at it in a mirror, and sometimes I put a mat on the painting. My difficulty here is that after I have been looking at the painting for some time, I cannot be sure what is on the paper and what is in my mind. So, I deliberately structure a different view to help me to see better. An evaluator might benefit from that trick. Another person could be asked to review the evaluation plan during its implementation to see that nothing has been missed.

Critiquing the Painting

When a picture is finished a mat is cut. Then I like to set it aside for awhile. After a few days I go back to it to see if it needs anything. Sometimes this critiquing can be aided by another person. My two sons were excellent help when they were living at home. They had an excellent sense of composition. I could show them a completed picture and their reactions almost invariably pinpointed sections of the painting that needed something. Perhaps a section was a little too light, some darks were needed for emphasis, or for balance. Perhaps a dash of color was needed.

Additional critiquing help can be found in a book called *Watercolor Your Way* (Schmalz, 1978). Although the title makes it sound like a how-to-do-it book, it isn't. Rather, it is devoted to helping the watercolor painter learn how to critique his or her own painting. This book is an excellent tool. The matrix made of Whitney's eight design principles and seven design elements is also useful. Both of these present checklists of things to look at and ways of looking at the completed picture to spot its inadequacies.

This is another respect in which painting has important meaning for the evaluator. When a report is nearly completed it should be checked using tools that might point up its weaknesses. The evaluation standards being developed by Stufflebeam's joint committee (1980) are one such tool. A paper by Sanders and Nafziger (1976) presents a checklist of things to be considered in an evaluation design. This checklist would also be useful at the end of an effort. The evaluation design prepared earlier for the evaluation now being reported would be another tool for this end-of-project critique of the effort.

Finishing the Picture

The last phase in watercolor painting has two parts — making the modifications deemed necessary and possible in the critique phase and framing the picture. Some changes, some corrections, can be made in a watercolor (see Barbour, 1975). But making changes requires considerable knowledge about the process of watercolor painting and about the materials used.

The same is true for an educational evaluation. The best thing is to do it right the first time. But, if some changes are needed, some corrections can be made by an evaluator who thoroughly knows the evaluation process and the techniques used.

Finally, the picture is framed. This sounds simple and unthinking, but it isn't. Framing has a great effect on a painting. It can feature the painting or subdue it, enhance or diminish it. Again, there is a lot of cognitive knowledge involved in framing. There is also affect and psychomotor skill involved in creating a frame. (And those who have had something framed recently by a professional know that it costs money.)

In educational evaluation the packaging is important also. The report format needs to facilitate the achievement of the evaluation's purpose. A sloppy report will be accepted and treated lightly. Make the appearance of the report reflect the importance you want the evaluation client to ascribe to it.

A watercolor needs protection to be permanent. It cannot be cleaned, so the frame must protect it. Evaluators would do well to think about this. The products of evaluations need protection too. The information can be distorted, intentionally and unintentionally. Evaluators need to develop procedures that will protect their information. Stufflebeam (1975) has spoken about contracting for an evaluation in ways that include these matters in the negotiation process. We need more tools here.

Some Thoughts Before Summarizing

Before summarizing, two more points are raised by watercolor painting that have helped me to understand about evaluation. It is extremely important for the artist to learn to obtain and use evaluation regularly as an aid in doing a specific painting and as a way of expanding her or his expressive repertoire. Few artists survive who don't learn this. Schmalz's book, *Watercolor Your Way,* is without parallel in educational evaluation. It is an entire book that is devoted to showing a painter how to use evaluation to improve his or her work. Even worse, the educational practitioner is not taught to value criticism or evaluation but to fear it. Guba's maxim, "The purpose of evaluation is not to prove but to improve," isn't generally believed. We would profit from a concerted effort to help educators, both teachers and administrators, learn that evaluation can be a friend, that it can help improve performance and conditions of work. Of course, making evaluation beneficial will require considerable change in educational operations. In many cases, evaluation is perceived by teachers and administrators as a punitive, or potentially punitive, force. "It will help those [expletive deleted] do me in." As long as society projects the idea that people are less important than money, that evaluation's major purpose is to weed out and cast aside the laggard, we will hold evaluation's benefits in suspicion, and justifiably so.

A last point. Good watercolorists know that painting behavior is a composite of the cognitive, affective, and psychomoter skills. To get a particularly effective soft cloud shadow effect, I need to know that a mixture of ultramarine blue and burnt sienna has particles that are of two different sizes and weights. Thus, when I float that mixture on an already wet surface, the blue particles will drop to the surface of the paper and the brown particles will move a little bit as a result of capillary action (and gravity). It happens every time. To get that effect, I have to *feel* how wet the paper is and how much spread is wanted. And, I have to *be able to deliver* the paint mixture to the proper spot on the composition. Good watercolorists know that these three aspects of behavior are inexorably mixed in an action.

Knowing-feeling-doing are one. Each is separate but contributes to the whole. Good watercolorists know, as do Benjamin Bloom, David Krathwohl, and their colleagues, that we can separate behavior into these components for logical analysis, but that separation does not exist in the real world! In teaching people who would be watercolor painters, I do not try to get them to know the cognitive items independently of their feelings and psychomotor skills. They have to master composite behaviors.

Summary

Watercolor painting, carefully analyzed, has helped me to see educational evaluation more clearly. I hope this exposition has been helpful to you. Although there are many points of process similarity, three stand out for me. They have helped me to see that in preparation for evaluation, the design of an effort to be carried out is of extreme importance. Evaluation, like painting a watercolor, is situation-specific (including time, place, and activity) and the planning for it is not a trivial part of the process.

Watercolor painting also makes clear that one of evaluation's purposes, to provide information that helps an individual or group make a choice among a set of educational program options, is not well understood. Making a choice is a valuing activity. The individual who will make the choice has to determine in his or her mind, "What is the value of option A? Option B? Option C?" People value and ascribe value to things differently. Because of this, it is not my task as an evaluator to come up with *the* absolute statement describing the worth of options A, B, or C. Rather, it is my task to help the decision maker become clear about how he or she goes about valuing those options. Just as the watercolorist lets the viewer provide the details of the object being represented, the evaluator should let his or her client complete the statement regarding the worth of the options. To do otherwise assumes that there is but one truth about the value of a set of items, an assumption that can be true only if we all have the *same* value base and reasoning processes.

Finally, the effort to compare and contrast educational evaluation with my 25-year avocation shows me that it is extremely important to know and to be able to use a great deal of information about the evaluation process in general, about principles and guidelines for its use, and about what the process can and cannot do. To distribute effectively water-soluble pigment on paper so as to represent the violent crash of the surf against the rocks of the Oregon coast or to represent the peaceful swaying of the sea oats on the sand dunes of the Gulf coast, I have to have a large quantity of information about the medium, how it works, and about the subject matter, both cognitive and affective information. I also have to be able to control myself and the medium. Language fails me at this point. I can speak or write only one word at a time. In watercolor painting knowing, feeling, and doing are simultaneous. I suspect that this applies in evaluation as well.

I close with the words of John Pike: "Into each life some rain must fall, why not try a little watercolor?"

References

On Watercolor Painting

Barbour, A. J. *Painting the seasons in watercolor.* New York: Watson-Guptill, 1975.
Black, W., & Croney, C. *The watercolor painting book.* New York: Watson-Guptill, 1978.
Croney, C. *My way with watercolor.* New York: Watson-Guptill, 1973.
de Reyna, R. *How to draw what you see.* New York: Watson-Guptill, 1972.
Hill, T. *Color for the watercolor painter.* New York: Watson-Guptill, 1975.
Kautzky, T. *Ways with watercolor.* New York: Van Nostrand Reinhold, 1963.
Kautzky, T. *The Ted Kautzky pencil book.* New York: Van Nostrand Reinhold, 1979.
Pellew, J. *John Pellew paints watercolors.* New York: Watson-Guptill, 1979.
Pike, J. *Watercolor.* New York: Watson-Guptill, 1973.

Pike, J. *John Pike paints watercolors.* New York: Watson-Guptill, 1978. (a)
Pike, J. *John Pike audio-visual program.* Woodstock, NY: John Pike Products, 1978
   (b).
Schlemm, B. L. *Painting with light.* New York: Watson-Guptill, 1978.
Schmalz, C. *Watercolor your way.* New York: Watson-Guptill, 1978.
Szabo, Z. *Landscape painting in watercolor.* New York: Watson-Guptill, 1971.
Szabo, Z. *Zoltan Szabo paints landscapes.* New York: Watson-Guptill, 1977.
Whitney, E. A. *Complete guide to watercolor painting.* New York: Watson-Gutpill,
   1974.

On Evaluation

Cady, H. A conference on research in music education. Cooperative Research
   Project Report #6-1388, 1967. ERIC #ED013-973.
Joint Committee on Standards for Educational Evaluation. *Standards for evaluations
   of educational programs, projects, and materials.* New York: McGraw-Hill,
   1980.
Sanders, J. R., & Nafziger, D. H. *A basis for determining adequacy of evaluation
   designs.* Occasional Paper No. 20. Bloomington, IN: Phi Delta Kappa, Inc.,
   1976.
Stufflebeam, D. L. Informal presentation at the Snowmass, Colorado Conference on
   Evaluation, 1975.
Stufflebeam, D. L. et al. *Educational evaluation and decision making.* Itasca, IL:
   F. E. Peacock, 1971.